Table of Contents

at a Glance

D0838234

Turn to Page 1 of each chapter for a
DETAILED TABLE OF CONTENTS

PREFACE

Welcome to the *20th Anniversary Edition* of *Neonatal/Pediatric Respiratory Care: A Critical Care Pocket Guide*.

In the very first year of its publication, 1989, ***Neonatal/Pediatric Respiratory Care*** was selected among hundreds of books as the "Best Book of the Year" by ***Nurse Practitioner*®** magazine. In addition, upon his initial review of the book, Dr. Alan Fields commented, "This book may serve the respiratory therapist, nurse, or physician ... as well as *The Harriet Lane Manual* has served the pediatric house officer".

Since that time, Dr. Fields has graciously been one of the book's illustrious Co-Editors and over the last 20 years this book has become the standard quick-reference among Respiratory Therapists, Nurses, and Physicians all over the world.

Whether you are *a student in training*, an *experienced practitioner in a tertiary hospital*, or *a clinician in an outlying hospital* (needing a quick and fresh reminder of the best way to manage this patient until transport arrives), you will find this book extremely informative, comprehensive, up-to-date, and easy to reference. I trust it will be one of the greatest investments of your career.

ACKNOWLEDGEMENTS

First and foremost, I want to thank my Maker, God Almighty. Thank you, Jesus Christ, for Your leading and for allowing me this opportunity to play a small role in helping improve the lives of Your children.

Secondly, I would like to thank and welcome several new Assistant Editors to this new edition, as well as recognize the continued support of Dr. Goldsmith and Dr. Fields, for their many years of devotion and faithfulness to this book.

Finally, I would be remiss not to recognize the valuable assistance of Dr. Gordon Avery, author emeritus of Avery's ***Neonatology***, in helping edit the very first Edition of this book (much of which still exists today).

Thank you all very much!

Dana Oakes

1 Pre- and Postnatal Assessment

Prenatal Assessment

Age Definitions

Fetus	Before birth
Newborn	Birth to 1 week
Neonate	1 week - 28 days
Infant	28 days to 1.5-2 years
Child	1.5 years to 12 years (puberty)
Adolescent	Puberty to adult

Pulmonary Maturity

Lung Maturity Tests

Approx. Gest. Age	L/S Ratio[1]	PI[2]	PG[3]	Risk of RDS
< 32 wks.	1:1	Absent	Absent	> 90%
32-35 wks.	1:5/2	Present	Absent	≈ 50%
> 35 wks.	2:1	Present	Present	< 5%

1 Lecithin to sphingomyelin ratio. May be falsely high or falsely low (see Table next page). L/S ratio is accelerated by administration of betamethasone or in infants of mothers with diabetes (class D, F, R), heroin-addiction, PROM > 48 hrs, hypertension, abruptio placenta, placental insufficiency or infection.
2 Phosphatidylinositol (PI)
3 Phosphatidylglycerol (PG)
* The pulmonary system is considered mature when it can sustain extrauterine life.

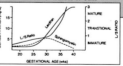

Figure reprinted with permission from Burgess, W. and Chernick, V. *Respiratory Therapy in Newborn Infants and Children*, 2nd Ed. Copyright 1986 by Thieme, Inc.

The L/S ratio takes 6-12 hours to obtain results. A comparable test, the TD_x Fetal Lung Maturity assay (FLM), measures lung surfactants relative to albumin, expressed as a surfactant/albumin ratio. (See next page.)

0-29 mg/g	Definitely immature
30-50 mg/g	Risky
50-70 mg/g	Treat with caution
Greater than 70 mg/g	Small likelihood for RDS

Asssessment of Fetal Maturity by Amniotic Fluid Assay*

Test	Result (in Normal Pregnancy)	Comment
L/S Ratio	Sphingomyelin concentration exceeds lecithin until 26th wk. Lecithin concentration exceeds sphingomyelin by 35-36 wk.	L/S ratio > 2.0 indicates fetal lung maturity. Falsely high L/S ratio when fluid is contaminated with maternal or fetal blood or vaginal secretions. Respiratory distress syndrome in spite of mature L/S ratio has been seen in diabetic pregnancies or after intrauterine transfusions.
PG	PG detectable beyond 35 wk. gestation.	Particularly useful in pregnancies complicated by diabetes mellitus. PG can eliminate false maturity by L/S ratio. PG is reliable even when contaminated with blood or vaginal secretions.
Shake test	After 36 wk. gestation, complete ring of bubbles present at 1,2 dilution of amniotic fluid in presence of ethanol.	A simple, inexpensive, reliable bedside screening test. Contamination with blood or meconium results in a false positive test result.
Fetal Lung Maturity assay (FLM)	At maturity, 70mg/g would indicate a very small likelihood for the development of respiratory distress syndrome.	Easy to perform. Relatively inexpensive. Fast turnaround time (less than 30 minutes). Reproducible. Done on a fluorescent polarimeter, a common clinical laboratory instrument.
Foam stability index	At maturity > 0.48	Quantitative measure of foam stability of surfactant and ethanol.

Test	Result (in Normal Pregnancy)	Comment
Lecithin concentration	At maturity lecithin: > 3.5 mg/100 ml phosphorus: > 0.1 mg/100 mL	Direct measure of primary phospholipid in surfactant
Saturated lecithin	At maturity > 500 mg/dL	Measurement after oxidation with osmium tetroxide
Osmolality	Near maternal plasma level (270 mOsm) at < 36 wk; value falls as term approaches (250 mOsm).	Value falls as a result of fetal urine contribution; reflects maternal electrolyte level; increases with fetal death.
Creatinine	1.5 mg/100 mL at < 36 wk, > 2.0 mg/100 ml at 36 wk. in 10%. > 2.0 mg/100 mL beyond 36 wk.	Values lower in diabetic women. Value depends on renal function of the infant, as well as muscle mass.
Protein	Protein value decreases as gestation progresses.	Value rises with fetal death, anencephaly, and other anomalies.
Bilirubin	13-30 wk. gestation, bilirubin remains at highest concentration. Falls to 0 by 36 wk. gestation.	Bilirubin in the unconjugated state. Origin a mystery. Elevated in toxemia, hydrops fetalis. GI obstruction, and anencephaly.

*L/S ratio, lecithin-sphingomyelin ratio; PG, phosphatidylglycerol.

Adapted from Harper, R. and Yoon, J. **Handbook of Neonatology**, 2nd Ed. Copyright 1987 by Yearbook Medical Pub. Inc.

Overview of Fetal Monitoring

	Assess	Frequency of assessments

FHR	Baseline rate
	Baseline variability
	Periodic changes
	Accelerations
	Decelerations
		Low risk patient:
		  active stage of labor – q 30 min.
		  2nd stage of labor – q 15 min.
		High risk patient:
		  active stage of labor – q 15 min.
		  2nd stage of labor – q 5 min.

Uterine Activity	Assess Frequency Duration Intensity Resting tone } of contractions	

Modes of assessment

	External mode *(abdominal)*	Internal mode *(intrauterine)* *Requires ROM + 2 cm dil.*
FHR	abdominal electrodes phonotransducer ultra- sound transducer	spiral electrode (ECG) fetal scalp electrode
Uterine Activity	Tocotransducer (meas- ures frequency & dura- tion) used in 1st stage of labor or with non- stress test or oxytoxin challenge test	Intrauterine Pressure Cath- eter (measures frequency, duration and intensity)

FHR Monitoring

Baseline = FHR in absence of uterine contractions (and between periodic rate changes).

normal range = 120-160 bpm

Abnormal rates:

	Causes	Clinical significance	Treatment
Tachycardia (> 160 bpm) (decelerations)	Early fetal asphyxia (see next page for causes)	ominous	Give O_2

Tachycardia (> 160 bpm) (no decelerations)	Fetal
	  anemia
	  hypovolemia
	  immaturity
	Maternal
	  anemia
	  fever
	  hyperthyroidism
	Intrauterine
	  infections
	Drugs
	  ß-sympathomimetics
	  Parasympatholytics
		usually benign	observe closely

Bradycardia (< 120 bpm) (decelerations)	Late fetal asphyxia*	ominous	give O_2
Bradycardia (< 120 bpm) (no decelerations)	Anesthetics Congenital heart block Maternal SLE Oxytoxin Propanolol (ß-blockers)	usually benign	observe closely

* Causes of fetal asphyxia

Reduced fetal oxygen supply:

Maternal — anemia, anesthetics, hemorrhage, hyper/hypotension, hyperthermia, supine position

Fetal — cord or head compression ($\downarrow$ HR)
placental separation
post maturity

Baseline variability

Normal = normal irregularity of the FHR
= 5-10 bpm (beat-to-beat or short term)
= 10-40 bpm (long-term or cycles)
= fetal well-being

	Causes	Clinical signif.	Treatment
Increased (> 15 bpm)	Fetal stimulation	benign	none
Decreased (< 5 bpm)	Sleep cycle	benign	none
	Analgesics (Demerol, Talwin, morphine)		observe with caution, stimulate fetus Δ maternal position D/C drugs
	Atropine		
	Arrhythmias		
	Anesthetics		
	Barbituates (Nembutal, Pento-barbitol, Seconal)		
	Narcotics		
	Tranquilizers (diazepam, Valium)		
No variability (smooth, flat baseline)	Severe fetal distress	ominous	above & if no variability remains, then obtain fetal ABG & consider prompt delivery

Baseline Variability

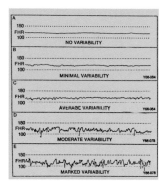

Reprinted with permission from Hon, *E. An Atlas of Fetal Heart Rate Patterns.* Copyright 1968 by Horty Press.

Periodic changes in FHR

Relationship between FHR and uterine contractions.

Normally, uterine contractions have no effect on FHR.

Transitory increases in FHR above baseline (accelerations) or decreases in FHR below baseline (decelerations) may occur concurrent with uterine contractions.

Abnormal Effect	Cause	Clinical significance	Treatment
Acceleration	Fetal movement	Fetal well-being	none
	Abdominal palpation or Vaginal exam	Benign	none
	Partial umbilical vein compression (ex. breech)	Usually benign but may become more severe as labor progresses	observe closely

Abnormal Effect	Cause	Clinical significance	Treatment
Deceleration Early (Type I)	Compression of fetal head against cervix	Benign	none or may use maternal atropine
Deceleration Late (Type ii)	↓ Placental perfusion: Compression of placental vessels - maternal position, oxytocin hyperstimulation, post mature syndrome Maternal diabetes, anemia, hyper/ hypotension Placenta previa Abruptio placentae	Ominous: uteroplacental insufficiency, fetal hypoxia, fetal stress, potential neurological damage	administer O$_2$, (8-12 lpm via face mask) obtain fetal ABG, change maternal position, elevate legs, D/C oxytoxin. consider early delivery if persists.
Variable (Type III)	Compression of umbilical cord:		
	FHR > 80 lpm, < 30 sec duration	mild	common & benign
	FHR 60-80 bpm, 30-60 sec duration	moderate	change maternal position
	FHR < 60, > 60 sec duration	repetitive moderate or severe	administer O$_2$, (8-12 lpm via face mask); obtain fetal ABG; amnioinfusion? immediate delivery?

Fetal HR Decelerations

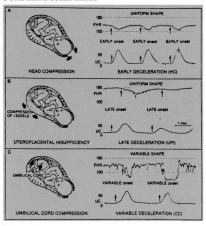

Summary of Fetal Monitoring

Reassuring Pattern	Non-Reassuring Pattern (Warning)
FHR baseline normal (120-160 bpm)	FHR baseline outside normal
Average baseline variability	Progressive ↓ in baseline variability
Early decelerations	Fetal pH 7.15-7.25
Mild variable decelerations	
Accelerations	
Fetal pH 7.25-7.30	

Ominous Patterns
Severe bradycardia
Prolonged deceleration
Severe variable decelerations (< 70 bpm for > 30 sec)
Late decelerations
Fetal pH < 7.15

Fetal Biophysical Profile (FBP)

Variable	Score	
	Normal = 2	Abnormal = 0
Fetal Breathing Movements (FBM)	One episode > 30 sec. during a 30 min period	absence for 30 min
Fetal Movements (FM)	presence of ≥ 3 discrete limb or trunk movements in a 30 min. period	< 3 movements in 30 min
Fetal Tone (FT)	presence of ≥ 1 episode of active extension of a limb or spine with immed. return to flexion in a 30 min. period	absence of FT in 30 min.
Amniotic Fluid Volume (AFV)	largest pocket of fluid > 1 cm diameter	pocket diameter < 1 cm
Non-Stress Test (NST)	Reactive (positive); > 2 FHR accelerations of ≥ 15bpm for ≥ 15 sec. during a 30 min. period and associated with FM.	Nonreactive (negative): < 2 FHR accelerations associated with fetal movement in a 30 min. period

FBP is an assessment of fetal well-being using ultrasound.

If the 1st four variables = 8, then the 5th variable (NST) is not performed.

If points lost are FBM, FM or FT, then the exam is repeated following nourishment given to the mother.

If points lost are only due to FBM (FM + FT is normal, and NST is reactive), this may be due to their periodic occurrences.

Any total score of < 8 is abnormal and action is required.

   8-10 — normal infant, low risk for chronic asphyxia.

   4-6 — suspected chronic asphyxia, delivery indicated.

   0-2 — strong suspicion of chronic asphyxia, immediate delivery.

Clinical Notes:

FM → ↑ FHR → positive NST.

A negative (nonreactive) NST is usually followed by a contraction stress test (CST) to determine cause.

CST: Contractions are stimulated by nipple manipulation or oxytocin (OCT). Late decelerations of FHR are a positive CST.

Negative NST + negative CST =
fetal sleep or maternal narcotics or sedatives

Negative NST + positive CST =
uteroplacental insufficiency (prolonged hypoxia)

Clinical Note:

There is a direct correlation between low FBP scores and fetal distress, fetal acidosis and hypoxia, low apgar scores, and perinatal mortality.

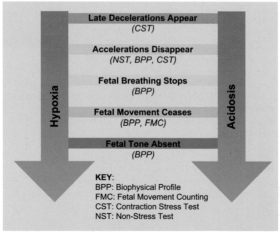

Late Decelerations Appear
(CST)

Accelerations Disappear
(NST, BPP, CST)

Fetal Breathing Stops
(BPP)

Fetal Movement Ceases
(BPP, FMC)

Fetal Tone Absent
(BPP)

Hypoxia

Acidosis

KEY:
BPP: Biophysical Profile
FMC: Fetal Movement Counting
CST: Contraction Stress Test
NST: Non-Stress Test

Reprinted with permission from *Clinical Obstetrics and Gynecology*, V. 30, #4, 1987.

Fetal/Neonatal Blood Gas Monitoring

	Scalp Blood				Cord Blood		Arterial Blood				
	Early labor	Mid-labor	Full cerv dil.	Before delivery	Umbilical artery	Umbilical vein	4 min.	8 min.	16 min.	32 min.	64 min.
Indications	FHR <100 or >160 bpm (Persistent or recurring) Presence of meconium				Ominous FHR Apgar <7 Birthwgt <1500 gm Meconium staining Intrapartum distress Early neonat. distress		Apgar <7 Post partum distress Early neonatal distress				
Normal Values pH	7.30	7.30	7.28	7.26	7.24	7.32	7.20	7.24	7.30	7.32	7.36
P_{CO_2}	25	45	49	50	43	38	46	40	35	35	34
P_{O_2}	20	21	19	17	13	28	53	62	68	70	70
Base deficit	6	5	6	7	9	7	10	9	8	6	4
Clinical Notes	Taken before birth. Capillary puncture is performed on fetal scalp (or presenting part) via endoscope up vaginal canal. (See Pg. 6-4)				Within 15 min. after birth. Puncture of umbilical artery or vein in the cord attached to the placenta after clamping.		Arterial puncture or arterial line sampling. (See Pg. 6-2 or 6-6)				

Overview of Normal Changes in ABGs During Birth

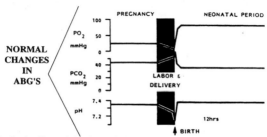

NORMAL
CHANGES
IN
ABG'S

Reprinted with permission from Schreiner, R. and Kisling, J. *Practical Neonatal Respiratory Care.* Copyright 1982 by Raven Press.

Abnormal Fetal ABGs	
Fetal pH:	
7.30-7.35	Early labor (should be within 0.05 of maternal pH)
7.25-7.35	Normal labor
7.15-7.25	Worrisome (repeat q 10 min.)
< 7.15	Potential asphyxia and metabolic acidosis (prompt delivery may be required)

FETAL DISTRESS

pH < 7.10
pCO_2 > 60
pO_2 < 20
BE > -15

Cardiopulmonary Changes at Birth

Body Structure	Before Birth	After Birth
Ductus arteriosus	Shunts blood from PA → aorta (bypassing the lungs)	Closes functionally within min.-hrs. (days in premies); due to O_2, metabolism of PGE2 by lungs and release of bradykinin and histamine. Permanent closure by 2-4 mos (to ligament)
Ductus venosus	Shunts blood from placenta to IVC (bypassing the liver)	Closes and becomes a ligament (exact timing and cause unknown).
Foramen ovale	Shunts blood from RA to LA (bypassing RV and lungs)	Functionally closes within min.-hrs. due to ↑ pressure (LAP > RAP) caused by ↑ pulm. flow and ↑ SVR. Anatomically seals approx. 3 mos.
Umbilical arteries and veins	Carries blood to and from placenta, respectively	Clamped (functional closure in minutes) and become ligaments in 2-3 months.
Pulmonary arteries	Carry only 10% of blood flow (3.5 mL/ Kg/min) ↑ PVR (= 60 mmHg) due to vessels tortuous, kinked and constricted.	Dilates to carry 130% of cardiac output, ↓ PVR (<25 mmHg) due to ↑ PaO_2, lung expansion, fluid elimination, muscle atrophy, and release of vasodilators (bradykinin).
Systemic circulation	Low pressures in left atrium, ventricle and aorta	↑ SVR, ↑ left ventricular volume work.

1-15

PRENATAL CIRCULATION

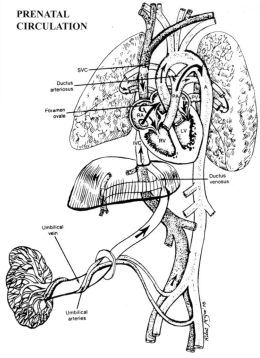

Reprinted with permission from Whaley and Wong, **Nursing Care of Infants and Children**. Copyright 1983 by the C.V. Mosby Co.

POSTNATAL CIRCULATION

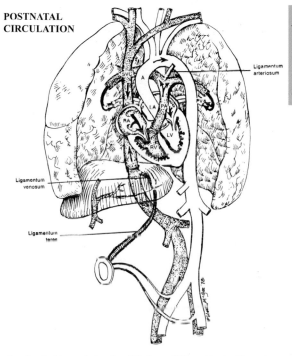

Ligamentum arteriosum

Ligamentum venosum

Ligamentum teres

Reprinted with permission from Whaley and Wong, *Nursing Care of Infants and Children.* Copyright 1983 by the C.V. Mosby Co.

Postnatal Assessment

Newborn Vital Sign Ranges	
RR	30-60 bpm
HR	120-160 bpm
BP	<u>60-80</u>
	40-50 mmHg

Mean BP should be ≥ gestational age.

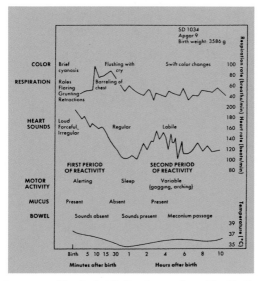

A summary of the physical findings in normal transition (the first 10 hours of extrauterine life in a representative high-Apgar-score infant delivered under spinal anesthesia without premedication).
From Desmond, M. et al: *Pediatric Clinics of N.A.* 13:656, 1966.

APGAR SCORING

Apgar scoring is done at 1 min. and 5 minutes after delivery.

A more rapid, immediate, and efficient assessment is the evaluation of the newborn at birth using NRP criteria (see pg 1-21). Intervention should not wait for the assignment of a score.

SIGN	SCORE		
	0	1	2
A Appearance (color)	Blue, pale	Body pink Extremities blue	Completely pink
P Pulse (heart rate)	Absent	Below 100	Above 100
G Grimace (reflex, irritability to suctioning)	No response	Grimace	Cough or sneeze
A Activity (muscle tone)	Limp	Some flexion	Well flexed
R Respiration (breathing efforts)	Absent	Weak, irregular	Strong cry

Apgar, V et. al: Evaluation of the Newborn Infant, *JAMA* 168:1985-88,1958.

Expanded Apgar Score Form*:

Comments:	Scoring Item:	# Minutes				
		1	5	10	15	20
	Oxygen					
	PPV/NCAP					
	ETT					
	Chest Compressions					
	Epinephrine					

* Proposed use by The American Academy of Pediatrics and the American College of Obstetricians and Gynecologists, 2006

NRP Guidelines:

- Do not wait for the 1 minute Apgar to initiate resuscitation when needed.
- Apgar scores should not be used to dictate resuscitative actions.
- Apgar scores should be performed every 5 minutes until ≥ 7 (up to 20 min).
- If no heart rate after 10 min of complete and adequate resuscitation efforts (and no evidence of other causes of compromise), discontinuation of resuscitative efforts may be appropriate.

AAP & ACOG Guidelines:

- Factors that may influence the Apgar score are:

Congenital anomalies	Hypovolemia	Resuscitative efforts
Drugs	Immaturity	Trauma
Hypoxia	Infections	

- The significance of the Apgar score in preterms is unknown.
- It is inappropriate to use the Apgar score alone to diagnose asphyxia.
- The 5 minute score is helpful in assessing recovery from depression, the effectiveness of any interventions, or a subsequent turn for the worse.
- Low Apgar scores are not useful for predicting future neurologic handicaps unless ≤ 3 at 10-15 minutes of age.

Neonatal Resuscitation Algorithm

Birth (1)

Term Gestation?
Amniotic Fluid Clear?
Breathing or Crying?
Good Muscle Tone?

→ YES (2) →

Routine Care (provide warmth, clear airway, dry, assess color)

↓ No

Airway (3)*

Position: clear airway
Provide warmth
Dry, stimulate, reposition

Evaluate (4) RR, HR, Color

* Endotracheal Intubation may be considered at several steps

Apneic Gasping or HR < 100

Breathing HR>100 but cyanotic

Breathing HR > 100 Pink →

Observational Care

Give O₂(5) → **Persistent Cyanosis**

Breathing (6)*
Provide Positive Pressure Ventilation

HR < 60

HR > 60

Effective Ventilation HR > 100 Pink →

Postresuscitation Care

Compressions (7)*
Administer Chest Compressions

HR < 60 → **Epinephrine +/or Volume***

1-21

SILVERMAN/ANDERSON SCORE

	UPPER CHEST	LOWER CHEST	XIPHOID RETRACT.	NARES DILAT.	EXPIR. GRUNT
GRADE 0	SYNCHRONIZED	NO RETRACT.	NONE	NONE	NONE
GRADE 1	LAG ON INSP.	JUST VISIBLE	JUST VISIBLE	MINIMAL	STETHOS. ONLY
GRADE 2	SEE-SAW	MARKED	MARKED	MARKED	NAKED EAR

Score 10 = Severe respiratory distress
Score ≥ 7 = Impending respiratory failure
Score 0 = No respiratory distress

From Silverman, W. and Anderson, D.: *Pediatrics* 17:1, 1956. Copyright American Academy of Pediatrics.

Terminology

Term Infant = 37-42 weeks gestation
Preterm Infant = < 37 weeks
Postterm Infant = > 42 weeks

Low-birthweight (LBW) = < 2500 gms
Very low-birthweight (VLBW) = < 1500 gms
Extremely low-birthweight (ELBW) = < 1000 gms

ASSESSMENT OF GESTATIONAL AGE

**Classfication of Newborns (Both Sexes)
By Intrauterine Growth and Gestational Age**

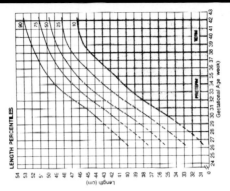

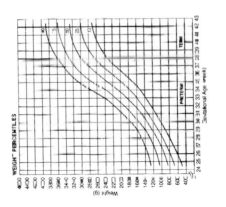

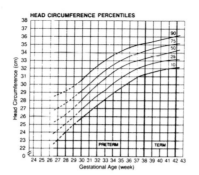

HEAD CIRCUMFERENCE PERCENTILES

Classification of Infant*	Weight	Length	Head Circ
Large for Gestational Age (LGA) (>90th percentile)			
Appropriate for Gestational Age (AGA) (10th to 90th percentile)			
Small for Gestational Age (SGA) (<10th percentile)			

*Place an "X" in the appropriate box (LGA, AGA or SGA) for weight, for length and for head circumference.

References

1. Battaglia FC, Lubchenco LO: A practical classification of newborn infants by weight and gestational age. *J Pediatr* 1967; 71:159-163.
2. Lubchenco LO, Hansman C, Boyd E: Intrauterine growth in length and head circumference as estimated from live births at gestational ages from 26 to 42 weeks. *Pediatrics* 1966; 37:403-408.

Reprinted by permission from Dr. Battaglia, Dr. Lubchenco, *Journal of Pediatrics* and *Pediatrics*

Maturational Asessment of Gestational Age (New Ballard Score)

Ballard JL, Khoury JC, Wedig K, et al: New Ballard Score, expanded to include extremely premature infants. *J Pediatr* 1991; 119:417-423.

Neuromuscular Maturity

	-1	0	1	2	3	4	5
Posture							
Square Window (wrist)	>90°	90°	60°	45°	30°	0°	
Arm Recoil		180°	140°–180°	110°–140°	90°–110°	<90°	
Popliteal Angle	180°	160°	140°	120°	100°	90°	<90°
Scarf Sign							
Heel to Ear							

(continued next page)

1-25

Physical Maturity

	-1	0	1	2	3	4	5
Skin	sticky friable transparent	gelatinous red, translucent	smooth pink, visible veins	superficial peeling &/or rash, few veins	cracking pale areas rare veins	parchment deep cracking no vessels	leathery cracked wrinkled
Lanugo	none	sparse	abundant	thinning	bald areas	mostly bald	
Plantar Surface	heel-toe 40-50 mm: -1 <40 mm: -2	>50mm no crease	faint red marks	anterior transverse crease only	creases ant. 2/3	creases over entire sole	
Breast	imperceptible	barely perceptible	flat areola no bud	stippled areola 1-2mm bud	raised areola 3-4mm bud	full areola 5-10mm bud	
Eye/Ear	lids fused loosely: -1 tightly: -2	lids open pinna flat stays folded	sl. Curved pinna; soft; slow recoil	well-curved pinna; soft but ready recoil	formed & firm instant recoil	thick cartilage ear stiff	
Genitals male	scrotum flat, smooth	scrotum empty faint rugae	testes in upper canal rare rugae	testes descending few rugae	testes down good rugae	testes pendulous deep rugae	
Genitals female	clitoris prominent labia flat	prominent clitoris small labia minora	prominent clitoris enlarging minora	majora & minora equally prominent	majora large minora small	majora cover clitoris & minora	

Maturity Rating

Score	weeks
-10	20
-5	22
0	24
5	26
10	28
15	30
20	32
25	34
30	36
35	38
40	40
45	42
50	44

Reprinted by permission of Dr. Ballard and Mosby-Year Book, Inc.
Perform at < 12 hours of age - score 2x by 2 different examiners.

2 Transport

Chapter Contents

Transport

Procedure for *Referring* Hospital

Indications

* From level I hospitals to Level II or III

  These are suggested guidelines by Amer. Acad. of Pediatrics, 2007; ***Guidelines for air and ground transport of neonatal and pediatric patients***, 3rd Ed. and are not all-inclusive. The decision to transport should be based on the patient's projected needs and the ability of the hospital to meet those needs.

Neonatal Conditions

Gestational age < 34 wks.

Birth weight < 2000 gm

Resp. distress:

  ≥ 40% to abolish cyanosis

  PaO_2 < 60 in 40% O_2

    (<2000 gm) (Level III)

  PaO_2 < 60 in 60% O_2

    (>2000 gm) (Level III)

  Persisting metabolic acidosis after 2 hrs. (< 7.20)

  Persisting respiratory distress after 1 hr.

  Progressive increasing respiratory distress

  Any condition requiring ventilatory support > 1 hr.

Birth asphyxia or shock:

  Apgar < 3 @ 1 min.

  Apgar < 5 @ 5 min.

Meconium aspiration:

  below cords. @ birth,

  with resp. distress, > 40% O_2 needed or air leaks.

Cardiac disorders with persisting cyanosis

Congenital malformations (requiring investigation or surgery, eg. diaphramatic hernia)

Hypoglycemia

Hypovolemia

Infants of diabetic mothers (IDM)

Seizures

Hemolytic disease

Sepsis or meningitis

Infants of mothers on hazardous drugs

Neonates requiring more than routine care or observation

Maternal Conditions

Obstetric

PROM (@ < 34 wks. or < 2000 gm expected)

Premature labor (< 2000 gm expected)

Probable birth (< 2000 gm expected)

Severe preeclampsia

Multiple gestation

IUGR with fetal distress

Third trimester bleeding

Rh isoimmunization

Premature dilation of cervix

Medical

Infections (which may result in premature birth)

Hepatitis, Influenza, Pneumonia, Others

Organic heart disease (Class III or IV)

Diabetes mellitus (poorly controlled)

Thyrotoxicosis

Renal disease ($\downarrow$ fx or $\uparrow$ BP)

Drug Overdose

Any severe illness

Hypotension

Surgical

Trauma or surgery which may result in premature labor or
    require intensive care

Acute abdominal emergencies

Thoracic emergencies requiring ICU or surgery

S.T.A.B.L.E. Additional Suggestions

The goal of all neonatal transport teams is to transport a well-
    stabilized infant,

This is best done by transporting the mother prior to delivery (when
    possible).

When not possible, efforts should be made to have qualified teams
    present at birth.

Minimally, team members should have NRP certification - ideally,
    team members will have S.T.A.B.L.E. certification

(see stableprogram.com for more information on certification)

Inter-Hospital Communication

The referral hospital should call for transport *as soon* as the need is apparent (or if anticipated).

The following info should be provided to the receiving hospital when the request is made:

Neonatal Patient	Maternal Patient
Gestational age	Reason for admission and transfer
Weight	Perinatal history
Perinatal history	Age
Vital signs	Date of last menstrual period
Respiratory activity	Est. date of confinement
O2 needs	Gravida, para, abortions
Ventilation needs	Relevant health problems
RR and depth/pattern	Blood type
Cardiac status	I&O
HR	Amniocentesis results
BP	Therapies & drugs administered
Temperature	Group B Strep status
Color	Maternal vital signs
Lab results	Fetal position/assessment
Blood glucos or Chemstrip	Cervical exam (if contracting)
ABGs	
HCT	
X-ray findings	
Types of lines in place	
Therapies & drugs administered	
Reason for transfer	

Adapted from *Guidelines for Perinatal Care* (AAP & ACOG), 6th ed., 2007, American Academy of Pediatrics

Stabilization

Maternal Stabilization

Hemodynamic support

Initiate tocolytics, anticonvulsants or antihypertensive agents as indicated.

Initiate treatment for active bleeding, preeclampsia, or rapidly progressive labor.

The possibility of delivery or the development of an acute crisis in transport should be minimized.

If maternal transport is not possible it is advisable to have the transport team present at delivery to assist in the initial stabilization.

Newborn Stabilization

Overview of Care (in relative order of importance)

Main Goals:	Prevent/Correct
Respiratory care.............	Asphyxia, hypoxia, hypercarbia
Thermal support.............	Hypothermia
Hemodynamic support...	Hypovolemia, hypotension
Glucose homeostasis......	Hypoglycemia
Acid-base balance..........	Acidosis

Transport

Respiratory Care

Airway Ensure open airway.
Suction prn (80-100 mmHg)

Oxygenation

Indications (see Pg 8-2)

Keep PaO_2 50-80 mmHg (see pg 8-2) or give just enough to relieve central cyanosis if no ABG's available.

Keep O_2 Sat > 85%

Note: In term or post-term infants with PPHN may want to keep PaO_2 > 100 mmHg or SaO_2 > 95%.

O_2 should be delivered as accurately as possible (blender or venturi).

A hood inside an incubator is better than flooding the incubator.

The FiO_2 should be analyzed continuously.

Use warm & humidified gases (cold gases will decrease body temp).

Use CPAP if indicated (pg 9-2) & available (do not use in Meconium Aspiration, CDH or other air-trapping).

Ventilation

Keep $PaCO_2$ 40-50 mmHg (permissive hypercapnia now widely used).

Manual ventilation — <u>always</u> use with a pressure manometer in line & keep PIP as low as possible to still achieve adequate chest expansion and breath sounds.

Indications for intubation and mech. vent.
(see pgs 6-15 & 10-2).

Do not use ventilators unless designed for neonatal/pediatric use.

Thermal Support

Immediately place in neutral thermal environment (see pg 7-3)

Use warmer, double wall incubator, plastic heat shield or plastic blankets as indicated and available.

Use warm water bottles cautiously and avoid direct skin contact.

Do not use gooseneck lamps.

Minimize time outside incubator.

Use portals only for manipulation.

Keep abdominal skin temp 36—36.5°C (see Page 7-3)

Correct hypothermia — to heat up, use an environmental temp of max 1.5° C > abdominal temp.

Signs & Symptoms of Hypothermia	Hypoxia ↓ peripheral perfusion ↑ PVR Hypoglycemia Metabolic acidosis

Hemodynamic support

Maintain pulse

Maintain systolic BP:	Ex: > 40 mmHg (1 Kg) > 50 mmHg (2 Kg) > 60 mmHg (3 Kg)
BPsys = [wt(Kg) + 3]10	

Maintain HCT > 40%

if anemic: Begin cross-match procedure before transport
for emergency: use non-cross matched type O neg cells

Correct hypovolemia: 10 cc/Kg NS (first choice)
(Caution in RDS or meningitis)

2-6

Signs & Symptoms of Hypovolemia	Persistent ↑ in heart rate Skin gray, dusky, pale & cool ↓ capillary refill ↓ BP Weak femoral pulses ↓ CVP (via UVC) ↓ Output (< 1 mg/Kg/hr)

Vascular access: Peripheral IV may be adequate
A-line +/or CVP preferred
UAC — is most often used
UVC — is the quickest & easiest

Umbilical Line Placement	High	Low
UAC	T6-T8	L3-L4
UVC	T11-T12 (above dia-phragm, not in heart)	Should be placed high

Glucose Homeostasis

Maintain 40-120 mg/dl (provide continuous IV infusion)
Use D5W(< 1 Kg)
D10W (>1 Kg)
D5•2NS (>1 day & stable glucose)
Avoid hypertonic glucose solutions

Daily Fluid Requirements (cc/kg/day)	80	100
D5W (mg/kg/min)	2.5	3.5
D10W(mg/kg/min)	5.0	7.0

If normoglycemic: Preterm 4-6 mg/kg/min
Term 6-8 mg/kg/min
If hypoglycemic: Give 2cc D10W/kg push then
8-10 mg/kg/min and titrate.

Signs & Symptoms of Hypoglycemia	Apnea
	Convulsions
	Cyanosis
	Coma
	Hypotonia

High Risks for hypoglycemia

Premie	Stressed
SGA	IDM
LGA	Sepsis
RDS	Hypothermic
Asphyxia	Polycythemia

Acid-Base Balance

Respiratory acidosis — correct alveolar ventilation

Metabolic acidosis — correct oxygenation, ventilation and perfusion then give NaHCO₃ therapy if pH < 7.20, HCO₃ < 15 mEq/L and BD > 10 mEq (mEq NaHCO₃ = BD × 0.3 × Kg) (infuse < 1 mL/Kg/min)

Other

Urine output   place urine bag on all transports

X-rays   chest: Resp. distress or lung pathology

CHF

Diaphragmatic hernia

Esophageal atresia or T-E fistula

Abdomen: distention

Tubes & catheters: to check location

NG/OG Tubes   All patients should have stomach contents aspirated before transport.

The tube may be left in place for transport, or removed as indicated.

> *Absolute indications:*
> Diaphragmatic hernia
> Ventilation with bag & mask
> Nasal CPAP
> Bowel obstruction or ileus
> EA or T-E fistula
> Vomiting

Suspected sepsis/meningitis — obtain blood & other appropriate cultures and begin broad spectrum antibiotics.

Specific Clinical Problems

In addition to the above stabilization procedure, specific attention is given the following:

RDS — Intubate before transport. Controversial whether to give surfactant prior to transport (due to significant compliance changes). Consultation advised.

Diaphragmatic hernia — (See Pg 11-45)
Do not ventilate with bag/mask.
Intubate immediately, may wish to sedate and paralyze
Pass N-G tube (constant low suction).
Ventilate with minimal pressures.
Ensure adequate O_2 (usually 100% O_2), CO_2 & pH prior to departure (ABG, CBG, or VBG)

Cyanotic congenital heart disease — (see Pg 11-31)
Cautious use of O_2 —
$\downarrow PaO_2$ ($\downarrow FiO_2$ or $\uparrow$ altitude) may open shunt
$\uparrow PaO_2$ may close a pre-existing shunt

Communication with a pediatric cardiologist is advisable.

Air leaks — correct before transport (esp. air transport) (see Pg 6-30 and Barotrauma, Pg 11-4)

Signs & Symptoms of Pneumothorax	$\uparrow$ Hemithorax size
	Shift of heart sounds
	Sudden $\downarrow$ BP
	Sudden change in HR & RR
	Narrowing of pulse pressure
	$\downarrow PaO_2$
	Sudden $\downarrow$ size of ECG complex

Esophageal atresia (EA) & TE fistula — (see Pg 11-80)
X-ray to confirm (use radio-opaque tube)
Place catheter to drain any pouch (low intermittent Sx)
Positioning: T-E — HOB elevated on right side
EA — HOB down on right side
Keep infant from crying (if possible)
Do not use mechanical ventilation (if possible)

Heart failure — begin digitalis & diuretics

Seizures — Perform Chemstrip® before transport
                    Anticonvulsants if indicated
                        (Phenobarbitol, 20 mg/kg IV is first choice)

Intestinal obstruction
    Place NG tube with frequent suction
    Keep HOB elevated (esp. if distended)
    X-ray with contrast (remove contrast before transport)
    Obtain cultures and begin antibiotics

Open lesions (omphalocele, gastroschisis, myelomeningocele)
    Immediately pass NG tube
    Do not rupture sac
    Ensure against heat & fluid loss:
        Cover lesions with warm saline soaks (sterile) and cover
        lower body with sterile plastic bag
    Avoid contamination
    Obtain appropriate cultures & start antibiotics

Record		
Vital signs	Incubator temp
I&O	Ventilator parameters
Apgars	Drug therapies
Time of first urine and meconium	Signs & symptoms
Quantity of gastric aspirate	X-ray & lab reports
FiO_2 given	Histories

Preparations for Transport

Explain & obtain consent from parents, arrange for baptism (if desired) before transport

Prepare records & document copies for transport team:
    Mother & infant charts, history, physical exams, drugs & procedures given, lab results, X-rays, etc.

Prepare specimens for transport team:
    Mother's blood (5-10 cc), cord blood (5-10 cc), placenta (if requested by protocol)

Referring MD should remain with patient until transport team arrives to insure proper care and communication.

Preparation

Upon obtaining referral request:
Receiving hospital should discuss evaluation and stabilization plans with referring MD. (Primary focus of referral hospital should be supportive care rather than extensive diagnostic evaluations)
Obtain proper info
Give estimated arrival time (teams should be ready to go within 10 min.)

Delegate Transport Team:

The transport team should be experienced staff and not a local ambulance service with unqualified personnel.

Team member qualifications should match the needs of the patient (ie, a respiratory therapist should attend any respiratory distress, an MD is often not required, esp. if two-way communication is available).

Technical expertise available on each team should include the following:

Newborn pathology	Recognition and management of the following complications:
Identification of high risk factors & possible complications	
Resuscitation/relieve airway obstruction	Hypoxemia/asphyxia
	Hypercarbia
Manual/mechanical ventilation	Respiratory distress
Oxygenation	Air leaks
Intubation	(chest tube insertion)
Thermal support	Accidental extubation
ABG interpretation	Vomiting/aspiration
Arterial & venous catheter placement	Cardiorespiratory arrest
	Apnea of newborn
Estimation of gestational age	Hypothermia
Hemodynamic support	Hypoglycemia
Emergency drugs (indications & dosages)	Hypovolemia
	Types of shock
Transport procedures	Seizures

Arrange for Mode of Transport

Factors to Consider in Selecting Transport Mode
Travel Time (should be under 2 hours one way)
Distance (ambulance <100 miles, helicopter 100-250 miles, fixed wing >250 miles)
Terrain (traffic congestion affects ambulance, helicopters can reach remote areas & avoid traffic)
Weather
Availability of vehicle & crew
Landing sites for air transports/need for ambulance on landing?
Space available (often limited in helicopters & small planes)
Interior lighting (possible for night flights?)
Two-way communication available (cell or satellite phone?)
Noise level (often excessive via air)
Vibration & rotational forces (may be issue in helicopters)
Pressurization of aircraft (fixed wing - maybe, helicopters - no)
Adequate O_2, air & suction available
Cabin temp needs to be monitored/controlled - air + ground
Ability to assess patient +/or perform procedures, eg. intubation, suction, etc. (vibration makes it difficult to observe chest expansion; noise makes it impossible to auscultate; turbulent forces and cramped quarters make it difficult if not impossible to perform procedures; aircraft just can't "pull over")
Will monitoring equipment interfere with aircraft navigational equipment?
Electrical hookups available with adequate grounding?
  12V/DC, 110V/AC with inverters — ambulances, helicopters, and light aircraft
  24-28 V/DC (AC Inverters?)— larger aircraft
  110 V/AC 400 HZ — jet aircraft
  110V/AC 60 HZ — household
  (Voltage and amp differences may affect motors [infusion pumps] and digital timers [ventilators])

Check Supplies and Equipment
O_2 supply: check pressures (Carry 2X the calculated O_2 requirement (see next page, and Pg 2-18)
Necessary wrenches/adaptors for O_2 connections

The O_2 supply required for mechanical ventilators requires the dialed-in flowrate plus the flowrate required to run the vent (check vent specs in operator's manuals).

Check all batteries (all electrical equipment should have sufficient battery backup for the <u>entire duration</u> of the transport including unexpected delays.) Check all electrical equipment for functioning & accuracy.

Warm incubator.

Duration of oxygen supply from cylinders

Duration of flow at various cylinder presures				
Flow rate (LPM)	2,000 psi	1,500 psi	1,000 psi	500 psi
E Cylinder: approximate minutes of flow				
2	280	210	140	70
4	140	105	70	35
6	93	70	47	23
8	70	53	35	17
10	56	42	28	14
12	47	35	23	12
15	37	28	19	9
H Cylinder: approximate hours of flow				
2	52	39	26	13
4	26	19	13	6
6	17	13	8	4
8	13	9	6	3
10	10	7	5	2
12	8	6	4	2
15	6	5	3	1

Adapted from Segal: *Transport of High Risk Newborn Infants.* Canadian Pediatric Society, 1972. Sherbrooke, Quebec.

Cylinder flow time Pressure in cylinder (Pcyl) × Conversion factor (CF)
$$\text{Cylinder flow time} = \frac{\text{Pressure in cylinder (Pcyl)} \times \text{Conversion factor (CF)}}{\text{flowrate (l/m)}}$$

$CF = \dfrac{\text{ft}^3 \text{ of cyl} \times 28.3}{\text{max Pcyl}}$

Cylinder Conversion Factors

Size	ft³	factor
A	2.7	0.035
B	5.3	0.068
D	12.6	0.16
E	22	0.28
G	186	2.41
H/K	244	3.14
M	128	1.65

Initial Evaluation and Stabilization of Patient

Evaluate:	Apply monitors:	
History	HR & RR	Assess primary diagnosis
Physical exam	Temp	Assess patient's condition
ABGs	BP	Assess presence or potential of compli-
X-rays	FiO_2	cating conditions
Lab	Pulse oximeter	
	IV	

Stabilize (See pages 2-3 through 2-7)

Complete any stabilization procedures not accomplished by the referring hospital. (The team should remember that the referring hospital personnel have probably performed to the best of their ability [regardless of pt's condition]). Each visit should present as a teaching and learning opportunity.

Stabilization prior to transport is probably the most important aspect of inter-hospital care. Patient deterioration enroute may not be detectable or treatable.

Stabilize as completely as feasible the following:

Temperature, ABGs (O_2, vent, pH), Vascular volume, Vital signs, and Glucose

Complete stabilization may not be possible but transport of an extremely unstable infant is usually contraindicated.

Just prior to leaving —

Intubate — if clinically indicated and any possibility of needing one enroute (prophylactic is sometimes advisable if by helicopter) (e.g., PGE infusion-related apnea) (x-ray to confirm position)

Tube Size (I.D. mm)	Patient Weight	Gestational Age
2.5	Below 1000 gm	Below 28 weeks
3.0	1000 - 2000 gm	28-34 weeks
3.5	2000 - 3000 gm	34-38 weeks
3.5 - 4.0	Above 3000 gm	Above 38 weeks

Reprinted with permission from ***Neonatal Resuscitation Textbook, 2000.***

Transport

ET tube positioning: 1000 gm - 7 cm @ lip
2000 gm - 8 cm @ lip
3000 gm - 9 cm @ lip
Ensure ET tube is well secured.

1-2-3-4 Rule	
1 x ETT size =	ETT Size
2 x ETT size =	NG, Foley, Sx cath size
3 x ETT size =	ETT depth
4 x ETT size =	Chest-tube size

Ensure airway clear — suction if indicated

Initiate mechanical ventilation (on transport ventilator) — if
any possibility of needing it enroute

Mechanical ventilation is preferred over manual ventilation

Self-inflating bags are safer and more consistent than flow-
inflating bags.

A pressure manometer is <u>always</u> used.

The mechanical ventilator ideally should be powered &
controlled by compressed gas (low consumption) and
provide all modes including continuous flow, CPAP,
PEEP & IMV

Chest tube placement (or Heimlich valve) — should be
inserted before transport, if indicated. Note: gas expansion
may occur via air transport.

Ensure transport incubator is warm — should begin heating
when first leave for referring hospital (use AC power
whenever possible).

Prior to Departure.

Ensure adequate O_2/Compressed air supply

Ensure MV is properly adjusted

Obtain all documents & specimens (lab, x-ray, mom & cord
blood, etc.)

Call receiving hospital: Give brief explanation of baby's
condition and equipment needed upon arrival

Visit parents

Let parents see and touch child, if possible, and , leave
photo of child with the family, provide emotional support

Explain diagnosis, reason for transport, prognosis, likely
events and care, obtain consent forms, allow time for
baptism, leave info with family: names and #'s of doc-
tors and nurses, map, visiting hours/rules, assistance
groups, lodging, etc., instruct supporting family members to follow when feasible.

Notify receiving hospital of ETA

Transport (En Route)

A well-stabilized pt should require little intervention during
transport.

The patient should remain under constant observation.

Continuous monitoring (or q15 min checks) should include:

Infant	Ventilator	Maternal
Temperature	parameters	HR
HR & EKG	PIP or V_T	RR & pattern
RR & pattern	Rate	BP
BP	PEEP	Uterine
Color	IV therapy	contractions
Activity	O_2/Air	Cervical dilation
F_1O_2	pressures	Fetal HR
O_2 Sat		Deep tendon
Blood glucose		reflexes
(Chemstrip®)		IV therapy

If possible, have alternative referral sites or temporary stops
identified in case of vehicle malfunction or patient deterioration.

Physiological effects of altitude (non-pressurized aircraft)

   ↑ Altitude

     ↓ PiO_2 → ↓PaO_2 Increase FiO_2 to maintain SaO_2

         ↑PDA   or read table (page 2-18)

      Gas expansion (closed spaces) —

         Thoracic gas → air leaks

         Intestinal gas → distention › ↑ diaphragm, vomiting &
           aspiration

         Ensure NG tube is placed in all air transport patients

         Air space above IV bottle

           ↑ pressure → forcible infusion

           Keep vent port open. Use infusion pump or vacuum packed
            infusion bags.

   ↓ Altitude

     ↑ PiO_2 → ↑ PaO_2 → RLF Adjust FiO_2 accordingly.

      Gas contraction —

         Air space above IV bottle

           ↓ press → vacuum → hemorrhage into IV line (see
           above)

On arrival Assist with admission as indicated

              Call back referring hospital to notify of safe arrival

              Complete documentation and communication to staff

              Immediately restock transport supplies

              Evaluate transport

Transport

Altitude Chart

Altitude (ft)	Barometric Pressure (mmHg)	FiO₂ Required to Maintain Constant PaO₂ [1]									PiO₂ While Breathing: 0.21	0.40	0.60	0.80	1.0	
16000	412	0.41	0.59	0.78	0.98						76	146	219	292	365	184
14000	446	0.37	0.53	0.71	0.89						83	160	239	319	399	170
12000	483	0.34	0.49	0.65	0.81	0.98					91	174	262	349	436	157
10000	523	0.31	0.45	0.60	0.75	0.90					100	190	286	381	476	145
8000	564	0.29	0.41	0.55	0.69	0.83	0.96				108	207	310	414	517	135
6000	609	0.27	0.38	0.51	0.63	0.76	0.89				118	226	337	450	562	125
4000	656	0.24	0.35	0.47	0.58	0.70	0.82	0.94			127	244	365	487	609	116
2000	707	0.23	0.32	0.43	0.54	0.65	0.76	0.86	0.97		138	264	396	528	660	107
Sea Level	760	0.21	0.30	0.40	0.50	0.60	0.70	0.80	0.90	1.0	149	285	428	570	713	100

1) As compared to that required at sea level.

$PIO_2 = (P_B-47) (FiO_2)$

$PAO_2 = PiO2 - PaCO_2 (1.25)$

Resp Assessment

Five Parameters for Rapid Assessment of Breathing

Parameter	Mild	Moderate	Severe
Mental Status	Normal	Agitated	Lethargic
Color	Normal	Pale/mottled	Cyanotic
Air Entry	Normal	Moderately decreased	Markedly decreased
Grunting, Flaring Retracting	Absent/mild	Moderate	Severe
Respiratory Rate	Normal	Moderately increased	Markedly increased
Newborn	40-45	45-60	60+
6 mos-2 yr	30-40	40-50	50+
2-10 yrs	20-30	30-40	40+
> 10 yrs	20	20-30	30+

RESPIRATORY RATES

Age	Norm Rate/Min.	Bradypnea	Tachypnea
Newborn	30-60	< 30	> 60
Ist yr	24-40	< 25	> 40
1-4 yrs	20-30	< 20	> 30
4-6 yrs	20-25	< 20	> 25
5-12 yrs	16-20	< 16	> 20
> 12 yrs	12-16	< 12	> 16

Distinct chest excursion is often unclear, esp. in the small tachypneic infant. (Respiratory rate, therefore, is always best measured using a stethoscope.) Note, however, that the touch of the stethoscope will often increase respiratory rate! Count for a full 60 sec. to detect irregularities. Crying will ↑ resp. rate. Resp. may be > 50 for first hour or two after birth.

LUNG TOPOGRAPHY

The infant and child's lungs are situated in the chest the same as an adult. Hence the imaginary lines and thoracic cage landmarks are the same.

Inspection, palpation, percussion & ausculation are employed as with adults. Findings, however, are often of limited and questionable value in neonates (percussion is difficult, breath and bowel sounds may be transmitted more widely, upper airway BS may be misidentified as adventitious BS in lower airways).

A&P Characteristics of the Newborn's Respiratory System

Structure	Characteristic	Consequence
Nose	Obligatory nasal breathing	Poor tolerance to obstruction
Tongue	Relatively large	Neck extension may not relieve obstruction
Head	Relatively large	Anterior flexion may cause airway obstruction
Epiglottis	Relatively large & U-shaped	More susceptible to trauma and forms more acute angle with vocal cords
Larynx	More anterior and cephalad	Intubation more difficult
Cricoid	Narrowest portion of airway	↑ Resistance with airway edema or infection. Acts as "cuff" during tracheal intubation.
Trachea	Small diameter (6 mm), high compliance	↑ Resistance with airway edema or infection. Collapses easily with neck hyperflexion or hyperextension.
Alveoli	↑ Closing capacity No pores of Kohn	↑ Air trapping and ↓ collateral circulation of air
Pulmonary vessels	↑ PVR	Very sensitive to vasoconstriction by hypoxia, acidosis & hypercarbia
Chest wall	↑ Compliance due to weak rib cage; ↑ A-P diameter; Ribs horizontal	Breathing is all diaphramatic (abdominal). FRC determined solely by elastic recoil of lungs. Chest wall collapses with neg. pressures.
Work of breathing	Increases at lower rates plus poor respiratory muscles	↑ RR equals early sign of respir distress
Regulation of breathing	Response to ↓O$_2$ is minimal; Response to ↑CO$_2$ is minimal in premie	Tolerates hypoxia poorly. Apneic spells.

Resp Assessment

Additional A & P Characteristics of Premature Infants

- ↓ # & size of alveoli
- ↓ surfactant
- ↑ alveolar/capillary distance
- ↓ gas exchange surface
- ↓ resp. muscle mass
- ↓ work of breathing endurance
- ↑ chest wall compliance
- ↓ nutritional reserves
- ↓ CNS control of respiratory system

Respiratory Distress

Signs of Respiratory Distress (and/or Inadequate Ventilation)	
Apnea	Hyperexpansion of chest
Bradycardia	Marked retractions
Bradypnea	Mottled color
Breath sounds decreased	Nasal flaring
Central cyanosis	Responsiveness change
Drooling (child)	SpO_2 decreased
Dyspnea or labored breathing	Stridor
Gasping	Tachycardia
Grunting	Tachypnea
Hemoptysis	Weak/ineffective cry
Hypercarbia	Weak muscle tone
Hypoxemia	Wheeze
Irregular pattern	↑ T_I or ↑ T_E

Differential Diagnosis of Respiratory Distress

Signs of Upper Respiratory Tract Involvement

Acute:	Non-acute:
Barking cough (see page 11-40)	Cough
Cyanosis	Ear ache
Drooling	Hoarseness
Hoarseness	Nasal congestion
Stridor	Sore throat
Retractions	
Supraclavicular	
Suprasternal	
↓ BS	
↑ T_I	

Signs of Lower Respiratory Tract Involvement

Acute:	Chronic:
Coarse Crackles	Cough
Cough	Chest pain
Cyanosis	Hemoptysis
Dyspnea	Hyperexpansion
Grunting	
Nasal flaring	
Retractions	
Intercostal	
Subcostal	
Tachypnea	
Wheezing	
Chest pain	
Hemoptysis	
Hyperexpansion	
↓ BS	
↑ T_E	

Signs of Airway Obstruction (see page 11-7)

Differential Diagnosis of Respiratory Distress in the Newborn by Common Causes

Pulmonary Disorders

Pulmonary:	Extrapulmonary
RDS or HMD	*Vascular*
TTN	PPHN
Meconium aspiration (MAS)	CHD
Group B — strep pneumonia	CHF
Barotrauma	PDA
Pneumothorax	Anemia
PIE	Polycythemia
Bronchopulmonary dysplasia	Hypovolemia
(BPD)	*Metabolic*
Diaphragmatic hernia	Asphyxia
T-E fistula	Acidosis
Upper Airway obstruction	Acites
Choanal atresia	Hypocalemia
Pierre-Robin	Hypoglycemia
Vascular rings	Hypothermia
Ribcage abnormalities	
Lobar emphysema	*Neuromuscular*
Pulmonary hemorrhage	Apnea of prematurity
Drugs - intoxification or	Maternal drugs
withdrawal	Cerebral hemorrhage
	Cerebral edema
	Muscle disorders
	Seizure disorders
	Phrenic nerve damage
	Meningitis

Differential Diagnosis of Respiratory Distress in the Newborn by Characteristics of Onset

Onset	Sudden	Gradual or Progressive
Birth	Pneumothorax	HMD
	Apnea	TTN
		PPHN
	Asphyxia	Pneumonia (group B streptococci, etc.)
	Maternal drugs	Meconium aspiration
	Choanal atresia	Congenital heart disease
	Diaphragmatic hernia	Hypoplastic left heart syndrome
		Transposition
		Pulmonary atresia
		Lung hypoplasia
0–7 days	Pneumothorax,	Pneumonia
	pneumomediastinum	Congenital intrathoracic lesions
	Apnea	Congenital heart disease
	Prematurity	Hypoplastic left heart syndrome
	CNS hemorrhage	Coarctation
	Sepsis	Ventricular defect
	Hypoglycemia	Tetralogy of Fallot
	Pulmonary hemorrhage	Patent ductus arteriosus
	Aspiration	Endocardial cushion defect
		Malposition
		Distended abdomen

Adapted from Hay, W., et al., *Current Diagnosis and Treatment in Pediatrics*, 18th ed., 2007, Lange/McGrawHill.

Differential Diagnosis of Respiratory Distress by Acute Signs *	Apnea	↓HR	Cyanosis	↓Muscle Tone	Grunting	Flaring	Retractions	Stridor	↑RR	Wheeze	BS	Other
Apnea	‡	‡									(↓)→	
Asphyxia	‡	‡	‡	‡								
Bacterial Pneumonia	+	‡			‡	‡		‡			→	Fine rales
Choanal atresia		‡					+	‡				
Diaphragmatic Hernia	+	‡										Scaphoid abdomen
Maternal Drugs	‡		‡	+								
Meconium aspiration	+	+	+		+	+		‡		→		Coarse rales & rhonchi, staining
Pneumothorax		‡		+	+	+		‡		→	→	Asymmetrical excursion BS or same side
RDS (HMD)		‡		‡	‡	+		‡		→	→	Fine rales
TTN								‡		→		Coarse rales & rhonchi

*The presence (or absence) of each sign often depends on the severity of the disease. Usually the greater the severity, the greater the number and intensity of the signs.

Differential diagnosis of respiratory distress in some specific disease states

	RDS	PPHN	Group B Strep	TTN	MAS
Gestation	Usually preterm	Often term	Preterm or term	More often term	Usually post-term
Perinatal history	APH, IDM, rhesus	Asphyxia, aspirin in pregnancy	Uterine inertia Asphyxia, PROM	IDM, C/S, asphyxia	Asphyxia, IUGR
Clinical features	Grunting prominent Gradual deterioration	Cyanosis prominent Sudden deterioration	Shock prominent Early apnea Pulmonary hemorrhage	RR > 60, Mild distress	Meconium staining Overinflated chest Progressive deterioration
Effect of oxygen	Improvement	Cyanosis unchanged	May improve	Improvement	May improve
Blood gases	Hypoxemia Raised PCO_2 Mixed acidosis	Marked hypoxemia Low or normal PCO_2 Metabolic acidosis (R) Radial/aorta difference	Hypoxemia, Metabolic or mixed acidosis	Mild hypoxem. Low or normal PCO_2 Mild metabolic acidosis	Hypoxemia Metabolic acidosis
Chest X-ray	Underinflation Reticulogranular mottling Air bronchogram	Overinflation Clear lung fields Cardiomegaly	Coarse infiltrates Collapse or mimic RDS	Overinflation Streaking ↑ Pulm. vasc. Pulm. edema Sl cardiomegaly	Coarse infiltrates Overinflation ± pneumothorax

continued next page

Resp Assessment

	RDS	PPHN	Group B Strep	TTN	MAS
Echocardiogram	RPEP/RVET ↑ or N LPEP/LVET N	RPEP/RVET ↑↑ LPEP/LVET often ↑	RPEP/RVET MAY ↑ LPEP/LVET N or ↑	RPEP/RVET N or ↑ LPEP/LVET ↑	RPEP/RVET N or ↑ LPEP/LVET N or ↑
Treatment	CPAP helpful MV	CPAP unhelpful MV, INO or tolazoline	Penicillins, blood transfusion, MV	Oxygen MV CPAP	Airway suction at birth, may need MV, CPAP unhelpful

Adapted from Halliday, H. etal, *Handbook of Neonatal Intensive Care.* Copyright 1981 by Bailliere Tindall LTD.

Respiratory Monitoring

Respiratory Rate

Impedance pneumography — monitors the change in electrical impedance, between two electrodes on the chest, brought about by chest excursions.

Indication — to monitor resp. rate, depth and apnea.

> **Caution**: This is a motion detector and cannot distinguish between breathing and artifact movement (seizure, obstructive apnea, etc.)

Do not use as a sole monitor in obstructive apnea. It should be augmented with transcutaneous, end tidal CO_2 monitoring or pulse oximetry.

> Electrodes are best placed in R & L midaxillary line opposite each other. Change electrode site q day.
> Set sensitivity to detect only effective breathing movements.
> *Increased baseline signal* = air (increased depth, pneumothorax, emphysema).
> *Decreased baseline signal* = liquid (consolidation, atelectasis, effusion)

Oxygen Monitoring

Transcutaneous O_2 pressure ($PtcO_2$ or $TcPO_2$) =
See AARC CPG, "Transcutaneous O_2" in Appendix

Definition — a non-invasive estimate of PaO_2

$$PtcO_2 \approx PaO_2$$

Indications —

Diagnosis, clinical management and early identification of cardiorespiratory problems.

Prevention of hypoxia or hyperoxia.

Evaluate effects of clinical procedures (suctioning, CPT, ABG stick, change in position, etc.)

Monitor effects of apnea, R-L shunts, crying or breath holding.

Determine optimal CPAP or ventilator settings.

Monitor for complications (apnea, airway obstruction, pneu-

mothorax, ventilator malfunction, ET tube position).
PaO$_2$ estimate during transport.
Determine "regional" O$_2$ tension.
Decrease need of frequent ABG sticks.

> Note: Best used in neonatal care (poorer correlation exists
> with age due to ↑ skin thickness).

Technique — a heated Clark electrode placed on the skin surface
measures O$_2$ diffusion from "arterialized" blood flow.

Procedure — (Refer to operator's manual for specific details)

Preferred sites:	Preferred heat range:
Anterior chest, abdomen, back, inner thigh. Older child: upper or forearm, forehead, scrotum Avoid bony prominences and extremities.	43°C-45°C: 43°C Premature infant 44° C Term infant & child 45° C Older child

Note: *Chest in infants < 1 Kg may not have adequate skin flow.*

Change electrode position regularly q2-6 hrs. (see user's manual).
(In infants < 1500 gm, may need to change electrode more often
to prevent burns.)

Advantages —

Decreases the need for frequent ABG sticks.
Continuous monitoring:

Monitors trends in clinical condition (apnea, hyperoxia/
hypoxia)

Indirect detection of shock, shunting, hypotension,
external cooling, pneumothorax, mucous plugging,
extubation, etc.

Provides real time indication of effects of procedures and
therapies

Instant response (15-90 sec.) (after 20 minute warm-up)
No sampling errors
No blood loss
Minimal complications

Precautions —

An accurate prediction of PaO_2 when PaO_2 is < 90 mmHg, normal blood pressure, good local perfusion and patient temperature are within normal limits.

TcPO₂ readings should be above ductus until ductus has closed (esp. if concerned with hyperoxia to eyes).

Not a substitute for ABG's

The relation between $PtcO_2$ and PaO_2 must be established for each patient, upon each electrode change and periodically checked per hospital protocol.

Record $PtcO_2$ at time of ABG withdrawal.

Blisters may form from too high a temp on site not changed regularly.

Keep electrode temp as cool as possible while still maintaining good correlation with PaO_2.

Immediately evaluate reason for poor correlations (may be early sign of sepsis, shock or NEC).

Insure calibration is done away from O_2 sources.

Calibrate at same temp as used on skin.

Keep membrane temp constant.

Do not place electrode under patient (pressure will decrease the blood flow).

Severe retractions may draw air under electrode.

Note: PtcO₂ is dependent on barometric pressure.

Interpretation $PtcO_2 \approx PaO_2$

Maintain $PtcO_2$ at 50-80 mmHg (assuming normal hemoglobin content and no cardiac failure.

Usually $PtcO_2 < PaO_2$, but may be higher (↑ temp shifts oxyheme curve to ®). (Eliminate cause of poor correlation)

When comparing PaO_2 and $PtcO_2$, insure both values obtained either above or below the ductus.

May underestimate PaO_2 in chronic pts (eg: BPD)

Use two electrodes in infants with suspected R → L shunt through a PDA (one on ® shoulder, preductal; the other on the lower abdomen or thigh, postductal). The difference in value reflects the proportion of shunt.

Perfusion monitor — the heating channel can be used as an indication of perfusion to the area. (i.e., blood flow removes heat.)

↑ Blood flow → ↑ heat energy (elect. current) to warm area → PtcO2.
↓ Blood flow → ↓ heat energy (elect. current) to warm area → PtcO2.

↓↓ $PtcO_2$ with norm PaO_2 = circulatory failure
↓↓ $PtcO_2$ with ↓ PaO_2 = respiratory failure

Causes of Poor Correlation of $PtcO_2$ with PaO_2 and $PtcCO_2$ with $PaCO_2$ *
ABG sample error
Air bubbles under electrode (↑ $PtcO_2$) (↓ $PtcCO_2$)
Crying during stick
Decreased BP
Decreased CO
Drugs: Vasoconstrictors or vasodilators
Halothane or nitrous oxide (↑ $PtcO_2$)
Tolazoline (↓ $PtcO_2$)
Hypothermia (< 35°C)
Improper calibration or warm-up time
Improper temp (electrode)
Membrane perforation or protein buildup
Motion artifacts
PaO_2 < 30 mmHg or > 70 mmHg
R-L Shunting
Severe acidosis (< 7.05) (PaO_2); (< 7.30) ($PaCO_2$)
Severe anemia
Site —
Inadequate perfusion, edema, hematoma, obesity, thick skin
Decreased skin perfusion:
shock, local ischemia, vasoconstriction, peripheral shunt

* Therapist must be thoroughly familiar with the user's manual to include proper electrode application and skin preparation, calibration technique, machine error and drift, alarms and troubleshooting procedures.

Resp Assessment

Oximetry

SaO₂ and SpO₂ Monitoring

See AARC CPG "***Pulse Oximetry***" in Appendix

SpO_2 may be a poor indicator of SaO_2. SpO_2 values may vary between
various models of oximeters. Hence, do not interchange oximeters
on the same patient.

Definition — Measure of arterial O_2 saturation

Indications — Conditions which may lead to rapidly
changing O_2 saturations

Techniques — *Noninvasive pulse oximetry (SpO_2)*
Passing the light source through an ear, nose
bridge, finger, forehead, or toe.

> Note: Sensors should be placed where blood
> flow is not diminished.

Invasive oximetry (SaO_2)
The light source is inserted into an umbilical or
peripheral artery via catheter

> Note: Arterial oximetry is performed infre-
> quently in children.

Procedure — Refer to the oximeter operator's manual

Interpretation — Maintain SaO_2 (SpO_2) 90-92% (variable
depending on patient's condition and altitude)
SpO_2 85-92% in VLBW infants is shown to
decrease O_2 toxicity (CLD, ROP)

> SaO_2 < 90% is usually indicative of
> hypoxemia
> SaO_2 > 92% may indicate hyperoxemia
> (especially for the neonate)

Caution — Trends are more important than absolute values.
Baseline correlations should be made with

PaO$_2$ and/or SaO$_2$ (CO-oximetry).

Pulse oximetry alone may not indicate hyperoxemia. With a reading of < 92%, however,
hyperoxemia is unlikely.

Clinical Notes —
Hyperventilation (ex. PPHN) → left shift of oxyhemoglobin
curve → normal sat = ↓ PaO$_2$.
Hence mild ↓ SaO2 may indicate severe ↓ PaO$_2$.

In neonate with PDA:
Monitor upper extremities if desire to monitor LH and
ascending aorta SaO$_2$.
Monitor lower extremities if desire to monitor RH, pulmonary artery and descending aorta SaO$_2$.

Institute appropriate ventilation and oxygenation quickly and
early for ↓ SaO$_2$.

Advantages & Disadvantages of Oximetry	
Advantages	*Disadvantages*
Accurate even with ↓ CO, ↓ BP or ↓ body temp	Accuracy affected by: jaundice, patient movement, skin pigment or thickness, regional blood flow, shock, carboxyheme or metheme, lights, anemia
Continuous monitoring of clinical trends, procedures and therapies	
Decreases need for frequent ABG sticks	Clot formation/embolism (invasive)
Direct, continuous SaO$_2$	Infection (invasive)
Infrequent repositioning required	Movement artifacts (shivering, seizures)
Infrequent sampling errors	
Instant response time	Won't detect hyperoxia (esp. SpO$_2$ > 94%)
Monitors pulse rate	
Virtually no risk (noninvasive)	

Do not repeatedly adjust FiO$_2$ up and down to try and maintain SpO$_2$ within acceptable range.

Keep alarm levels at 85% (low) and 93% (high)

May keep high alarm at 94% for larger VLBW.

↓SpO$_2$ (low alarm)

First, check HR, respiratory effort, appropriate pulse wave, motion artifacts, and how low for how long?

If ↓SpO$_2$ due to apnea or handling, try increasing RR, PEEP, PIP, tactile stimulation or manual ventilation before ↑FiO$_2$.

If ↑FiO$_2$, ↑ 2-5% at a time, and observe for 10 minutes for SpO$_2$ stability.

↑SpO$_2$ (high alarm)

↓FiO$_2$ as fast as necessary, but never more than 2% to 5% at a time, and only if the SpO$_2$ is a "stable" high.

Resp Assessment

Troubleshooting the Pulse Oximeter

	Possible Cause	Recommended Action
? Inaccurate SaO$_2$	Excessive patient movement	Quiet patient, if possible. Check security of sensor; replace if necessary. Move sensor to different site. Change type of sensor used. Use ECG signal synchronization. Select a longer (10-15 sec) averaging time, if possible.
	High carboxyhemoglobin or methemoglobin levels	Measure dysfunctional hemoglobin levels. Measure arterial blood gas. Do not place sensor on same side as indwelling arterial catheter or blood pressure cuff.
	Reduced arterial blood flow	
	Electrocautery interference	Move sensor as far as possible from cautery cable; change sites if necessary. Check sensor; replace if damp. Place oximeter plug into a different circuit from cautery unit.
	Excessive ambient light (surgical lamps, heating lamps, bilirubin lights, bright fluorescent lights, direct sunlight, dark fingernail polish, dark pigmented skin)	Cover sensor with opaque material.

Loss of pulse signal	Constriction by sensor	Check sensor; move to a different site or change type of sensor used.
	Reduced arterial blood flow	Same as above.
	Excessive ambient light	Same as above.
	Anemia	Check patient's hemoglobin. Warm monitoring site and replace sensor.
	Hypothermia	Check patient's condition including vital signs.
	Shock (hypotension, vasoconstriction)	
Inaccurate pulse rate	Excessive patient motion	Same as above. Move sensor to a different site.
	Pronounced dicrotic notch on arterial waveform	Check ECG leads; replace if necessary.
	Poor quality ECG signal	Same as above
	Electrocautery interference	

Resp Assessment

Reprinted with permission from Daily, E.K. and Schroeder, J.S. *Techniques in Bedside Hemodynamic Monitoring, 4th Ed.* Copyright 1989 by C.V. Mosby Co., St. Louis.

$S\overline{v}O_2$ Monitoring

Definition — Measure of mixed venous O_2 saturation.

$$S\overline{v}O_2 \approx O_2 \text{ demand (consumed by body tissue)}$$

Note: $S\overline{v}O_2$ does not correlate well with SaO_2, PaO_2, or CO, especially in critically ill patients.

Indications — Conditions of rapidly changing or unstable cardio-pulmonary function ($S\overline{v}O_2$ changes often precede significant changes in hemodynamics)

3-19

Techniques — *Intermittent sampling* — blood gas from the distal port of a PA catheter.
Continuous monitoring — a fiberoptic catheter is attached to a PA catheter and an oximeter.

Procedures — Refer to Oakes' ***Hemodynamic Monitoring: A Bedside Reference Manual***, and/or the oximeter operator's manual.

Interpretation $S\bar{v}O_2 \approx O_2$ demand (consumed by body tissue)

Normal $S\bar{v}O_2 = 60 - 80\%$

(O_2 supply = O_2 demand)

$S\bar{v}O_2 > 80\% = O_2$ supply > O_2 demand (consumption)
$S\bar{v}O_2 < 60\% = O_2$ supply < O_2 demand (consumption)

Causes of ↑ ***SṽO₂***
1. ↑O_2 delivery [↑ CO (anxiety, septic shock, CO therapy), (↑ CaO_2 (excessive O_2 therapy))]
2. ↓ O_2 demand (hypothermia, induced muscle paralysis, anesthesia, coma, septicemia)
3. L → R shunt
4. Mechanical interference

Causes of ↓ ***SṽO₂***
1. ↓ O_2 delivery [↓ CO (arrhythmias, hypovolemic shock, CHF), ↓ CaO_2 (anemia, hemorrhage, hypoxemia)]
2. ↑O_2 demand (agitation, pain, suctioning, CPT, bathing, (↑ WOB, burns, shivering, seizures, sepsis, hyperthermia)
3. R → L shunt
4. Mechanical interference

Clinical Note
↓ SṽO2 ≤ 5% = maybe clinically insignificant
↓ SṽO2 ≥ 10% for 3 min. (10 min. following positional change) = impending deterioration. An immediate evaluation of the patient's O_2 supply/demand status, catheter position and/or calibration is indicated.

Transcutaneous CO_2 pressure (PtcCO_2 or TcPCO_2)*

Definition — a non-invasive estimate of PaCO_2.

$$PtcCO_2 \sim PaCO_2$$

Indications — Prevention of hyper or hypocapnia

Monitor ventilator therapy (manipulations of PIP, PEEP, ET tube plugging, leaks, V_D/V_T)

Monitor effects of clinical procedures and complications (hyperventilation, muscle paralysis, status asthmaticus)

PaCO_2 estimate during transport

Decrease need of frequent ABG sticks

Evaluate respiratory drive

Technique — a heated Severinghaus (pH) electrode placed on the skin measures CO_2 diffusion from "arterialized" blood flow.

Procedure — (Refer to operator's manual for specific details.)

Preferred site: same as PtcO_2, see pg 3-11

Preferred heat range: 42°-44°C

(Unheated PtcCO_2 probably correlates with PvCO_2)

Change electrode site q 3-4 hrs.

Advantages and Precautions —

same as PtcO_2, see pg 3-11

Interpretation — PtcCO_2 ≈ PaCO_2

Usually PtcCO_2 > PaCO_2 by 2 - 20 mmHg

May overestimate PaCO_2 in chronic pts (eg: BPD)

Less sensitive to changes in skin perfusion than PtcO_2.

↓ CO, ↓ perfusion or acidosis → ↑ PtcCO_2 and less correlation with PaCO_2

Reliable indicator of shock state: PtcCO_2 >> PaCO_2.

See Page 3-14 for other causes of poor correlation.

* See AARC CPG in Appendix.

Resp Assessment

End Tidal CO$_2$ Pressure (Pet CO$_2$)

Definition — A measure of end-tidal CO$_2$ as an estimate of PaCO2:

$$PetCO_2 \approx P_ACO_2 \approx PaCO_2$$

Indications — Similar to PtcCO$_2$ (see previous page)

Technique — End-tidal (exhaled) CO$_2$ is collected from the ET tube or a catheter in the nose and measured via mass spectrophotometer or infrared monitor.

Procedure — Refer to operator's manual

Interpretation — PetCO$_2 \approx P_ACO_2 \approx PaCO_2$

In normal conditions, PetCO$_2$ is a close approximate to PaCO$_2$. (See next page). Trends are more important than absolute values. Not as useful a monitor as PtcCO$_2$ in newborns.

See AARC CPG, "Capnography/Capnometry During Mechanical Ventilation" in Appendix.

See Oakes' *Clinical Practice Pocket Guide to Respiratory Care* for detailed information on capnography and capnometry.

Changes in correlation between $PetCO_2$ and $PaCO_2$ can indicate changes in underlying respiratory physiology. PetCO2 is inaccurate in presence of:

1. A-a CO_2 gradient:
   Severe respiratory disease (eg RDS)
   $$V < Q \rightarrow PetCO_2 < PaCO_2 \approx PaCO_2$$
   Pulmonary embolus or ↓ CO
   $$V > Q \rightarrow PetCO_2 \approx PaCO_2 < PaCO_2$$
2. ↑ Deadspace ventilation
   Rapid and shallow breathing
   $$PetCO_2 < PaCO_2 \approx PaCO_2$$
3. ↑ Alveolar ventilation
   Hyperpnea —
   $$PetCO_2 \approx PaCO_2 < PaCO_2$$

During resuscitation, a very low $PetCO_2$ may be due to poor CO or ET tube misplacement.

A sudden ↓ $PetCO_2$ may indicate extubation or a plugged tube.

Respiratory vs Cardiac Diagnosis

Respiratory Disease	Cardiac Disease
↑ RR before ↑ HR	↑ HR before ↑ RR
Symptoms within first 2 days of birth	Symptoms delayed until 3-5 days after birth
↑ $FiO_2 \rightarrow$ ↑ PaO_2 (unless PPHN)	↑ $FiO_2 \rightarrow$ no significant ↑ PaO_2
CXR → atelectasis, infiltrates, air leaks	CXR → lung fields normal, very dark, or ↓ pulmonary blood flow
ECG → RVH	ECG → ↑ P wave +/or LVH

4 Cardiovascular Assessment

Chapter Contents

Emergency Cardiovascular Signs		
Age	*HR*	*BP sys*
Newborn	< 80	< 50
0-2 yrs	< 80	< 60
2-5 yrs	< 60	< 70
> 5 yrs	< 50	< 90
Heart Arrhythmias		

Clinical Note

Bradycardia is the most common pediatric arrhythmia. The
most common causes are hypoxia or vagal stimulation
(eg. suctioning).

Always check for an oxygenation, airway and/or gas exchange problem.

Profound or persistent bradycardia (in the absence of reversible hypoxia) is ominous and indicates impending arrest.

Physical Exam

Inspection:
Level of consciousness —
Glasgow coma score
—see Pg. 5-3
Body size & shape
Skin—pale/cyanosis
Symmetry of chest
Chest pulsations
Respiratory rate & pattern
see Pg. 3-2
Tachypnea
Dyspnea/PND
Orthopnea
Neck vein distention
Clubbing, Squatting,
Sweating

Palpation:
Peripheral perfusion -
capillary refill time
Pulse —
Peripheral equality
(femoral vs. brachial)
Heave
Thrill
Liver (hepatomegaly)
Spleen (splenomegaly)
Edema
Skin—Warm/cold/clammy/
dry

Percussion
Lung
Heart borders

Ausculation
Heart sounds - Rate/rhythm,
Murmurs
BP in arms & legs see
Pg 4-6

General Assessment — "Good vs. Bad"

Pediatric health care providers should be able to determine when a child "looks good" or "looks bad."

Assess	"Good"	"Bad"
Activity level	Active and moves all extremities	Inactive
Capillary refill	Brisk	Prolonged
Color	Pink mucous membranes and nailbeds	Pale mucous membranes and nailbeds
	Consistent skintones	Mottled skintones or gray pallor or cyanosis
Eye contact	Good	Poor
Feeding behavior	Good	Poor
Muscle tone	Good	Flaccid
Peripheral pulses	Strong	Diminished
Position of comfort	Easily able to find	Unable to find
Response to pain	Normal	Diminished
Response to stimuli	Responsive	Unresponsive
Responsiveness	Alert	Diminished
Temperament on arousal	Normal	Irritable
Temperature of extremities	Warm	Cool
Vital signs	Normal or "appropriate"	Abnormal or "inappropriate"

Note: Correlate clinical and hemodynamic parameters with the child's general appearance. Obtain resting values before touching and stimulating the child. Then compare with parameter values following stimulation.

Blood Flow Through Normal Heart

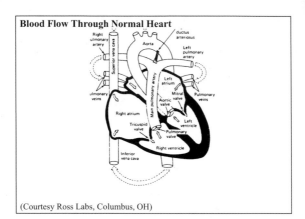

(Courtesy Ross Labs, Columbus, OH)

Heart Rate

Normal Heart Rates in Children*

Age	Awake heart rate (per min)	Sleeping heart rate (per min)
Neonate	100-180	80-160
Infant (6 mo)	100-160	75-160
Toddler	80-110	60-90
Preschooler	70-110	60-90
School-age child	65-110	60-90
Adolescent	60-90	50-90

* Always consider patient's normal range and clinical condition. Heart rate will normally increase with fever or stress. Adapted from: Gillette PC and others: Dysrhythmias. In Adams FH and Emmanouilides GC (eds): *Moss' heart disease in infants, children, and adolescents*, ed. 4, Baltimore, 1989, Williams & Wilkins.

Heart Rate by Pulse:

Pulses in the small newborn are often taken via the brachial or femoral arteries (radial may be too small). Count for a full 60 sec. Crying will increase HR. Palpation rate may vary from actual HR. Best way is to listen at PMI with stethoscope (or watch EKG monitor) while palpating the peripheral pulse and compare.

Abnormal Pulses and Possible Etiologies

Type	Possible Etiologies
Absent (in legs)	Coarctation of aorta
Weak	Dehydration Hypovolemia Shock
Weak (with slow upstroke)	Aortic stenosis Coarctation of aorta Congestive cardiomyopathy
Bounding pulse (rapid & strong)	↑ ICP PDA Systemic A-V fistula Anemia — may cause Aortic insufficiency — sudden Hypotoxicosis — collapse
Pulsus alternans (regular rhythm with alternating strong and weak beats)	Myocardial failure
Pulses pardoxicus (weak on inspiration, strong on expiration) MEDICAL EMERGENCY	Cardiac tamponade Constrictive pericarditis Pericardial effusion Severe RDS Severe air trapping
Dicrotic (double pulse; strong/weak)	Fever Toxemia
Pulsus bigeminus (2 beats close together - coupled)	PVCs

Blood Pressure

Normal Blood Pressure in Neonates and Children *

Age	Systolic pressure (mm Hg)	Diastolic pressure (mm Hg)
Birth (< 750 g)	34-54	14-34
Birth (1000 g)	39-59	16-36
Birth (1500 g)	40-61	19-39
Birth (3 kg)	50-70	25-45
Neonate (96 hr)	60-90	20-60
Infant (6 mo)	87-105	53-66
Toddler (2 yr)	95-105	53-66
School age (7 yr)	97-112	57-71
Adolescent (15 yr)	112-128	66-80

* Blood pressure ranges taken from the following sources: *Neonate:* Versmold H and others: Aortic blood pressure during the first 12 hours of life in infants with birth weight 610-4220 gms, Pediatrics 67:107, 1981. 10th-90th percentile ranges used. *Others:* Horan MJ, chairman: Task Force on Blood Pressure Control in Children, report of the Second Task Force on Blood Pressure in Children, *Pediatrics* 79:1,1987. 50th-90th percentile ranges indicated.

Estimation of Median and Lowest Acceptable Systolic Blood Pressure in Children

Median (50th percentile) systolic blood pressure:
90 mmHg + (2 × age in years) = _____ median systolic BP

Lowest (5th percentile) systolic blood pressure:
70 mmHg + (2 × age in years) = _____ lowest systolic BP

Clinical Note:

Normal BP varies with age

Correct cuff size is important for accuracy (length of inflatable
bladder should be *no less* than 90% of upper arm
circumference).
(See Pg 4-10)

Detection of weak systolic signals may be improved with
Doppler cuffs. (See Pg 4-11)

Infants < 2 yrs — can obtain systolic BP by palpation or
automated oscillometric device.

Trends are more important in the critically ill child.
Use the same method each time.

Document: BP

Extremity used

Method used

$\overline{BP}$ = 1/3 S + 2/3 D (should be ≥ gestational age in neonates)

BP often higher by 20 mmHg in leg than arm (> 1 yr. age)

Crying & agitation will affect BP

AORTIC BP
(during 1st 12 hrs after birth)

MEAN AORTIC & PULSE PRESSURES
(during 1st 12 hrs. after birth)

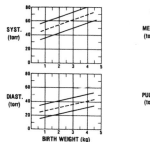

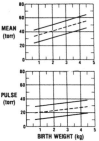

Reprinted with permission from Versmold, H. etal: *Pediatrics* 67:607. Copyright 1981 by Amer. Acad. of Pediatrics.

BP in Boys

BP in Girls

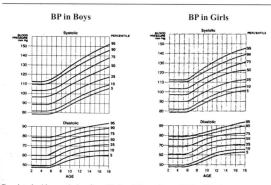

Reprinted with permission from National Heart, Lung & Blood Institute's Task Force on BP Control in Children. *Pediatrics* 59:797, 1977.

Indirect (Non-Invasive) Blood Pressure Measurement

(see Pg. 4-13 for Invasive)

AUSCULTATION OF ARTERIAL PRESSURE

Technique –

Place arm at level of heart, place BP cuff around upper arm, place stethoscope over brachial artery. Inflate cuff to 20-30 mmHg above suspected BP sys. Deflate cuff slowly (≤ 3 mmHg/sec).

BP sys = appearance of sounds.

BP dia = change in character or muffling of sounds (diastolic 1) or cessation of sounds (diastolic 2).

Note: Some clinicians and AHA recommend recording 3 levels:
> BP sys / BP dia (1)/BP dia (2)

When 2 points are recorded:	When 3 points are recorded
BP sys = appearance	BP sys = appearance
BP dia (2) = cessation	BP dia (1) = change
	BP dia (2) = cessation

Measurements should be taken with arm at heart level. Pulse sounds are best heard with the bell of the stethoscope. Baseline measurements should be made in both arms. (> 15mmHg difference may indicate an obstructive lesion in aorta or subclavian arteries.)

Sources of Error in Indirect Blood-Pressure Measurements

Problem	Effect on Blood Pressure	Precaution
Defective manometer 1. Air leaks 2. Improper valve functions 3. Dirty tubing 4. Loss of mercury	Falsely low values	1. Check level of mercury at zero cuff pressure 2. Check for clear definition of meniscus 3. Verify that pressure holds when tightened.

(continued on next page)

Problem	Effect on Blood Pressure	Precaution
Inappropriate cuff size **1. Too narrow** **2. Too wide**	1. Falsely high values 2. Falsely low values	Verify appropriate size cuff
Cuff applied loosely	Falsely high values owing to ballooning of bag and narrowing of effective surface	Apply cuff snugly
Cuff applied too tightly	Inaccurate reading owing to impedance of flow through artery	Apply cuff snugly without undue pressure
Rapid deflation of cuff	1. Falsely low values owing to inaccurate detection of beginning of sounds, or 2. Falsely high values owing to inadequate equilibration between cuff pressure and manometer pressure	Deflate cuff at rate of 2 mm Hg/sec-3 mm Hg/sec
Active or crying patient	Variable	Recheck when patient is quiet

Reprinted with permission from Fletcher, M. etal. *Atlas of Procedures in Neonatology.* Copyright 1983 by J.B. Lippincott Co.

Appropriate Size Blood Pressure Cuff *

	Range of dimensions of bladder cm	
Cuff Name	Width	Length
Newborn	2.5-4.0	5.0-10.0
Infant	6.0-8.0	12.0-13.5
Child	9.0-10.0	17.0-22.5
Adult	12.0-13.0	22.0-23.5
Large adult arm	15.5	30.0
Adult thigh	18.0	36.0

* Selection of proper size is dependent on the size of the extremity, not cuff name. (From "Report of the Task Force on Blood Pressure Control in Children," Pediatrics, 59 (suppl.): 801, May 1977. Used by permission)

DOPPLER

Indication: To obtain accurate systolic arterial pressure.

Procedure: Apply cuff (see pg. 4-9).

Add gel to probe.

Place probe on artery below cuff.

Turn on Doppler.

Listen for pulsatile hissing sound.

Inflate cuff rapidly until hiss stops.

Lower pressure slowly until hiss reappears (systolic pressure).

Record pressure and which extremity was used.

Signs of Poor Perfusion In Infants and Children

Change in responsiveness:

Irritability, confusion, stupor, coma

Cool Skin

Delayed capillary refill

Diminished pulses

Evidence of organ failure

Metabolic acidosis or increased serum lactate

Oliguria (urine volume < 1 ml/kg/hr)

Pale or mottled color

Tachycardia

Late signs. ↓ BP + ↓ HR

Nonspecific Signs of Distress in Neonates:

Apnea

Hypoglycemia

Temperature instability

Clinical Note:

Hypotension (↓ BP) is a very late sign of cardiorespiratory distress. Arrest is imminent.

Circulating Blood Volume in Children

Age of the child	Blood volume (ml/kg)
Neonates	85-90
Infants	75-80
Children	70-75
Adults	65-70

Clinical Note:
> It is critically important to accurately measure and record blood volumes drawn or lost during clinical procedures. Careful attention must be paid to all stopcocks and tubing connections to prevent blood loss.

Cardiac Output

Normal Pediatric Cardiac Outputs and Stroke Volumes

Ranges of normal cardiac output in children at different ages			
Age	Cardiac output (L/min)	Heart rate	Normal stroke volume
Newborn	0.8-1.0	145	5 ml
6 mo	1.0-1.3	120	10 ml
1 yr	1.3-1.5	115	13 ml
2 yr	1.5-2.0	115	18 ml
4 yr	2.3-2.75	105	27 ml
5 yr	2.5-3.0	95	31ml
8 yr	3.4-3.6	83	42 ml
10 yr	3.8-4.0	75	50 ml
15 yr	6.0	70	85 ml

Clinical Notes:

CO: Infant at birth = 400 mL/kg/min
Infant after 1st few weeks = 200 mL/kg/min
Adolescent =100 mL/kg/min

CI: Child = 3.5 - 5.5 L/min/m^2
Adolescent - 2.5 - 4.0 L/min/m^2
(CI < 2.5 = ↓ CO at any age)

SV: Neonate = 1.5 mL/kg/beat
Adolescent = 60 -120 mL/kg/beat

CARDIOVASCULAR MONITORING

Non-Invasive

Heart rate — see Pg. 4-4
Blood pressure — see Pg. 4-6

Invasive

Pediatric differences affecting invasive monitoring

• *Small vessels* — hence small catheters and easy occlusion.
• *Small measurements* — hence small errors can result in significant variations from actual.
• *Small blood volume* — hence small blood loss can be significant, fluid overload is a very real probability, and small blood samples should be taken.
• *Vigorous movement of extremities* — require restraining and careful positioning and monitoring of tubings, connections and catheters.
• *Immunologically immature* — hence at a greater risk of infection.
• *Intellectually less able to understand what is going on* — hence extra careful comforting and explanation is often required.

Clinical Notes.

Hemodynamic monitoring in children requires very careful calibration and maintenance of the monitoring equipment. Extreme caution is required during insertion, blood withdrawal and maintenance of IV, CVP or PA lines. *Absolutely no air* can be allowed to enter the lines because it may be shunted via R → L intracardiac shunt and enter the systemic circulation *All newborns and infants less than 3 months are assumed to have R → L shunts, as well as children with cyanotic congenital heart disease.*

4-13

Arterial Line (A-Line) Monitoring

Indications:	**Insertion sites (arteries):**
Continuous monitoring of arterial BP. Monitor effects of vasoactive medications. Frequent ABG/blood sampling.	Umbilical (newborns) Radial Femoral Dorsalis pedis Posterior tibial Axillary **Note:** *Temporal A-lines are not recommended in neonates or children.*

Equipment, Insertion, Maintenance, Infection Control, Drawing a Blood Sample, Pressure and Waveform Variations — refer to Oakes' ***Hemodynamic Monitoring: A Bedside Reference Manual***.

Interpretation:

Arterial Pressure — see Pg. 4-6 for normal BP values.

A-line BP is usually more accurate than cuff BP and is usually 5-20 mmHg higher than cuff BP.

Wide variations may exist, however, due to vasomotor changes, vascular obstructions or quality of Korokoff sounds.

Arterial Waveform (identical to adult)

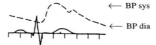

← BP sys
← BP dia

<u>Systolic press</u>: Top of wave (indicative of systemic circ.) <u>Diastolic press</u>: Bottom of wave (indicative of coronary circ.) <u>Mean press</u>: (indicative of renal & cerebral circ.)

Monitor for pressure and waveform variations.

Precautions:

Ideally, "nothing" should ever be administered via a-lines except hypotonic or isotonic flush solution.

Periodically correlate values with cuff pressures.

Always monitor extremity for color, temperature and sensation.

Carefully chart "I+O" (flushes & withdrawals) in small infants.

Never manually irrigate a clotted line.

Syringe pumps, over high pressure bags, are often preferred in infants.

If a high pressure bag is used, insure infusion pressure is greater than vascular pressure being monitored.

High pressure lines (> 60 mmHg) need 2 mL/hr infusion rate to keep lines patent.

Low pressure lines (< 60 mmHg) need only 1 mL/hr infusion rate.

Keep drawing and flushing to a minimum: Blood to be reinfused may be done via central line rather than back into the small vessel line.

Pigtail or squeeze chambers provide large, unknown quantities of flush fluid. Frequent flushes may cause fluid overload in children or back flushing into cerebral circulation.

Complications to watch for:

↓ or absent pulse	Infection
Blanching at site	Spasm (ischema)
Bleedback	Thrombosis/embolus
Electric microshock	Trauma (nerves)
Fluid overload	
Hemorrhage	

Troubleshooting the A-Line

Problem	Possible Causes	Correction/Prevention
Artifact, noise or fling	Catheter whip	Avoid excessive catheter length. Try different tip position.
	Electrical interference	Have Bio-med dept. check.
	Hyperresonance	Dampening device
	Patient movement	Limit patient movement.
Dampened waveform	Air bubbles in system or catheter	Aspirate catheter and/or flush system.
	Blood clot on catheter tip or in system	Aspirate clot with syringe
	Catheter tip against vessel wall	Check for free backflow of blood. Reposition catheter tip if needed.
	Compliant tubing	Use less compliant tubing.
	Improper zero or calibration	Recheck zero and/or calibration.
	Incorrect stopcock position.	Check stopcock position.
	Loose connection	Insure tight connections.
	Loss of counter-pressure from bag	Insure proper pressure in pressure bag.
	Loss of IV solution	Replace IV bag.
	Tubing kink	Correct external or internal kinks.

Problem	Possible Causes	Correction/Prevention
Low reading	Incorrect zero and/or calibration	Recheck zero and/or calibration.
	Loose connection	Check connections.
	Transducer level too high	Recheck transducer and patient positions
	Altered tip location	Check position under fluoroscope and/or x-ray and reposition.
High reading	Fast continous flow	Reduce IV flow
	Incorrect zero and/or calibration	Recheck zero and/or calibration
	Transducer level too low	Recheck transducer patient positions
	Altered tip location	Check position under fluoroscope and/or x-ray and reposition.
No waveform	Complete occlusion of catheter	Attempt to aspirate clot If can't, remove catheter.
	Incorrect zero and/or calibration	Recheck zero and/or calibration.
	Incorrect monitor settings	Check monitor settings.
	Incorrect pressure range setting	Check monitor settings.
	Kink in catheter	Reposition
	Loose connection	Check all connections.
	Monitor/amplifier off	Switch power on.
	Stopcock off to patient	Adjust stopcock.

continued on next page

	Possible Causes	Correction/Prevention
Poor infusion of IV or unable to flush	Blood clot at tip	Aspirate clot
	Kink in tubing	Connect external or internal kinks.
	Pressure bag improperly inflated	Inflate pressure bag.
	Stopcock not open	Open stopcock.
	Catheter tip against wall	Reposition catheter.
Waveform drift	Kink in electrical monitoring cable	Replace cable.
	IV solution temperature change	Allow for temperature equilibration.

Central Venous Pressure (CVP) Monitoring

Indications: Assess cardiac function and right heart pressures

Assess intravascular volume status and venous return.

Fluid and drug administration (large volumes, vasoactive drugs and/or hypertonic solutions).

Insertion sites (veins)

External/internal jugular

Subclavian or femoral

Basilic/cephalic veins in arm

UVC (making a comeback in popularity)

<u>Catheter tip placement</u> should be at junction of vena cava and atrium.

Confirm position by all of the following:
Catheter length
Pressure waveform
X-ray
O_2 saturation (high if in left atrium via F.O.)

*Equipment, Insertion technique, Maintenance, Drawing a
Blood Sample, Measurement technique, Pressure and
Waveform Variations* — refer to Oakes' *Hemodynamic
Monitoring: A Bedside Reference Manual.*

Interpretation:

Pressures: Normal mean value = 0-6 mmHg

Note: Trends are more important than absolute
values. All measurements are made at end-
expiration. Normal fluctuations should not
exceed 3-4 mmHg.

Waveform: (identical to the adult)

NORMAL VENOUS WAVE

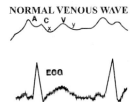

Monitor for pressure and waveform variations

Precautions and Clinical Notes

Never leave the system open to air (bubbles must not
enter the line), insure stopcock is below level of ®
atrium when blood samples are withdrawn.

Danger of coronary or cerebral infarct if air or clots
enter left heart via foramen ovale or septal defect.

Infusion pumps may increase pressures and change
waveforms.

The effect of assisted vent. on CVP is influenced by:
Lung compliance and resistance
Mean airway pressure
Acid-base balance
Myocardial contractility
Amount and distribution of intravascular volume

Sudden increase in CVP may indicate tension pneumothorax or reaccumulation of air after chest tube
is clamped.

Complications to watch for

Arrhythmias	Fluid overload
A-V fistula	Hemorrhage
Bleedback	Infection
Brachial plexus injury	Pneumo/hemothorax
Cardiac perforation and	Thoracic duct injury
tamponade	Venous puncture
Embolism/Thrombosis	

Troubleshooting the CVP Line

Same as A-line (Pg. 4-16), plus:

Problem	Possible Causes	Correction/Prevention
Fluctuations	Respirations	Normal
	Heart beat	Abnormal - tip has migrated into RV
	Positive pressure ventilation	Ensure readings are taken at end-expiration

Pulmonary Artery Pressure (PAP) Monitoring

Indications: Assess cardiac function:

Right heart — pressure and waveforms and valve function.

Left heart — CO and indirect pressures.

Assess pulmonary function:

Pressures, flow (PVR), oxygenation ($P\overline{v}O_2$, $S\overline{v}O_2$, $\dot{D}O_2$, $\dot{V}O_2$).

Diagnosis, management and treatment of heart and lung disorders.

Assess blood volume and fluid status.

Monitor therapeutic interventions (O_2, fluid and drugs).

Contraindications: Large intracardiac shunts, serious dysrhythmias, severe coagulopathies, very low CO or when risk > benefits.

*Equipment, Insertion technique, Maintenance, Measurement
technique, Pressure and Waveform Variations, Clinical
Problems in obtaining accurate PA Catheter measurements,
and Ventilatory effects on hemodynamic pressures* — refer
to Oakes' *Hemodynamic Monitoring: A Bedside Reference
Manual.*

Interpretation:

Measurement Obtainable with a PA Line

Measured	Derived	Note: All invasive parameters may be obtained with the combination of an A-Line and a PA line (thermodiulution)
CO	CI	
CVP	CvO_2	
HR	$C\bar{v}O_2$	
RADP	LV (function,	**A-Line**
PASP	curve)	**+**
PAWP (LAP,	LVSW	**PA Line parameters**
LVEDP)	LVSWI	**Derived**
pl̄v	PAMP	
pH$\bar{v}$	PVR	a-vDO₂ MDO₂
$PvCO_2$	PVRI	a-$\bar{v}DO_2$ M$\dot{V}O_2$
P$\bar{v}CO_2$	RVSW	$Ca-vO_2$ O_2ER
PvO_2	RVSWI	$Ca-vO_2$ $\dot{Q}_s/\dot{Q}_T$
P$\bar{v}O_2$	SV	CPP SVR
RAP (RVEDP)	SVI	$\dot{D}O_2$ SVRI
SvO_2	SW	$\dot{V}O_2$
S$\bar{v}O_2$	SWI	

Pressure	Normal Value
CVP (RAP)	0-6 mmHg
PASP	15-25 mmHg
PADP	8-15 mmHg
PAMP	10-15 mmHg
PAWP	4-12 mmHg
PADP-PAWP gradient	0-6 mmHg

Note: All pressures measured at end-expiration.
      Newborn variations from; above: PASP=50,
      PADP=30, PAMP=38

Waveforms:

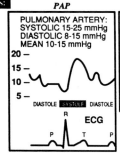

PAP

PULMONARY ARTERY:
SYSTOLIC 15-25 mmHg
DIASTOLIC 8-15 mmHg
MEAN 10-15 mmHg

20 —
15 —
10 —
5 —

DIASTOLE SYSTOLE DIASTOLE

ECG

P R T P

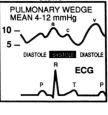

PAWP

PULMONARY WEDGE
MEAN 4-12 mmHg

10 —
5 —

DIASTOLE SYSTOLE DIASTOLE

a c v

ECG

P R T P

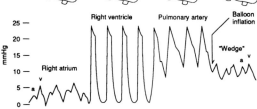

25 —
20 —
15 —
10 —
5 —
0 —

mmHg

Right atrium

Right ventricle

Pulmonary artery

Balloon inflation

"Wedge"

a v

a v

For Wedging Protocol, Verifying a True Wedge Position, Guidelines to Prevent Balloon Rupture, Drawing a Blood Sample from a PA Line, Complications and Troubleshooting - Refer to Oakes' *Hemodynamics Monitoring: A Bedside Reference Manual*

Cardiac Output (CO) Monitoring

Indications:

Assessment of: LV function
Perfusion status
Hemodynamic status
Response to therapies

Calculation of CI and other
hemodynamic parameters:

Hemodynamic parameters obtained from CO measurement			
CI	SV	SVR	PVR
CO	SVI	SVRI	PVRI
EF	SW		
	SWI		

Methods of CO measurement, Thermodilution procedure, Interpretation of Thermodilution curve, Potential Sources of Error, Causes of decreased or increased CO and Troubleshooting CO measurements — refer to Oakes' *Hemodynamic Monitoring: A Bedside Reference Manual.*

Catheters are inserted directly into heart chambers during cardiovascular surgery and brought out through the chest wall.

Left Atrial Line

Indications:

Monitor pressure in left atrium to obtain LVEDP and determine left ventricular function.

Monitor volume status.

Obtain pulmonary venous blood.

Perform contrast echocardiography in suspected L-R shunts.

> Caution: danger of coronary or cerebral infarct if air or clots enter heart via line.
>
> Check q hr. for air bubbles or clots.
>
> Never infuse medications, fluids or blood products.
>
> Monitor heart sounds closely.
>
> Take readings q hr. and at end expiration.
>
> Never manually irrigate the line.

Interpretation:

Norm LAP = < 12 mmHg

LAP ≈ LVEDP

(assuming normal mitral valve and function)

LAP = PA diastolic and PAWP (if no pulm. hypertension)

$$(PVR = \frac{PAMP - \overline{LAP}}{CO})$$

Troubleshooting Left Atrial Pressure Monitoring Problems

Problem	Cause	Action
Blood clot	Inadequate flow of solution	Notify physician immediately. Do not attempt to flush or aspirate the catheter.
Waveform is of poor quality or unobtainable	Loose connection in system	Quickly check system for proper connections.
	Blood clot on catheter tip	Notify physician immediately.
	Improper position of catheter	Do not attempt to flush or aspirate the catheter.

Right Atrial Line

Indications:

Substitute for RA port of a pulmonary artery catheter.

Obtain RA pressures

Infusion line for medications or fluid

Thermodilution port (injectate)

Interpretations/Precautions/Complications —

see CVP pg 4-19

Pacemaker

Indication — A-V conduction blocks causing decreased CO.

Types — External

Fixed rate (asynchronous)

Demand (fire when patient rate less than set limit)

AV sequential — provide both A & V impulses in sequence (DVI mode)

DDD mode— "physiologic pacing" now available

Placement —

Transvenous — wire threaded through a large vein.

Epicardial — wire inserted through anterior chest wall.

Components of demand pacemaker

Output = amt of current delivered to myocardium.

Use lowest possible to maintain a constant capture of the heart.

Rate = pulses/min.

Fixed rate: set rate higher.

Demand rate: lowest possible rate that will maintain adequate CO.

Sensitivity = minimum patient EKG signal that will initiate or inhibit pacemaker firing.

Full clockwise = demand.

Full counter-clockwise = fixed.

> **Complications to watch for**
> Arrhythmias
> Pulmonary embolism
> Heart perforation
> Electrical shocks
> Infection
> Hiccups

5 Neurological Assessment and Monitoring

Newborn

No single neurologic assessment is applicable to all newborns. Each assessment must be tailored according to the status and environment of the infant (i.e., resp. status, sepsis, nutritional status, gest. age, post-birth age, tubes, lines, ventilator hookup, monitors, IV boards, straps, light & noise intensity, temp, etc.).

Observe (prior to manual exam)
Spontaneous posture
Movement
State of consciousness
Signs of seizure activity

Infant states of consciousness*

* The most important element of an infant neuro exam because his reactions to all stimuli and his range of behavior are dependent on his state of consciousness. The state depends on hunger, nutrition, hydration and sleep-wake cycle.

State 1: Deep Sleep
Eyes closed, no eye movements; breathing regular; no spontaneous activity except startles at regular intervals.

State 2: Light Sleep
Eyes closed, rapid eye movements; small movements; irregular resp.

State 3: Drowsy
Some clinicians regard State 3 as a transition state, and hence only define 5 states.
Eyes opened or closed; activity level variable; reactive to sensory stimuli; state change after stimulation often occurs.

State 4: Alert
Eyes open; attention focused on stimulation; motor activity minimal.

State 5: Active
Eyes open; gross movements of limbs; stimuli cause increased activity; fussing may be present.

State 6: Crying
Last for at least 15 seconds.

Modified Glasgow Coma Scale for Infants and Children

	Child	Infant	Score
Eye opening	Spontaneous	Spontaneous	4
	To verbal stimuli	To verbal stimuli	3
	To pain only	To pain only	2
	No response	No response	1
Verbal response	Oriented, appropriate	Coos and babbles	5
	Confused	Irritable cries	4
	Inappropriate words	Cries to pain	3
	Incomprehensible	Moans to pain	2
	No response	No response	1
Motor response	Obeys commands	Normal spontaneous movement	6
	Localizes painful stimulus	Withdraws to touch	5
	Withdraws to pain	Withdraws to pain	4
	Decorticate posturing (abnormal flexion) in response to pain	Decorticate posturing (abnormal flexion) in response to pain	3
	Decerebrate posturing (abnormal extension) in response to pain	Decerebrate posturing (abnormal extension) in response to pain	2
	No response	No response	1
Total GCS score	≤ 7 = serious alteration of consciousness 8-12 = moderate disability. < 15 = concern for any patient with respiratory distress. Consider need for airway support.		

From *The Harriet Lane Handbook*, 18th ed., 2009, Mosby/Elsevier

Neurological

Descriptive Terms for Level of Consciousness

Alert — awake, oriented, and responds appropriately
Confusion — inability to think clearly. Impaired judgment.
Disorientation — beginning loss of consciousness. Disoriented to time, place.
Lethargic — sleepy, arouses easily, and responds appropriately.
Obtunded — awakens only with difficulty and then responds appropriately.
Stuporous — does not completely awaken, responds only to deep pain, withdraws or pushes you away.
Semicomatose — responds only to deep pain, exhibits reflex (decerebrate posturing).
Comatose — no response, no reflexes, and flaccid muscle tone.

Neurological Monitoring

Intracranial Pressure (ICP) Monitoring

Indication — to detect changes in ICP:

Examples:	Conditions	Procedures
	Cerebral edema	Mechanical ventilat.
	Encephalopathy	Intubation
	Hemorrhage	Suctioning
	Acute hydrocephalus	Patient positioning

Methods — see table below and Intracranial hypertension, Page 11-52

Ensure HOB slightly elevated
Ensure transducer at level of lateral ventricle (mid-temple)
Check at least q hr.
Do not check during any patient activity or movement

Neurological

Methods of ICP Monitoring

Method	Explanation	Advantages	Cautions
Intraventricular	Catheter inserted into ventricle	Sharp distinct waveforms Direct measure of CSF pressure Can withdraw CSF Compliance testing	Watch for hemorrhage, CSF leakage, infection and blockage by brain tissue or blood
Subarachnoid bolt	Hollow screw inserted into subarachnoid space	Easy to insert Does not invade brain tissue Accurate, direct measure	Waveform often dampened or blocked Cannot be used on infant < 10 mo. Watch for CSF leakage, infection and blockage
Subdural	Soft catheter inserted in subdural space	Easy to insert Does not invade brain tissue	Dampened waveform Easily blocked
Fontanel transducer	Noninvasive pressure sensitive transducer on open fontanel	Noninvasive	Only direct measure Fontanel must be open False high readings if in contact with bone or secured too tightly Measure in supine position Normal pressure 3-10 mmHg
Intraastral (Camino)®	Pressure tipped transducer placed subdural or intraparenchymal	Pressure transducer is within the cerebral vault More rapid & accurate response time	

Neurological

Intraventricular pressure method

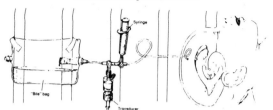

Subarachnoid and Subdural methods

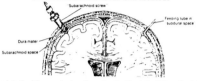

Figures reprinted with permission from Levin, D. etal, *A Practical Guide to Pediatric Intensive Care*, 2nd Ed. Copyright 1984 by the C.V. Mosby Co.

Interpretation —

Pressure —

	Normal	Abnormal
ICP	< 20 mmHg	> 20 mmHg
CPP	> 40-60 mmHg	< 40 mmHg

$$CPP = \overline{BP} - \overline{ICP}$$

$\overline{BP}$ = diastolic + 1/3 (systolic minus diastolic)

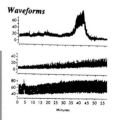

Waveforms

	Clinical Significance
A waves (plateau) Amplitude 50-100 mmHg Duration 5-20 min	Danger: decompensation ↑ $PaCO_2$, ↓ PaO_2, cerebral edema
B waves Amplitude 0-50 mmHg Frequency 1/2-2/min	Fluctuate with respirations, assoc. with sleep or coma
C waves Ampliiude 0-20 mmHg Frequency 4-8/min	Unknown

Neurological

Blood Sampling
(Note: Must follow OSHA standards for occupational exposure, see Pg. 7-11).

Arterial Puncture

Indication

To obtain an accurate ABG when no arterial catheter is in
place or a newborn preductal ABG is desired.

Contraindications — Coagulation defect, inadequate collateral
circulation, infection in sample area, circulatory compromise

Puncture sites

Radial (preferred)

Temporal artery (Newborns only)

Dorsalis pedis artery

Posterior tibial artery

Brachial — use only as a last resort

Femoral — use only in life threatening situations

Preductal sites
Right radial or
brachial
Temporal

Postductal sites
Umbilical (A-line)
Femoral
Posterior tibial
Dorsalis pedis

Variable sites
Left radial or
brachial

Procedure: Equipment

— Tuberculin syringe
(heparinized)

— 23-26 gauge needle or
scalp vein butterfly needle (heparinized)

Wash hands

Perform modified Allens test (radial artery site)

Elevate hand, occlude both radial and ulnar arteries, mas-
sage palm towards wrist, release pressure over ulnar
artery, look for color return to hand in < 10 secs., if
color return > 10 secs, do not use this radial artery

Shave hair if temporal site

Cleanse skin of pt. and palpating finger (use alcohol or
iodophor)

Palpate and stabilize artery (do not hyperextend the wrist)

Insert needle in direction opposing blood flow (transillumi-
nation may be used to visualize vessel) (See Pg 6-29)

Insert at an angle of 30° - 45° with bevel up
(radial/post. tibial art.)

Insert at an angle of 15° - 25° with bevel down
(temporal, dorsalis pedis or radial in small infants)

(A non-acute angle and bevel down helps prevent needle from
passing through the artery) (see Fig. next page)

Advance needle until artery is punctured (blood fills syringe hub or butterfly needle) or resistance is met (bone).

If resistance is met, slowly withdraw needle to a level just below the skin, move point of needle in an arc and try again.

If infant cries hard or holds breath, delay procedure.

When artery is punctured, gently withdraw blood desired (usually 0.2-0.3 cc, depending on ABG analyzer)

Withdraw needle and immediately apply pressure to site with sterile gauze. Hold for 5 min. or until bleeding has completed stopped.

Remove air bubbles from syringe, cap, mix blood with heparin, label and analyze immediately (only place on ice if glass syringe).

Verify peripheral blood flow.

Complications
Arterial spasm or laceration
Blood loss
Carpal tunnel syndrome
Infection
Hematoma
Nerve damage
Thrombosis/embolus

Sources of Error
Crying ($\downarrow PCO_2$)
Venous sample ($\downarrow PO_2$, $\uparrow PCO_2$)
Too much heparin ($\downarrow PCO_2$)
Too much air exposure ($\Diamond PO_2 \downarrow PCO_2$, $\uparrow PH$)
Procedure or analysis error
Hypo or hyperthermic patient

15°-25°

45°

Reprinted with permission from Fletcher, M.A. etal. *Atlas of Procedures in Neonatology.* Copyright 1983 by J. B. Lippincott Co.

Interpretation/Assessment

Normal ABG Values

	Birth	1 hour	1 day	Infant	Child
pH	7.20-7.30	7.30-7.35	7.35-7.40	7.35-7.45	7.35-7.45
pCO$_2$	45-55	35-40	35-40	35-45	35-45
	< 60	60-80	70-100	80-100	80-100
HCO$_3$	20-24	20-24	20-24	22-26	22-26

Heel Stick

("ARTERIALIZED" —
CAPILLARY BLOOD GAS SAMPLING)
Indications and Contraindications (See AARC CPG in Appendix)

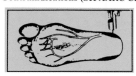

Puncture sites

> Heel (posterio-lateral or medial, see Fig) — preferred in preterm infants
>
> Fingers and toes (lateral aspects of distal phalanges — both older infants and children (not preferred in young infants)

Procedure

> Warm puncture site to 40-42°C (104°F) for 3-5 min.
>> Use towel, diaper, bath, heel warmer, or warm pack that is warm, *not hot*, to touch.
>>> Do not use if temp is > 110°F.
>
> Wash hands (or use antibacterial gel)
>
> Cleanse area with alcohol or iodophor
>
> May apply thin layer of petroleum jelly to bead blood
>
> Puncture with a 2.0 mm lancet. (Never slash or use a scalpel.)
>> Employ a quick perpendicular stab. Avoid previous puncture sites. Do not use posterior heel curvature or antero-medial aspect of heel.
>
> Discard 1st drop of blood (wipe off with gauze)
>
> Milk area *gently* if needed. Excessive squeezing will result in contamination with venous blood and interstitial fluid.

Place heparinized capillary tube at downward angle as close to
    puncture site as possible. Avoid unnecessary exposure to air.
    Avoid collecting air in tube.
Collect 0.2-0.3 mL (40-140 µl for microsampler)
Apply pressure to puncture site with dry gauze for 5 min or until
    bleeding stops. Apply bandaid.
Place small metal mixing rod into each tube and seal ends.
Mix with a magnet and analyze.

Interpretation

PcO_2 usually ≈ 10 mmHg lower than PaO_2
    (when PaO_2 < 60-70 mmHg)
PcO_2 unreliable when PaO_2 > 60-70 mmHg/poor perfusion,
    first 24 hours of life.
If PcO_2 > 50 mmHg, obtain a PaO_2 to assess actual oxygenation.

> It is possible to have a low PcO_2 and an unacceptably high
> PaO_2 (hence ↑ risk of ROP or BPD)
> It is also possible to have a high PcO_2 and an unacceptably
> low PaO_2 (hence risk of hypoxic damage)
> PcO_2 must be periodically correlated with an arterial gas or
> oxygen saturation monitor

$PcCO_2$ and pH usually correlate well with arterial $PaCO_2$ and pH
CBG may be used in combination with SaO_2 or SpO_2 to give a
more complete analysis.

Complications to watch for

False readings leading to too high or too low oxygenation may
be due to:

Inadequate warming	Calcaneous osteochrondritis
Circulatory stasis	Calcified heel nodules
Contamination	Cellulitis
Exposure to air	Hemorrhage
Inapprop. technique	Infection
Too much heparin	Laceration
Machine error	Nerve injury
	Scarring

Arterial Line Sampling

Procedure

Wash hands and use aseptic technique

Wipe stopcock with alcohol (if flush syringe present, close
   stopcock to syringe, remove and cap or discard)

Attach sterile syringe (3-5 cc)

   Close stopcock to IV flow

   Withdraw fluid from line until blood is obtained/ fills line.

   Turn stopcock to 45° angle.

   Remove, cap, and set aside syringe.

Attach second sterile syringe (1 cc heparinized)

   Turn stopcock to block IV flow.

   Withdraw blood sample (0.2-0.5 mL).

   Turn stopcock to 45° angle.

   Remove syringe.

   Prepare sample:

      Remove air bubbles.

      Roll syringe to mix with heparin.

      Label and send for analysis.

      Place in ice (only if a glass syringe)

Attach first sterile syringe (3-5 cc) (contains line fluid with
      drawn).

   Aspirate any air from port and tap so bubbles rise to top of
      syringe.

   Infuse fluid slowly (allow no air bubbles to enter line).

   Close stopcock.

Flush line.

   Flush with IV soln or attach a flush syringe.

   Use minimum amount of flush.

Record amounts withdrawn and flushed in.

Complications to watch for

False low reading (PDA present and line sample is post-ductal)

A right radial or temporal puncture is recommended periodically to monitor true O_2 to brain.

Arterial spasm or perforation

Hemorrhage

Thrombosis or embolus

Infection

Airway Management

Manual Ventilation

Types
    Bag and mask
    Bag to ET tube

> Give 100%, same FiO_2 as receiving or 10% higher depending on indication.

Indications
    Apnea/respiratory failure/arrest
    Impending respiratory failure
      Support until mech. ventilation
    Oxygenation (before, during and after)
    Suctioning
    Intubation
    Hyperventilation (to lower PVR)
    Turning baby, when on MV (during disconnect)

Procedure
    Assemble bag and connect to O_2:
      with reservoir ≈ 100%
      without reservoir ~ 40%
      or connect to blender for exact %
      connect pressure manometer
    Set O_2 now to 10-15 l/m
    Clear patient's airway
    Place in sniffing position (do not hyperextend neck of infant)
      (see Fig. next page)
    Attach bag to pt. (via mask or ET tube)
    Gently compress bag
      Watch for visible chest rise. ***Do not deliver volumes greater than needed to produce visible chest rise***.
      Listen for breath sounds with stethoscope (listen in axillary area bilaterally)
      Watch pressure on manometer (if already on ventilator — use same pressure)
    Pop off valves are controversial:
      As a general rule they are beneficial and protective of the pt.
      They are recommended when the clinician is inexperienced.

A bag without a pop-off may be required to ventilate a pt. with low lung compliance or resuscitation at birth (first few breaths)

A bag & mask should always be ready <u>at the bedside</u> of every sick infant or child. Check for proper function often.

If no response to bagging, check:
O_2 conc., delivered	BS
Connections	Chest expansion
Mask Fit & Seal	Pressure generated
Neck position	O_2 Line Connection

May use hand-controlled ventilatory device which delivers preset pressures and PEEP (Neopuff™).

BAG-MASK POSITIONING IN THE INFANT

Correct:

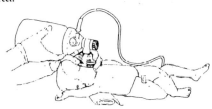

Overextension:

Overflexion:

Reprinted with permission from Schreiner, R. and Kisling, J. *Practical Neonatal Respiratory Care.* Copyright 1982 by Raven Press.

Suctioning Procedure

See AARC Clinical Practice Guideline in Appendix

Indications

Evidence of Secretions	Changes in Neonatal State
Visible secretions in tube Audible course, wet, or ↓ BS Palpation of wet, coarse vibrations thru chest wall	↑ agitation, irritability, restlessness Hypertonic/hypotonic Listless, lethargic

Changes in Vital Signs	Changes in O₂ and Ventilation

Changes in *respiratory pattern*:
↑ WOB (retractions, grunting, flaring), tachypnea, apnea
Changes in *cardiac pattern*:
↑ HR or ↓HR
	Desaturations (< 90%) or labile
	  saturations on SpO₂
	Skin color changes – pale, dusky,
	  cyanotic
	Changes in ABGs – ↑ PaCO₂,
	  ↓ PaO₂, respiratory acidosis
	↑ PIP on MV and ↑ high-pressure
	  alarms

*From Merenstein, G. and Gardner, S: *Handbook of Neonatal Intensive Care*, 5th Edition, Mosby, 2002.

Contraindications – Suction of pharynx and below in patient with epiglottitis with no ET tube in place.
Note: Routine suctioning is rarely indicated; suction only when necessary.

General Precautions
Must follow OSHA/CDC standards for occupational exposures.

When suctioning, ensure:
- cardiorespiratory monitoring,
- proper catheter size (see page 6-20),
- proper suction pressures (see next page),
- adequate oxygenation and ventilation of the patient before, during and after procedure,
- sterile technique,
- O₂ concentration is <u>returned to pre-suction setting</u> following procedure,
- proper ventilating pressure (a pressure manometer connected to the resuscitator is *essential* when suctioning infants).

Two people are recommended when suctioning infants or active children.

Suction *only* when catheter is being withdrawn.

Never force catheter (esp. infants).

Always *stop* procedure immediately if ↓ HR or cyanosis.

Suction only as needed or as ordered.

Procedure

Examine patient (BS, RR, respiratory pattern, SpO$_2$, color, HR, BP, ECG, peripheral perfusion).

Explain procedure to patient if old enough to comprehend.
Set up monitors if not already present.

Set up suction equipment:
Wash hands, adjust vacuum pressure: (ensure suction line occluded).

> **60-80 mmHg, infant**
> **80-100 mmHg, child**

Set up suction kit:
Select proper catheter size (See page 6-14). Open kit with aseptic technique. Fill basin with sterile water or saline, open 5 mL vial of NS. Don sterile glove. Connect catheter to suction tubing. Determine catheter insertion distance.

> **Nose-to-Ear to-Clavicle, or see page 6-14**

Prepare patient:
Clear mouth and nose with bulb syringe, if needed, when no ET tube is in place.

Note – mouth should always be suctioned first in infants to prevent aspiration of oral contents by reflex when the nose is suctioned.

Note position of ET tube if present.

Oxygenate and ventilate patient.
Approximately 10 breaths with ventilator or manual resuscitator connected to a blender and manometer. Use same PIP if already being ventilated, or use minimal pressure needed to achieve good chest expansion. Do not hyperinflate any patient with active lung injury.

Note – if a bronchial plug is suspected, just oxygenate, suction once, then ventilate.

O_2 concentration:

Match FiO_2 pt. already receiving for premature infants.
Give 10% to 20% higher for all others.
Give 100% only when necessary (e.g., PPHN).

Consider instilling normal saline (NS) and manually ventilate only
when indicated by thick secretions that threaten airway patency
(the practice of routine instilling of saline is now discouraged, but
may be life-saving if airway patency is threatened).

0.2-0.5 mL, infant; 1-3 mL child

Suctioning Procedure Continued Via Technique:

Perform ET or Trach Tube SX

Moisten catheter with sterile water.

Insert catheter without suction the predetermined length (see Fig. next page) (shallow sx = to tip of ET tube).

Apply suction and withdraw catheter. (Do not rotate catheter up or down).

Observe patient and monitors.

Limit suction time to 5 sec. (Limit total time catheter in ET tube to 10 sec.)

Oxygenate and ventilate

3-4 quick breaths then several breaths at a normal rate.

Adjust O_2 conc if needed (i.e., cyanosis or $\downarrow SaO_2$)

Ascultate to ensure bilateral BS

Rinse catheter with sterile water.

Repeat if necessary — For thick secretions, may instll saline lavage (few drops up to 3 ml for older child — 0.5 ml max for neonates) and manually ventilate several times to disperse it.

Caution: Do not repeat if HR, BP, color, SaO_2, EKG, or respirations have not returned to normal.

Head rotation is now contraindicated

Note: Sx past carina is *not* recommended in premies.

After trachea is cleared, suction mouth first, then nose.

Rinse and dispose of supplies.

Return ventilator and/or resuscitator to original O_2 conc.

Wash hands and record info (date, time, sputum description, adverse effects).

Perform Naso or Orotracheal SX[1]

Position patient's head.

Sniff position for infants

Hyperextend neck for older child

Moisten catheter or apply water soluble jelly.

Gently insert catheter without suction at a 90° angle to face (close to nasal septum if naso).

Insert through vocal cords only during inspiration.

Gentle pressure over larynx may be helpful.

Continue as outlined in box on left.

Perform pharyngeal SX

Moisten catheter with sterile water, or apply water soluble jelly.

Insert catheter into pharynx via mouth first (then repeat via nose).

Apply intermittent SX and withdraw catheter.

Note: Closed tracheal suction systems have different procedures for use.

See AARC CPG, *Nasotracheal Suctioning*, in Appendix

6-13

Suction Catheter Sizes

Intubated Patient *	
ET Tube (mm I.D.)	Catheter Size (Fr.)
2.5	5
3.0	6.0
3.5	8.0
4.0	8
4.5	8
5-7	10
7.5-8	12
8-8.5	14

Nonintubated Patient	
Age	Catheter Size (Fr.)
Newborn	5-6.5
6 mo.	8
1 yr.	8-10
2 yrs.	10
5 yrs.	12
> 10 yrs.	12-14

*CPR Standards included

CATHETER INSERTION DISTANCES

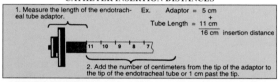

1. Measure the length of the endotracheal tube adaptor.

Ex. Adaptor = 5 cm
$$+$$
Tube Length = 11 cm
16 cm insertion distance

2. Add the number of centimeters from the tip of the adaptor to the tip of the endotracheal tube or 1 cm past the tip.

Complications to watch for

Accidental extubation

Apnea/atelectasis

Aspiration

Broncho/laryngospasm: wheezing stridor

Cardiac arrhythmias

Change in ICP

Hypotension

Hypoxemia: too little O_2
  Cyanosis
  Bradycardia — infants
  Tachycardia — older child

Hyperoxia: too much O_2

Hyper/hypocarbia: $TcCO_2$

Infection: aseptic tech.

Trauma:
  Hemorrhage
  Air leaks (bronchopleural fistula)

Endotracheal Intubation

Indications (see also CPR Guidelines Ch 13, and AARC CPG, ***Management of Airway Emergencies***, in Appendix)

Ventilation

Ventilatory failure (or resuscitation)

Bag and mask unsuccessful or undesirable (diaphramatic hernia, meconium aspiration)

Oxygenation ($FiO_2 > 0.5$)

Obstruction (upper airway, Pierre-Robin)

Protection (from aspiration — cuffed tubes only)

Secretions (pulmonary toilet)

Emergency:	Orotracheal is preferred
Elective*:	Nasotracheal may be used

* There is little agreement as to preference of route of intubation in neonates.

Anatomic Considerations for Infant Intubation

- Larynx more anterior and cephalad (C-4)
- Tongue relatively large
- Short neck
- Epiglottis is longer, stiffer and protrudes at 45° angle
- Trachea is short (easy for bronchial intubation)
- Elevation of hyoid bone may precipitate apnea
- Nasal lymph tissue may prevent nasal intubation
- Cricoid ring is narrowest point of airway

Equipment:

Cardiorespiratory monitor, SaO_2 monitor.

Laryngoscope with extra batteries and bulb

Blade — see Page 6-20 for size; style is by preference (straight is usually preferred for < 8 years of age)

ET tubes — see Page 6-20 (see next airway)

— Use tubes with uniform diameters.

Age	ET Tube Type
Neonates	Uncuffed
1-10 years	Uncuffed or Cuffed
10+ years	Cuffed

Stylet
Bag and mask with manometer and adjustable O_2 source.
Suction apparatus plus catheters (see previous page) and
    Yankauer
Magill forceps (naso only)
Sterile water or lubricant
Fixation device (scissors, tape, benzoin, etc.)
Syringe
Gloves and goggles

Procedure — Orotracheal

Assemble and prepare equipment:

Ensure scope light, suction, and bag & mask works.
Select 2-3 tube sizes, check cuff function.
Cardiorespiratory monitoring is a must.
Heat source for infant.

Prepare patient

Infant and child < 2 yrs.
  Do not flex neck; Head should be on a flat surface.

Older child (> 2 yrs.)
  Sniff position (place towel or small blanket under shoulders
    to flex neck); do not hyperextend.

Suction oro- and nasopharynx if needed

Ventilate and oxygenate: **Do not Hyperinflate any patient**
    For 1 minute if possible **with Active Lung Injury!**
    Use enriched O_2
      (100% is most commonly used)
    Pressure: 20-30 cmH$_2$O

> ***Do not manually ventilate if:***   meconium aspiration
>   diaphramatic hernia
>   upper airway obstruction

Monitor vital signs and SpO$_2$.

Intubate

Position self at patient's head
Hold scope in *left* hand
Open mouth with fingers (not blade)
Insert blade into *right* side of mouth
Move blade to center of mouth, pushing tongue to the left
Slowly advance blade and lift epiglottis until larynx is
    visualized

If esophagus is seen first, withdraw blade slightly

Position curved blade into vallecula and lift
Position straight blade under top of
  epiglottis & lift
Visualization may be improved by:
  1. Suctioning of pharynx
  2. gentle "lifting" of the scope
  3. gentle pressure on the hyoid
     bone

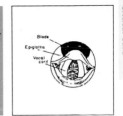

Insert ET tube into *right* side of mouth using *right* hand and
  pass alongside of blade (not through the blade groove)
Advance tube 1-2 cm through cords ***while maintaining
  visualization.*** (No further than half the distance from vocal cord to carina (see table below).

Correct position is:	1-2 cm above carina (children) midway between carina and clavicle in small infants

Note: A stylet may be used but ensure it is at least 1
       cm back from ET tube tip.

Hold tube in place (note position) and
  gently withdraw laryngoscope
Inflate cuff (larger tubes)
Attach bag, ventilate and oxygenate
  (same as above)
Secure tube: There are many good
              techniques. A simple one
              is pictured on page 6-22
Cut tube 1 cm above tape (after confirm-
  ing x-ray)
A small leak should exist around cuffless
  tubes. (@ 10 cm pressure)

Cord to Carina Length (cm)	
Birth	4.0 (Term infant)
6 mo.	4.2
1 yr.	4.3
1 1/2 yr.	4.5
2 yr.	5
3 yr.	5.3
5 yr.	5.6

Stop procedure if bradycardia (< 60 bpm in infant, < 80 bpm in child) arrythmias, cyanosis, or significant ↓SpO_2. Do not repeat until parameters return to prior status.
Never force the ET tube.
Prevent hypothermia in infants during the procedure.
Ensure proper tube size:

Cuffless tube: proper size equals a small leak with 10-20 cm of ventilating pressure.

Position confirmation by x-ray is a necessity.
Always note head position during x-ray.
Avoid excessive head motion - see page 6-23.

Cautions —
Do not hyperextend neck in infants.
Always visualize ET tube going into the glottis.

Glottis — black verticle (triangular) slit with white cords
Esophagus — muscular horizontal slit

Never attempt procedure for more than 20 sec at a time.
Always use a manometer when bagging infants.

Confirm position by:
Auscultation of chest (equal BS) <u>and</u> stomach
Chest excursion (bilateral)
Improved color
Improved heart rate and rhythm } Should improve
Improved SpO_2 within seconds
End tidal CO_2 or esophageal detector
No gastric distention, vapor in tube
Stat x-ray

Procedure — Nasotracheal
Same as orotracheal with following exceptions:
ET tube is lubricated with H_2O soluble lubricant
ET tube is inserted via nose
Keep orotracheal tube in place (if already present): when the nasotracheal tube is just above the glottis, have an assistant pull the oral tube out, apply gentle pressure to hyoid bone and advance the tube through the cords. A Magills forceps is often cumbersome in neonate but may be used to guide the tube.

Complications to watch for:

Insertion
Apnea
Arrhythmias/↓BP
Aspiration (gag reflex): vomitis,
  blood, tooth.
Bronchospasm
Laryngospasm
Hypoxia (max 15 sec)
Trauma (poor technique):
  hemorrhage, broken teeth,
  spinal cord damage.
Vagal stimulation

Improper Position
Esophagus, pharynx, right
  mainstem, beveling at carina.

Cuff
Leak: not enough air, tube
  to small, hole in cuff or
  balloon,↑ tracheal diameter
  (malacia).
Over-inflation: Necrosis
  (tracheomalacia), tracheal
  stenosis, fistula, vessel rupture, cuff herniation

Improper Care
Contamination, desiccation,
  oral/nasal necrosis

**Accidental
Extubation**

Obstruction
Cuff herniation, kinking, secretions.

Body Response
Airway perforation, atelectasis,
  barotrauma, cord paralysis,
  edema, granulomas, pneumonia, sepsis, subglottic
  stenosis.

**Additional
Complications of Trach Tubes**
Hemorrhage, infection,
  laryngeal nerve damage,
  pneumothorax, subQ emphysema

Intubation Equipment Sizes

	ET Tube Size[2]		Insertion Distance (cm from upper lip)[1]		Trach Tube	Suction Catheter	Blade	Mask Size
	ID (mm)	OD (Fr.)	Oral	Nasal				
Newborn								
< 1000 gm	2.5	12	6-7	7-8	000	5	0	1 small
< 2000 gm	3.0	14	7-8	8-9	000	6	0	1
< 3000 gm	3.5	16	8-9	10-11	00	6-8	1	1
> 3000 gm	4.0	18	9-11	11-14	00	6-8	1	1
6 mo.	3.5-40	16-18	10-12	14-16	00-1	6-8	1-2	1
1 yr.	4.0-4.5	18-20	12	16	0-2	8-10	1-2	2 med
2 yr.	4.0-5.5	22-24	12-14	16-17	2	8-10	1-2	2
2-4 yr.	4.5-6.0	24-26	12-15	16-18	2-3	8-10	2	3
4-7 yr.	5.0-6.5	26-28	14-16	17-19	3-4	10-12	2	3
7-10 yr.	6.0-7.0	28-30	15-17	18-21	4	10-12	2	3
10-12 yr.	6.5-7.5	30-32	17-20	20-23	4-5	10-14	2	3
12-16 yr.	7.0-8.0	32-34	17-21	22-24	5-6	12-14	3	4 large

1) These are general guidelines only. Considerable variation exists among the literature concerning exact sizes and lengths. Current CPR standards are included in these ranges.

2) Correct ET Tube Size: The most reliable ET tube size estimate is using a body length based resuscitation tape for children under 35 kg (e.g., Broselow™ Tape).

Adequacy of ventilation is a major determinant for proper size. Correct size should allow for a minimal air leak at a PIP of 20-30 cmH$_2$O.

AHA recommendations: uncuffed tubes for neonates, cuffed or uncuffed for ages 1-10, and cuffed for > 10 yrs. Cuff pressures should be kept < 20 cmH$_2$O.

ET tube size approximations:

$$Uncuffed = \frac{age\ (yrs) + 4}{4}$$

$$Cuffed = \frac{age\ (yrs)}{4} - 3$$

In newborns and infants, their little finger may be a close approximation to the correct ET tube size (ID) (Croup or other narrowing may require a smaller tube).

3) Insertion Distance to lip:

a) Weight in kg ÷ 6. (E.g., 1 Kg = 7 cm, 2 Kg = 8 cm, 3 Kg = 9 cm) Add 1 cm for nasal tubes.

b) ETT ID x 3

c) Child > 2 yrs = $\frac{age\ (yrs) + 12}{2}$

Orotracheal Vs. Nasotracheal Intubation

	Orotracheal	Nasotracheal
Advantages	Quicker & easier	More easily secured
	Less movement with head movement	Less extubations
		Better oral hygiene
	Less contamination of trachea	More comfortable
		Less tracheal erosion
Disadvantages	More difficult to secure (more movement)	More movement with head movement
	Stimulate oral secretions	Nasal necrosis
	May cause cleft palate	Sinus and eustachian tube blockage
	Affects subsequent primary dentition	More difficult to insert
	Extubation	Post extubation atelectasis more common

Sample Tube Fixation Procedure

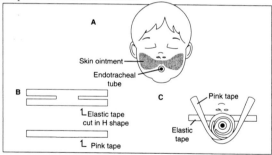

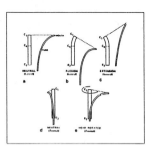

Endotracheal Tube Movement

The position of the endotracheal tube in the newborn child varies considerably with the position of the head.

a. Neutral position, lateral view.
b. Flexion, lateral view: Tube tip moves toward carina.
c. Extension, lateral view: Tube tip moves away from carina
d. Neutral position, frontal view.
e. Lateral rotation, frontal view: Tube tip moves away from carina.

Reference: Donn, S.M., and Kuhns, L.R.: *Pediatr. Radiol.,* 9:37, 1980.

Direct Digital Tracheal Intubation in Neonates

Indications: Resuscitation of apneic neonate in delivery room or nursery, when ventilatory assistance required only for short period of time.

Equipment Woven DeLee ET catheter (#10 Fr premie, #12-14 Fr term)
O$_2$ source
Suction

Procedure

Place pt's head in neutral position.

Insert index finger into mouth with tip of finger sliding along tongue (use fifth finger for small infants < 1500 gm).

Locate larynx (beyond epiglottis)

Insert catheter along palmar surface of finger to tip of distal phalanx.

Place thumb on infant's neck just below cricoid.

Gently steady larynx with thumb and finger.

Advance catheter through glottis (using tip of finger to guide) for about 1 cm.

Leave finger in mouth to hold catheter during resuscitation.

Gently inflate infant's lungs with clinician's breath.

This procedure is easier to perform in an apneic baby (reflexes are
lessened and larynx lax).
Do not insert past 1 cm (bronchial puncture may occur).
Breathe gently and watch chest expansion.
Experience required.

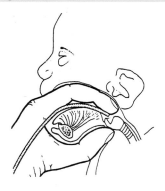

Reprinted with permission from Woody, N., *J. Pediatrics* 23:903. Copyright
1968.

Extubation

See AARC CPG, ***Removal of the Endotracheal Tube***, in Appendix.

Indications

Resolution or improvement of condition which necessitated
intubation. Ensure patient stability:

Pulmonary	CNS
O_2 therapy < 40% Minimal CPAP (2-4 cm H2O)? Vent rate < 4-10 bpm? Adequate ABG's No acute changes in secretions	No apnea Good reflexes (gag, swallow, cough) Adequate muscle strength
Cardiovascular	**Metabolic**
Adequate CO (good BP, per- fusion and urine output) Arrhythmias under control. Adequate HCT	No metabolic imbalances (glucose, Na, K, etc. Positive nitrogen balance.

Procedure

Preparation	Removal
Withhold oral feedings 4 hrs prior.	Remove tape.
Obtain chest x-ray and ABG's.	Ventilate for several breaths (use same O_2 as patient receiving or 100%)
Place patient on cardiorespiratory monitor (if not on one)	Deflate cuff.
Obtain bag, mask and suction equipment.	Withdraw tube at peak of large inspiratory breath.
Empty stomach.	Suction nose, mouth and pharynx if needed.
Suction ET tube, bag ventilate, then suction pharynx.	Place in FiO_2 0.05-0.1 higher than previously delivered.

Postcare:

Keep intubation equipment available. Be prepared for immediate reintubation.

NCPAP in neonates decreases need for reintubation.

Assess clinical status closely:

Watch for stridor, retractions, cyanosis, ↑ RR.

Obtain ABG in 20 minutes (or follow SaO_2).

Obtain chest x-ray 2-4 hours post-extubation.

Aerosol racemic epinephrine (0.25-0.5 ml of 2.5% in NSS) may be given either prophylactically or in case of stridor.

Heliox therapy for stridor?

Dexamethasone may be given 8-24 hours prior to extubation and 24-48 hrs. post-extubation (? effectiveness).

Keep NPO for 6-8 hrs. (or until patient can phonate).

Tracheostomy

Indications

ET tube not possible (anatomic or physiologic) or desirable	Long-term need
Epiglottitis	Long-term ventilation
Congenital malformations	CNS disorders
Upper airway obstruction	Failure to wean ET tube
Burns or trauma	(↓ dead space)
Upper airway bypass	

Removing a Trach

Procedure is the same as changing a trach except instead of inserting a new one, the stoma is covered with sterile gauze and taped in place.

Monitor closely the patient's ventilation and oxygenation.

Post-op Care

Monitor closely in an NICU or PICU setting for 24 hrs.

Watch closely for:	
Tube patency	Changes in
Tube position	secretions
Sub Q emphysema	Pneumothorax
Frank hemorrhage	Aspiration
	Cuff herniation

A trach that bounces with each heartbeat means it could be rubbing the inominate artery and result in hemorrhage.

Suction PRN: q 10-15 min. may be necessary at first

Cleaning:

q. shift (and PRN) Remove and clean inner cannula (if present). Change dressings and ties (two-person procedure to prevent extubation).

q. day   clean trach site with hydrogen peroxide and sterile H_2O using sterile swabs.

Note: Avoid accidental extubation in 1st 7-10 days post tracheostomy until tissue planes have scarred. Reintubation through stoma may be very difficult. May need to orally intubate.

Ensure standby equipment is present:

Obturator, Extra trach tube and ET tube, Small curved forceps, Bag and mask, Suction equipment, Intubation equipment

Complications of trach (See Page 6-19)

Procedure for Changing a Trach Tube

Indications
    Obstruction
    Crusted secretions
    Irritated neck

NOTE: Do not change for 10-14 days post-trach until surgical planes are healed.

Equipment
    Replacement tube (and next smaller size) with obturator and neck ties in place
    Manual resuscitator with O_2 source
    Suction equipment

Procedure
    Explain procedure to patient.
    Ensure patient has not just eaten.
    Ensure sterile technique.
    Position patient supine or slightly elevated with a small shoulder roll.
    Cleanse surrounding area.
    Oxygenate, suction trach and upper airway.
    Reoxygenate.
    Cut ties and remove trach tube.
    Quickly insert new tube with obturator.
        (Pull ↓ slightly on skin below opening to enlarge hole.)
    Hold tube in place while removing obturator.
    Secure trach ties (leave one finger width loose).
    Suction and oxygenate if needed.
    Document

Procedure for Accidental Extubation
Position patient with head hyperextended.
Provide O_2 flow toward stoma (if necessary).
Pull on stay sutures and using sterile forceps grasp the tip of a sterile trach tube and insert into stoma.
Ventilate with bag to check for proper insertion. ***Do not use
excessive force*** if note resistance to airflow (high risk for
pneumothorax or pneumomediastinum due to insertion in
false lumen). Remove tube if resistance felt.
Auscultate for equal breath sounds (if none heard, remove tube).
    If tube cannot be easily inserted:
Insert suction catheter into stoma and slide trach tube over it into
stoma.
If still unable, consider orotracheal intubation.
Notify physician.

Cricothroidotomy (Cricothyrotomy)

Indication complete upper airway obstruction that is unresponsive to standard treatment techniques.

Technique — Hyperextend neck, position larynx as far anterior as possible.

Insert 20 gauge needle percutaneously through the cricothyroid membrane.

Aspirate with syringe to verify proper position.

Insert large bore catheter-over-needle cannula (14 gauge).
Direct cannula caudally at 45° angle. Aspirate again.

Advance catheter into trachea, remove needle, aspirate a third time.

Connect cannula.

Reprinted with permission from Nichols, D et al., *Golden Hour - Handbook of Advanced Pediatric Life Support*. Copyright 1991 by Mosby-Yearbook.

Transillumination

Chest Transillumination

Purpose Immediate diagnosis of pneumothorax or pneumopericardium in infants

Technique

Turn out overhead lights.

Place light probe tip on anterior chest in several locations.

Move from side to side to compare translucency.

A pneumothorax will show as an area of hyperlucency on the affected side and in the areas of collected air.

Emergency thoroacentesis may be performed if needed.

Confirm by x-ray before chest tube placement.

Caution: Inappropriate light source or filter may cause burns

Radial Artery Transillumination

Purpose Locate radial artery for sampling or cannulation in infants.

Technique

Turn out overhead lights.

Place light probe tip directly opposite puncture site (back of wrist).

Artery appears as dark, pulsating linear structure with indistinct edges.

Emergency Thoracentesis

Definition/Purpose

Needle tap into pleural space for emergency removal of air or fluid.

Technique

Position patient in supine or semi-fowlers.

Locate 4th IC space at anterior axillary line.

Clean skin with alcohol and/or iodine.

Attach 18 gauge needle (child) or 21-23 butterfly gauge (infant) to a 3-way stopcock and 20 ml syringe.

A flexible cannula may replace the needle once the puncture is made.

Insert needle just over superior margin of lower rib at 90° angle.

Once needle is under the skin, have assistant apply gentle negative pressure to syringe plunger.

Advance needle, usually a decrease in resistance and a flow of air into the syringe occurs as the pleura is punctured.

Hold needle as still as possible.

When syringe is full, turn off stopcock, remove syringe and empty it.

Reconnect syringe to stopcock and repeat until air flow stops.

Close monitoring of vital signs is essential during procedure.

Remove needle and cover site with petroleum gauze and small dressing.

Obtain stat chest x-ray.

This procedure is often followed by a permanent chest tube

Caution: Needle should be removed if patient coughs repeatedly.
Do not leave needle in place when procedure is
finished.

Complications

Pneumothorax
Hemothorax
Infection

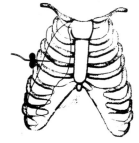

Chest Tube Insertion

Evacuation of pneumothorax or large pleural-fluid collection.

Equipment

- pediatric cut-down set tray
- thoracic catheter
- povidine-iodine solution
- sterile gown and gloves
- cap and mask
- waterseal drainage unit
- 3-0 silk suture
- cardiorespiratory monitor

Chest Tube Sizes (Fr)	
Newborn	8-12
Infants	10-16
1-5 yr	16-20
5-10 yr	20-28
>10yr	28-42

From *The Harriet Lane Handbook*, 2007, Mosby, Inc.

Technique

Assemble equipment (prepare drainage unit and open trays).
Position and restrain patient (ensure NTE if infant)
Ensure continuous cardiorespiratory monitoring.
Use sterile surgical technique (gown, glove, cap and mask).
Clamp distal end of catheter.
Pinch proximal end of catheter with curved hemostat.
Prepare insertion site (scrub and drape) (Do not block heat source)

> **Emergency (not x-ray confirmed) — 2nd IC space,**
> **midclavicular line**
> **X-ray confirmed — 3rd to 5th IC,**
> **mid to anterior axillary line**

Note: Posterior placement is desired to evacuate fluid.

Make superficial incision (1 cm long, upper border of lower rib).

Separate muscle tissue (use small hemostat).

Puncture the pleura with the curved hemostat (and catheter) (push downward and away from lung tissue).

Note: Remove patient from ventilator during insertion to reduce risk of lung puncture.

Slowly release and remove hemostat.

Slowly advance catheter to desired length (at least 3 cm. beyond last opening in catheter).

Connect distal end of catheter to water seal drainage unit and turn on low suction (60-80 mmHg).

Remove distal end clamp (ensure all connections are secure).

Secure catheter with purse-string suture.

Apply occlusive dressing (vaseline gauze and sterile dressing).

Obtain x-ray.

Document.

Figure reprinted with permission from Levin, D., etal. *A Practical Guide to Pediatric Intensive Care*, 2nd Ed. Copyright 1984 by The C.V. Mosby Co.

Landmarks for chest tube insertion. A) Diagnosis <u>not confirmed</u> by x-ray.
B) Diagnosis is <u>confirmed</u> by x-ray.

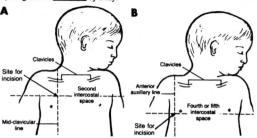

Insertion of Chest Tube

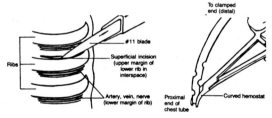

Above diagrams reprinted with permission from Meier, P. and Paton, J. Clinical
Decision Making in Neonatal Intensive Care. Copyright 1984 by Grune and Stratton.

Securing the Chest Tube

Reprinted with permission from Fletcher, M. etal. *Atlas of Procedures in Neonatology.*
Copyright 1983 by J.B. Lippincott Co.

Care of Chest Tube	Removal of Chest Tube
Secure tubing to bed to avoid tension.	Indications — no bubbling for 24 hrs.
Milk the tubing q 1 hr. (for fluid)	no pneumothorax on x-ray.
Observe for changes in air flow or fluid vol or color.	Technique-clamp tube or H$_2$O seal
Monitor patient's vital signs.	Wait 12-24 hrs.
Watch for resp. distress, cyanosis, or HR changes.	Obtain chest x-ray.
Transport of patient:	If no reaccumulation has occurred, then remove tube.
Clamp tube with hemostat if drainage system will be elevated above insertion site.	Remove tube during expiration — draw the ends of the purse-string suture together.
Use portable suction system if tension pneumothorax is present.	Immediately cover puncture hole with petroleum jelly gauze and plain gauze.
Never clamp a chest tube without an order.	Apply sterile dressing.
	Monitor vital signs and obtain x-ray in 1-2 hrs.

Complications to watch for

Perforation of lung or major vessels (pneumo/hemothorax).

Nerve damage — intercostals or phrenic.

Tube misplacement

    Tip impinging on aorta will cause hypotension.

    Placement too low may injure liver, spleen or kidney.

    If most proximal fenestration is not inside pleural cavity, subcutaneous emphysema may result.

    Improper placement may fail to relieve tension pneumothorax.

Equipment malfunction

    Leaks

    Blockages

    Incorrect suction pressures

Infection (empyema)

Pericardiocentesis

Indication
Emergency treatment of cardiac tamponade

Technique
Sedate patient, if time allows.
Position patient in semi-fowlers and restrain.
Cleanse subxiphoid area with antibacterial and drape area.
Anesthetize area with 1% lidocaine.
Connect chest lead (V) of ECG to metal hub of an 18-20
      gauge spinal needle with an alligator clip.
Attach limb leads as usual.
Attach needle to 2- or 3-way stopcock and large syringe.
Insert needle into left xiphoid-costochondral junction.
      Direct it posterior and superior towards the tip of the
         left scapula.
      Use a hemostat on needle to prevent deep penetration.
A distinct "POP" is encountered when pericardial sac is
      punctured.
Monitor vital signs closely.
If epicardium is entered, an injury current (ST-T
      waveshift, see Fig.) will be seen on ECG. Withdraw
      needle slightly.
Use stopcock and syringe to aspirate pericardial air or
      fluid. (As little as 2cc may relieve tamponade.)
When finished, remove needle. Cover site with dressing.
Monitor vital signs for several hours.
Obtain chest x-ray and post-tap ECG strip.

> **Complications to watch for**
>   arrhythmias
>   pneumothorax or cardium
>   coronary artery injury
>   myocardium laceration

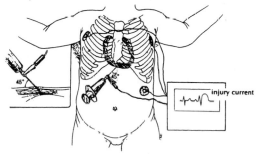

Reprinted with permission from Levin, D.L. etal. *A Practical Guide to Pediatric Intensive Care*, 2nd Ed. Copyright 1984 by the C.V. Mosby Co.

Umbilical Artery Catheter (UAC) Placement

Indications

Respiratory failure or cardiovascular collapse in the newborn infant where percutaneous attempts for vascular access have failed.

Purpose

Frequent ABG sampling or SaO_2 monitoring.

Continuous BP monitoring.

Infusions of parenteral fluids and medications.

Note: Umbilical catheters should be removed ASAP.

Equipment

Antiseptic (povidine-iodine) solution.

Sterile drapes, gauze pads, mask, gown and gloves.

Hemostats, scissors, scalpel, needles, sutures (3.0 silk).

10 mL syringe filled with normal saline, 3-way stopcock.

Heparinized infusion solution (1 unit/ml).

Umbilical catheter (3.5 FR < 1500 gm, 5.0 Fr > 1500 gm).

Procedure

1. Place patient supine and restrain limbs.
2. Ensure proper oxygenation, ventilation and thermoregu-

lation.

3. Monitor HR during procedure.
4. Use sterile procedure to include hand washing, gloves, gown, mask.
5. Prepare catheter. Attach to stopcock and syringe.
6. Prepare cord stump and surrounding area with antiseptic and drape.
7. Place 3.0 silk tie around base of cord to make a purse string. Do not tighten.
8. Cut cord 1-2 cm above abdominal wall.
9. Locate vessels: 2 arteries (thick-walled and round), 1 vein (thin-walled and oval).
10. Dilate umbilical artery with small curved forceps.
11. Insert catheter and advance gently and slowly under constant tension to overcome resistance where the artery bends. A pulsatile blood return should appear after the second bend.
12. Advance catheter desired distance: (see Fig. 6-38):

> Low position — L3-4
> High position — T8

> Note: Advance catheter an extra 1-2 cm to allot for the stump height. Remember it is possible to withdraw catheter if advanced too far (after x-ray verification), but it cannot be advanced later if not in far enough (a new catheter would be required).

13. Confirm blood flow at final point.
14. Tighten purse string knot.
15. Secure catheter (see Fig. on next page).
16. Infuse heparin solution (unless contraindicated).
17. Verify position with abdominal x-ray.
18. Document.

Air embolization
Hemorrhage (vessel perforation, catheter dislodgement or
    leaks/disconnects)
Hypertension
Infection
Necrotizing enterocolitis
Thrombus formation
Vasospasm — arterial supply to one leg is compromised. Try
    warming contralateral leg. Remove catheter if blood supply
    does not improve adequately

UAC Placement

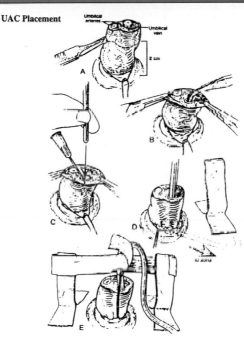

Reprinted with permission from: *Advanced Pediatric Life Support*, 1989. Copyright by The American Academy of Pediatrics and the American College of Emergency Physicians.

Catheter position determined from total body length. (Modified from Rosenfeld et al.) J. Pedia 96:735, 1980

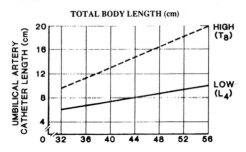

Umbilical Vein Catheter (UVC) Placement

Indications

Immediate access to a vein is needed for an emergency situation (ex. delivery room resuscitation).

Equipment and Procedure

Same as UAC placement except the umbilical vein is catheter-ized and the tip is placed in the inferior vena cava.

Chapter Contents

General Nursing

General Guidelines

At Birth

Dry with prewarmed towels (esp. head).

Keep warm with a radiant heater above & warm mattress below.

Wrap in a dry, warm blanket, swaddler or transparent plastic bag.

Keep baby away from drafts.

Resuscitation — use warm, humidified O_2 (cold O_2 in and warm CO_2 out of lung will rapidly $\downarrow$ body temp in small infants.

Use a radiant heat source over baby when with Mom in the delivery room.

Do not wash or bath newborn until temp is stable.

Term & AGA Newborns —

Monitor temp at birth and q4 hrs until normal and stable.

Premies or low birth weight —

Monitor temp continuously via thermistor (skin probe) or q. 1-3 hrs.

In Nursery or ICU

Newborns with stable temp

Place in bassinet at the following room temps:

Room Temperature Required to Provide Adequate Warmth for Neonates, Clothed & Covered in Bassinet, Draft-Free, 35-60% Humidity

Room Temperature

Birth Weight (kg)	29.5° C (85° F)	26.5° C (80° F)	24°C (75°F)
1.0	For 2 weeks	After 2 weeks	After 1 month
1.5	For 2 days	After 2 days	After 2 weeks
2.0		For 1 week	After 1 week
3.0		For 1 day	After 1 day

General Nursing

Place in a neutral thermal environment (NTE) (incubator or radiant warmer) (see NTE chart, 7-4)

NTE — environment (temp & humidity) at which minimal O_2 consumption occurs (when skin-environment temp differential is < 1.5°C.)

Minimize heat loss:

Infusions

If slow — OK at room temp.

If fast — warm to body temp.

Irrigation fluids, x-ray contrast, etc. - warm to body temp.

Preventing Heat Loss		
Mechanism	Examples	Prevention
Conduction (direct contact)	Cold sheet, scale, x-ray, table, hands, stethoscope	Use prewarmed blankets between surfaces. Use mattresses with poor heat conduction
Convection (air currents)	Cold O_2, air vents, windows, doors, cold room, transport (movement)	Use warm O_2* Insure warm rooms Avoid drafts Use prewarmed incubators or blankets for transport Use heat shield
Radiation (transfer without contact)	Cold incubator walls, room walls or windows	Do not place child near a cold wall or window Use secondary heat shield or swaddle in incubator Cover transport incubator to keep it warm when outside
Evaporation (liquid to vapor)	Wet skin from birth, bath, solutions, cooling of lungs from tachypnea or cold & dry air mixtures	Dry immediately Use prewarmed towels & blankets Do not bathe a newborn until temp is stable Wash & dry only small areas of skin at a time Prewarm solutions or soaks Use prewarmed & humidified O_2/air mixtures

Neutral Thermal Environment Chart

Age and weight	*	Starting temperature (°c)	Range of temperature (°c)
0-6 hours			
Under 1200 g*	500-800 g start @ 36.5°	35.0	34.0-35.4
1200-1500 g	800-1200 g	34.1	33.9-34.4
1501-2500 g	start @ 35-36°	33.4	32.8-33.8
Over 2500 g (and > 36 weeks)		32.9	32.8-33.8
6-12 hours			
Under 1200 g		35.0	34.0-35.4
1200-1500 g		34.0	33.5-34.4
1501-2500 g		33.1	32.2-33.8
Over 2500 g (and > 36 weeks)		32.8	31.4-33.8
12-24 hours			
Under 1200 g		34.0	34.0-35.4
1200-1500 g		33.8	33.3-34.3
1501-2500 g		32.8	31.8-33.8
Over 2500 g (and > 36 weeks)		32.4	
24-36 hours			
Under 1200 g		34.0	34.0-35.0
1200-1500 g		33.6	33.1-34.2
1501-2500 g		32.6	31.6-33.6
Over 2500 g (and > 36 weeks)		32.1	30.7-33.5
36-48 hours			
Under 1200 g		34.0	34.0-35.0
1200-1500 g		33.5	33.0-34.1
1501-2500 g		32.5	31.4-33.5
Over 2500 g (and > 36 weeks)		31.9	30.5-33.3
48-72 hours			
Under 1200 g		34.0	34.0-35.0
1200-1500 g		33.5	33.0-34.0
1501-2500 g		32.3	31.2-33.4
Over 2500 (and > 36 weeks)		31.7	30.1-33.2
72-96 hours			
Under 1200 g		34.0	34.0-35.0
1200-1500 g		33.5	33.0-34.0
1501-2500 g		32.2	31.1-33.2
Over 2500 g (and > 36 weeks)		31.3	29.8-32.8
4-12 days			
Under 1500 g		33.5	33.0-34.0
1501-2500 g		32.1	31.0-33.2
Over 2500 g (and > 36 weeks)			
4-5 days		31.0	29.5-32.6
5-6 days		30.9	29.4-32.3
6-8 days		30.6	29.0-32.2
8-10 days		30.3	29.0-31.8
10-12 days		30.1	29.0-31.4
12-14 days			
Under 1500 g		33.5	32.6-34.0
1501-2500 g		32.1	31.0-33.2
Over 2500 g (and > 36 weeks)		29.8	29.0-30.8
2-3 weeks			
Under 1500 g		33.1	32.2-34.0
1501-2500 g		31.7	30.5-33.0
3-4 weeks			
Under 1500 g		32.6	31.6-33.6
1501-2500 g		31.4	30.0-32.7
4-5 weeks			
Under 1500 g		32.0	31.2-33.0
1501-2500 g		30.9	29.5-32.2
5-6 weeks			
Under 1500		32.0	30.6-32.3
1501-2500 g		30.4	29.0-31.8

Reprinted with permission from Klaus, M. and Faranoff, A., *Care of the High Risk Neonate*, 3rd Ed. Copyright 1986 by W. B. Saunders Co.

* Keep ventilator circuit temperature at 35° - 37°C. For infants < 1000 gm, 37°C will be necessary to avoid cooling.

Hypothermia = axillary temp < 36.5° C
Hyperthermia = axillary or skin temp > 37.5° C

Effects of Cooling	*S & S of Cold Stress (in Newborn)*
Peripheral vasoconstriction	Bradycardia
Anaerobic metabolism	↓ resp. rate
Metabolic acidosis	Expiratory grunt
Pulmonary vasoconstriction	Lethargy
↑ pulm artery pressure	Feed poorly
↑ R → L shunting	Cold to the touch
Hypoxia	Edema of face and extremities
Apnea & bradycardia	
Hypoglycemia	
↑ O_2 consumption	
↓ Free fatty acids	
Norepinephrine release	

Rewarming a Cold Infant (core temp < 36.5°C)

Place in NTE

If servo: set control temp 1.5°C higher than skin temp
Remove sources of heat loss (see Table pg 7-3).
Administer calories (do not nipple feed if resp. distress). Follow blood glucose closely.
Administer O2 for hypoxemia.
Add additional heat source if needed.
Do not warm too rapidly (causes apnea, excess O_2 consumption & rebound hyperthermia) 0.5°C per hour is sufficient.

Incubators, Radiant Warmers and Heat Lamps

General Principles

Manual temp control
Thermostat control is adjusted to achieve desired <u>environmental</u> temp (NTE). See Table, (max 35.5°C, min 29.0°C)

Always check & record core temp of infant:
> q1 hr if unstable
> q3 hrs if stable

Servo temp control

Servo control is adjusted to maintain a constant <u>skin</u> temp
(normally 36-36.5°C)

Always check & record core temp of infant:
> q1 hr if unstable
> q3 hrs if stable

Do not use servo control to control core temp.

Never use an internal (rectal) probe. Skin temp is monitored by a skin probe (thermistor).
> As skin cools, probe cools & heater turns on or up to warm skin back up.
> As skin warms, probe warms & heater turns off (or down).

> **Preferred sites:**
> > Upper mid or left abdomen when supine.
> > Lumbar area when prone.

> <u>**Underheating**</u> may occur when:
> > Infant is lying on probe (probe warms, heater off).
> > Probe is not covered (receives direct heat from source).
> > > The probe should be shielded from the heat source by an alumninum foil pad, sponge or gauze.
> > Radiant source is blocked by worker's head, drapes, equipment, etc.

> <u>**Overheating**</u> may occur when:
> > Probe is loose or falls off (probe cools, heater on).
> > Probe is placed on cool distal extremity.
> > ↓ skin perfusion (skin cools, heater on)
> > > Caution: burns may occur.

Never completely cover the patient (eg. draping during surgical procedure). It blocks the heat.

Check capillary perfusion:
> q1 hr if unstable
> q3 hrs. if stable

Note: servo control will mask unstable temp (eg. sepsis).

Incubator

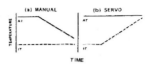

TIME

Thermal response of an infant who becomes hypothermia from sepsis with (a) manually controlled isolette or (b) servo-controlled isolette. Note the decreasing axillary temperature in a, whereas in b the axillary temperature is maintained by an increasing isolette temperature. Both patterns are higly suggestive of sepsis. (AT) axillary temperature. (IT) isolette temperature.

Reprinted with permission from Schriener, R. and Kisling, J. *Practical Neonatal Resp. Care*. Copyright 1982 by Raven Press.

General Nursing

Incubator
Advantages
Isolation from drafts
Stable temp control — best for small premies (< 1200 gm)
Isolation from outside infection
Humidified environment
(better heat conduction & less insensible water loss)
Disadvantages
Limited access
Wide temp swings during on-off cycle.
Infection from humidifier.
Slow rewarming after heat loss (door open)

Ensure O_2/air is delivered at same temp as environment:
>   NTE if manual
>   36° — 36.5°C if servo

Provide 50-75% humidity inside the incubator.
>   (Use external source — incubator reservoir is not
>   recommended)

Performing procedures:
>   Use portholes if possible (close immed. after use).
>   If door must be opened or prolonged procedures — use
>   an additional radiant heat source.

Keep incubators away from cold walls, windows, sunshine, drafts. To further ↓ heat loss:
>   Dress infant or if observation is needed use booties,
>   hats, diapers, and plastic tents.
>   Use a double wall incubator, plexiglass shield, bubble
>   blankets or line incubator with aluminum foil to ↓
>   radiant heat loss in infants < 1000 gm.
>   Use servo control only (not manual) when patient is
>   receiving phototherapy (keep skin temp 36-36.5°C).

Checking incubator:

Check mode —

>   Manual — compare thermometer reading with pt's axillary
>   temp.
>   Servo — Calibrate servo meter.
>   Set control temp (meter)
>   Check skin temp (meter)
>   Check axillary temp
>   Check probe placement
>   Check thermistor wire for kinks
>   Check O_2/air concentration, temp, humidity
>   Check power source & lamp

Radiant Warmer

Advantages
Quick & easy access
Good for performing procedures
Complete visibility
Rapid rewarming

Disadvantages
↑ Heat loss from drafts
(maybe too great for small premies)
↑ Insensible water loss
(maybe too great for small premies)
↑ Risk of infection (maybe too great for small premies)
↑ Radiant heat loss (maybe too great for small premies)

Warmers should be used with servo control only.
  Manual control is not recommended.
Ensure O$_2$ air is delivered at same temp (normally 36°-36.5°C).
Ensure alarms are on and functioning.
Ensure thermistor wire is not pinched.
Keeps warmer away from cold walls, windows, sunshine,
  drafts.
To further ↓ heat loss, dress infant in booties, hat and diaper.
Do not place oily substances on skin — may burn.

Checking radiant warmer:
Check power/lamp
Check probe selector or meter calibration
  (depends on brand)
Check set temp
Check skin temp
Check axillary temp
Check probe placement and wire for kinks
Check high/low alarm

Heat Lamp

Advantages & disadvantages — same as radiant warmer
Indications —
Ancillary heat source for open incubator
Infant in bassinette or on table

Precautions —

Keep lamp > 20" from infant.

Do not direct at incubator thermometer.

Set incubator thermostat on manual 33°-35°C.

Do not use servo control.

Cover eyes and male genitals.

Monitor core temp continuously if procedure > 10 min. or premie.

Do not place oily substances on skin.

Infection Control

General Guidelines *

Do not have direct contact with patients or clean equipment if have: skin lesions, draining wounds, acute resp. infection, fever, gastroenteritis, or other communicable diseases per hospital policy.

Remove all jewelry from hands and arms when scrubbing up & preferably do not wear.

Keep hair away from face and shoulders — cover hair if likely to touch patient or equipment.

Do not wear long sleeves (except clean or sterile cover gowns).

Wear mask if have URI or cold sore.

Cover scrubs/uniform with lab coat when leaving ICU.

Always wash hands between patients.

Patient Preparation

Aseptic procedures — clean skin with alcohol swabs (2 times in circular motion from center to periphery). Allow to dry. Repeat prior to each attempt.

Sterile procedures — wash & shave skin, apply antiseptic (3 sponges in circular motion, center to periphery)

Allow to dry.

Do not use iodine solutuion on newborn skin.

Do not use hexachlorophene on premature skin.

* Check hospital policy for variations.

Infection Control Guidelines

CDC Standard Precautions

Applies to:	1) All patients (regardless of diagnosis or infection status).
	2) Blood, all body fluids, secretions, excretions (except sweat), non-intact skin, and mucous membranes
Handwashing	Wash hands after touching blood, body fluids, secretions, excretions, or contaminated items (even if wearing gloves); immediately after removing gloves; between patient contact.; between tasks/procedures on different body sites of the same patient and when otherwise indicated. Use plain soap for routine handwashing and antimicrobial soap or waterless antiseptic for specific instances.
Gloves	Wear clean gloves when touching blood, body fluids, secretions, excretions, contaminated items, mucous membranes, and nonintact skin. Change gloves between tasks/procedures on same patient after contact within the infectious material. Remove gloves promptly after use before touching noncontaminated items or surfaces, and before going to another patient. Wash hands immediately after removing gloves.
Gowns	Wear a clean gown to protect skin and clothing from splashes or sprays of blood, body fluids, secretions, or excretions. Remove soiled gown as promptly as possible and wash hands.
Patient Care Equipment	Handle used equipment soiled with blood, body fluids, secretions, and excretions in a manner that prevents skin and mucous membrane exposure, contamination of clothing, and transfer of microorganisms to other patients and/or environments. Do not use reusable equipment for another patient unless cleaned/reprocessed appropriately. Properly discard single-use items.
Occupational Health and Blood-borne Pathogens	Use extreme caution when handling, cleaning, or disposing of needles, scalpels, and other sharp instruments or devices. Never recap, use both hands, or point towards the body any used needles; rather, use either a one-handed "scoop" technique or a mechanical device. Do not bend, break, manipulate, or remove used needles from disposable syringes by hand. Place used disposable syringes and needles, scalpel blades, and other sharp items in appropriate puncture-resistant containers; place reusable syringes and needles in a puncture-resistant container to be reprocessed. Use mouthpieces, resuscitation bags, or other ventilation devices as an alternative to mouth to mouth resuscitation.
Patient Placement	Use a private room for patients who contaminate the environment or who do not/cannot assist in maintaining appropriate hygiene or environmental control. Consult with infection control if a private room is not available.
Mask, Eye Protection, Face Shield:	Wear to protect eyes, nose, and mouth from splashes/sprays of blood/body fluids./secretions/excretions.

7-11

Transmission-Based Precautions

Additional precautions beyond Standard Precautions.

Applies to: Patients with known or suspected infections (or colonized) with pathogens that can be transmitted by airborne, droplet, or contact.

Airborne Precautions (Small particle airborne droplet nuclei)	**Patient Placement:** Private negative-pressure room with 6 to12 air changes/hr, plus either safe external air discharge or HEPA filtration. Cohorting acceptable or consult with infection control. Keep room door closed and patient in room. **Patient Transport:** Essential purposes only. Have patient wear a surgical mask. **Respiratory Protection:** Wear N95 respirator when entering room of patient with known/suspected infectious pulmonary TB. Persons immune to measles (rubeola) or varicella (chickenpox) need not wear respiratory protection. If possible, persons not immune to measles or varicella should not enter the room, or wear respiratory protection.
Droplet Precautions (Large droplets)	**Patient Placement:** Private room, cohorting acceptable, or separate patient from others (patients and visitors) by > 3 feet. **Patient Transport:** Essential purposes only. Have patient wear a surgical mask. **Mask:** Wear a surgical mask within 3 ft. of patient (or upon entering room).
Contact Precautions (Hand or skin-to-skin contact)	**Patient Placement:** Private room, cohorting acceptable, or consult with infection control. **Patient Transport:** Essential purposes only. If must be transported, minimize risk of disease transmission. **Gloves and Handwashing:** Wear clean gloves upon entering room. Change gloves after contact with infectious material. Remove gloves before leaving patient's environment and wash hands immediately with antimicrobial agent or waterless antiseptic. Then do not touch any potentially contaminated surface or item. **Gown:** Wear clean gown upon entering room if anticipate patient, surface, or item contact; if patient incontinent, has diarrhea, ileostomy, colostomy, or wound drainage not contained by a dressing. Remove gown before leaving room, then do not contact any potentially contaminated surface. **Patient Care Equipment:** Dedicate use of noncritical equipment to single patient or cohort. If shared, ensure adequately cleaned and disinfected before next patient use.

* Guideline for Isolation Precautions: Preventing Transmission of Infectious Agents in Healthcare Settings 2007. http://www.cdc.gov/ncidod/dhqp/pdf/guidelines/Isolation2007.pdf

Chapter Contents

Procedures

Oxygen Therapy

Indications

Hypoxemia (PaO_2 < 60 or SpO_2 < 90% on room air with or without cyanosis).

Respiratory distress with hypoxemia (do not administer for dyspnea if no hypoxemia).

Resuscitation

Asphyxia – use 100% O_2 initially, then adjust per PaO_2 or SpO_2.

Apnea, bradycardia, or hypercarbia (i.e., intermittent bag & mask ventilation) – use same FiO_2 that patient has been receiving (increase only if clinical condition warrants).

Cyanosis (central or generalized)

Use minimal concentration necessary to abolish cyanosis, then regulate per PaO_2/SpO_2 ASAP.

Cyanosis is a late and unreliable sign. It may not be noticeable until PaO_2 32-42 (fetal heme) or PaO_2 42-53 (adult heme). It is also a function of light conditions, individual perception, Hgb/HCT levels, perfusion, skin complexion, pH, temperature, PCO_2 and 2,3 DPG levels ($\downarrow$ DPG is often found in premies with resp. distress).

Therapeutic Goals

Use lowest FiO_2 possible for shortest time possible:

	Newborn	Infant	Child
PaO_2 (mmHg)	50-70	60-80	80-100
SpO_2 (%)	86-92	90-95	95-97

Correlate SpO_2 with ABG values q. 8-12 hours in unstable pts.

Treat O_2 as a drug.

The upper safe limit of PaO_2 remains unknown. Never exceed PaO_2 > 100 except with persistent pulmonary hypertension (PPHN).

Administer for as short a duration as possible.

Whenever the amount of O_2 to give is in question, err on the side of too much versus too little.

Do not routinely administer to well infants, either premature or term. Avoid excessive O_2 in premies.

Do not administer to premies for apnea only.

Keep patient in required FiO_2 while performing procedures even if only lasting for a minute.

Wean from O_2 as soon as improvement occurs.

Decrease by 5% increments or 0.5 lpm (exceptions are in patients with PPHN or BPD).

Speed of weaning depends on clinical condition.

Recommendation for Administering Oxygen

Guidelines for Perinatal Care, 6th Edition, American Academy of Pediatrics, American College of Obstetrics and Gynecologists, 2007.

O_2 should not be used without a specific indication (cyanosis, low PaO_2, or low O_2 Sat).

Other than resuscitation, O_2 should be monitored by regular assessments of PaO_2 and/or O_2 Sat.

The duration of time that O_2 may be administered without appropriate PaO_2 or O_2 Sat monitoring is contingent upon gestational age and severity of oxygenation deficit. In general, neonates < 36 weeks or with > 40% O_2 should be stabilized and transferred promptly.

BP, blood pH, and $PaCO_2$ should accompany measurements of PaO_2. For a preterm neonate, maintain PaO_2 at 50-80 mmHg (given normal Hgb and blood flow). Even with careful monitoring, PaO_2 may fluctuate outside this range.

Hourly measurement and recording of O_2 delivered to the neonate is recommended.

Except for emergencies, air/O_2 mixtures should be warmed and humidified.

Caution:

Hyperoxia may cause:

- Retinopathy of Prematurity (ROP) - see page 11-77
- Premature closure of Ductus Arteriosus in infants and CHD
- ↑ BP, ↑ SVR, ↓ CO in acyanotic CHD

Monitoring

PaO$_2$

q 10-30min................. after a change in FiO2 or vent setting.

q 4 hrs. .... infants or children with FiO2 > .40

q day........................... stable chronic lung disease

Frequency depends primarily on stability and status of the cardiopulmonary systems.

As often as indicated to determine needs and/or response to therapy.

Frequency may often be ↓ with continuous SpO2 monitoring.

Continuous SpO$_2$ monitoring is recommended for all sick patients (esp. premies). Caution: It is not to be used as a substitute for periodic PaO2 sampling.

> Note: In BPD patients > 30 days of age, the pulse oximeter appears to be more accurate than periodic ABGs.

FiO$_2$ (or liter flow)

q day and after a change in FiO$_2$ (or flow).

Continuous monitoring is recommended for premature infants.

Temperature of gas flow q day (with O$_2$ check) with hood, ET tube, or heated aerosol.

Recommended temperature of gas: 32°-37°C.

Humidity & condensation buildup with each O$_2$ check. Keep > 70% humidity. Keep 100% humidity with ET tube.

Oxygen Delivery Devices

Device	Liter Flow (% Delivered)	Comments	Complications
Nasal cannula*	0.1 - 6 -PM (21+ 50%)	Good for long term chronic disease states, best observation of complete child, pt. can eat & talk, efficient/ convenient, good pt. mobility, unable to deliver aerosol mist if desired. May deliver low-level CPAP @ 1-2 Lpm.	High flows may cause abdominal distention/rupture, need patient nasal passage; drying/irritation, easily dislodged, ↓FiO_2 as V_E increases.
Simple mask*	5-8 LPM (40-50%)	Good for short term delivery (eg. ER), good mobility, easy access to pt., to overcome fear they can play; diver, astronaut or pilot, interferes with eating.	General mask complications; Skin irritation, may aspirate vomitus, O_2 masks are easily and often removed by smaller children, children may be fearful or claustrophobic, ↓FiO_2 as V_E increases.
Partial rebreather	6-10 LPM (55-70%)	Same as simple mask, high FiO_2, flow should be sufficient to keep bag from deflating.	General mask complications: (See "Simple mask"), high FiO_2 complications if long term.
Nonrebreather	6-10 LPM (70-100%)	Same as partial.	Same as partial.

8-5

Device	Liter Flow (% Delivered)	Comments	Complications
Aerosol mask (face tent, or trach mask)	8-12 LPM (28-100%)	Face tent is more readily accepted than masks, high FiO_2 delivered and precise, can provide controlled temp of gas.	Face tent may deliver less accurate FiO_2, overheating, hazards of aerosol, (see Pg 8-10) General mask complications: (See "Simple mask"), high FiO2 complications if long term, near drowning from condensate.
ET Tube via T-piece (Briggs) CPAP, ventilator	$3x \dot{V}_E$ (21-100%) - depending on (device)	FiO_2 received is same as delivered.	ET tube easily occluded with secretions, Near drowning if condensation in tubing enters ET tube, overheating.

*FiO_2 will vary with patient's respiratory rate, tidal volume, and minute ventilation

Device	Liter Flow (% Delivered)	Comments
Air Entrainment Mask (Venturi)	Variable (24-50%)	Delivers exact O₂ conc. Air entrainment ports can be occluded by bed linen, pt. or clothes. General mask complications (see "Simple mask").

Air Entrainment Ratios				
O₂%	Air/O₂ ratio		O₂%	Air/O₂ ratio
24%	25/1		50%	1.7/1
28%	10/1		60%	1/1
30%	8/1		70%	0.6/1
35%	5/1		80%	0.3/1
40%	3/1			

Device	Liter Flow (% Delivered)	Comments
Hood or head tent	7-12 LPM (21-100% - usually a blender)	Primarily for infants and smaller children, simple, effective, precise O₂ provides large volume of O₂ around head so entire tidal volume is met, can deliver aerosol, good visibility of pt., easy access. Need to remove for feeding and care of head. Quick to overheat. (Keep O₂ 32°-34°C) Inadequate flow results in CO₂ buildup. Visibility reduced if large amounts of aerosol generated.

Hood/Head Tent continued next page

Procedures

8-7

Device	Liter Flow (% Delivered)	Comments	Complications
Hood/Head Tent (cont.)		(O_2 more stable with it on), FiO_2 recovery time is quick, can be used in isolettes, warmers or cribs, can continuously monitor FiO_2, prone position may be used, poor patient mobility.	Noise can lead to hearing impairment in infants.
Incubator (Isolette ®)	Varies by model	Used for smaller infants with temperature instability and for isolation purposes, good visibility. Most clinicians do not recommend this delivery system. Instead an O_2 hood or nasal cannula is used inside the incubator.	Imprecise O_2 concentration, difficult to maintain specific and uniform O_2 concentration, must change daily if the humidification system is employed (excellent source of micro-organisms), FiO_2 recovery time is slow, poor pt. access.

Device	Liter Flow (% Delivered)	Comments	Complications
High Flow Therapy Systems	Neonatal: 1-8 LPM Pediatric: 8-20 LPM Adult: 8-40 LPM (Delivers up to 100% O_2)	Used to deliver precise O2 and humidification from 80% to 100% RH at body temp (37o C) FIO2 is determined by analysis via bleed-in or blender. Beneficial in children with asthma, CF and post-surgical care where low-flow oxygen or other delivery systems is inadequate Can also be used in humidifying CPAP, improving pulmonary hygiene, tracheostomy management and in the treatment of rhinitis/sinusitis.	Use with a special nasal cannula to accommodate high liter flows. Recommended for neonatal and pediatric patients with oxygenation difficulties related to BPD, CF and other related pulmonary conditions where the PaO_2 < 55 mmHg or the O_2 Sat is < 88%, tachypnea present with retractions, mild apnea and/or bradycardia (as seen in apnea of prematurity or AOP).

See CPG, Selection of an Oxygen Device for Neonatal and Pediatric Patients —see Appendix

Aerosol and Humidity Therapy

Indications	Goals
Bronchial hygiene	Mobilize secretions
Administration of aerosolized drugs	Deliver medications
Continuous gas therapy	Humidify inspired gases

Contraindication	Precautions/Hazards *
Lack of patient tolerance	Bronchospasms

Physiological Effects	Obstruction from swelling of dried secretions
Hydrate inspissated secretions	Overmobilization of secretions
Maintain mucous blanket	Fluid overload
Improve cough stimulation	Contamination
Decrease airway inflammation	Near drowning from aspiration of condensate
Promote expectoration	Hypo/hyperthermia
Drugs — provide rapid and/or topical actions with decrease extrapulmonary effects	

Clinical Notes:
Aerosol and humidity therapy is essentially the same as for adults with greater attention paid to precautions and hazards.
*The smaller the child, the greater the risks.

See *Oakes' Clinical Practitioner's Pocket Guide to Respiratory Care* for indications, devices and procedures.

See AARC CPG, *Selection of an Aerosol Delivery Device for Neonatal and Pediatric Patients,* in Appendix

Bronchial Hygiene Therapy (Airway Clearance Techniques)

Indications for Bronchial Hygiene Therapy

Prevent Secretion Retention	Remove Copious Secretions
Acute respiratory failure	Allergens/irritants
Atelectasis	Asthma
Immobile patients	Bronchiectasis
Lung disease (BPD, CLD, etc.)	CLD (BPD)
Neuromuscular disorders	Cystic fibrosis
Post Op?	Infection

Signs & Symptoms of Need for Bronchial Hygiene

Symptoms	Signs
↑ Chest congestion	BS – abnormal, audible or ↓
↑ Cough (or ineffective)	↑ RR, ↑ HR
↑ SOB or WOB	↑ Respiratory tract infections and fever
↑ Wheezing	↓ SpO$_2$ or worsening ABG's
↑ or ↓ Sputum production	↓ Expiratory flow rates
	Secretions - ↓ or ↑, thick, or discolored
	Chest X ray changes

Note: The effectiveness of bronchial hygiene therapy is commonly determined by improvement of the above signs & symptoms

Selecting a Bronchial Hygiene Therapy or Combination Of*

Patient Concerns	Technique Factors
Ability to self administer is an important factor	Clinician skill in teaching the technique
Disease type and severity	Cost (direct and indirect)
Fatigue or work required	Equipment required
Patient's age and ability to learn	Physician/caregiver goals
Patient's preference and goals	Therapy effectiveness

* see **Bronchial Hygiene Selection Algorithm** (pg 8-13) and ACCP Reccomendations (pg 8-14)

Procedures

See Oakes' *Clinical Practitioner's Pocket Guide to Respiratory Care* for a detailed explaination of airway clearance techniques and lung expansion therapies, including:

1. Active cycle of breathing
2. Airway and chest oscillatory devices
3. Autogenic drainage
4. Breathing exercises (diaphragmatic breathing and strengthening)
5. Incentive spirometry
6. IPPB
7. Manual-assist devices
8. PEP therapy
9. Therapeutic coughing techniques

See page 8-15 for Chest Physical Therapy

Procedures

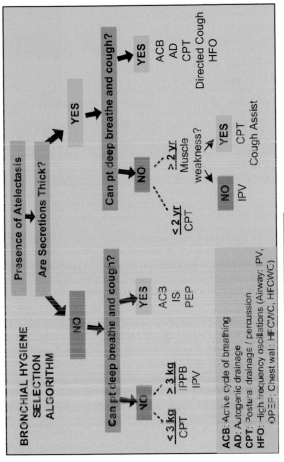

BRONCHIAL HYGIENE SELECTION ALGORITHM

Presence of Atelectasis

Are Secretions Thick?

YES

Can pt deep breathe and cough?

YES
- ACB
- AD
- CPT
- Directed Cough
- HFO

NO
- ≤ 2 yr: CPT
- > 2 yr: Muscle weakness?
  - YES: CPT, Cough Assist
  - NO: IPV

NO

Can pt deep breathe and cough?

YES
- ACB
- IS
- PEP

NO
- < 3 kg: CPT
- ≥ 3 kg: IPPB, IPV

ACB: Active cycle of breathing
AD: Autogenic drainage
CPT: Postural drainage / percussion
HFO: High frequency oscillations (Airway: IPV; OPEP; Chest wall: HFCWC, HFCWC)

Procedures

Adapted from:

Chatburn, RL: High Frequency Assisted Airway Clearance. *Respiratory Care*, 2007; 52 (9): 1232

Wilkins, RL, et.al: *Egan's Fundamentals of Respiratory Care*, 9th Ed, 2008, pgs918 & 942, Mosby.

8-13

Summary Recommendations by the ACCP*

Autogenic Drainage

Should be taught as an adjunct to postural drainage for patients with CF. It is a method to clear sputum because it can be performed without assistance and in one position.

Chest Physical Therapy

Recommended in CF patients as an effective technique to increase mucus clearance. The effects of each treatment are relatively modest and the long-term benefits are unproven.

Cough Assist

Mechanical cough assist devices are recommended in patients with neuromuscular disease with impaired cough, to help prevent respiratory complications.

Expiratory Muscle Training

Recommended in patients with neuromuscular weakness and impaired cough, to improve peak expiratory pressure, which may have a beneficial effect on cough.

High Frequency Techniques

Devices designed to oscillate gas in the airway, either directly or by compressing the chest wall, can be considered as an alternative to chest physiotherapy for patients with CF.

Huff Cough

Huff coughing should be taught as an adjunct to other methods of sputum clearance in patients with COPD and CF.

Manually Assisted Cough

Should be considered in patients with expiratory muscle weakness to reduce the incidence of respiratory complications.
Manually assisted cough may be detrimental and should not be used in persons with airflow obstruction caused by disorders like COPD.

PEP Therapy

Recommended in patients with CF over conventional chest physiotherapy, because it is approximately as effective as chest physiotherapy, and is inexpensive, safe, and can be self-administered.

Final Note:

"The effect of nonpharmacologic airway clearance techniques on long-term outcomes such as health-related quality of life and rates of exacerbations, hospitalizations, and mortality is not known at this time."

* Nonpharmacologic Airway Clearance Therapies: ACCP Evidence-Based Clinical Practice Guidelines, *Chest*. 2006; 129:250S-259S.

INDICATIONS	CLINICAL SIGNS TO WATCH DURING CPT
There are very few valid indications for CPT in infants and children (i.e., lobar atelectasis and cystic fibrosis) The routine use of CPT is controversial. Use may only be appropriate in select patients. See ACCP recommendations on previous page.	ABG's ($\downarrow$ SpO$_2$, $\uparrow$ TcCO$_2$) Airway patency (collapse of neonate's or over-mobilization of secretions) Aspiration BS — (before & after) Color HR and arrhythmias $\uparrow$ ICP Overall activity/mental status Resp. distress Resp. rate & depth (apnea in infants)

Procedures

Clinical Notes:

Postural drainage positions for infants and children are essentially the same as for adults. Only the methods employed to obtain those positions differ.

Percussion and/or vibration is commonly employed in conjunction with postural drainage and should be vigorous but never painful or injurious.

Oxygen requirements of the patient usually increase during CPT procedures, but should decrease following the procedure.

Always remember that a positional change may be either beneficial or detrimental to the patient's ABG's (esp. neonates). (Use SpO_2)

Avoid Trendelenburg in severely ill patients, & esp. premies.

Head-down position has been implicated in an increase of Gastro-Esophageal Reflux Disease (GERD).

Encourage deep breathing and cough during and immediately before each positional change. (There will be less of a rise in ICP if the patient is in an upright position during the cough.)

Neonates (esp. < 32 wk. gestation) are highly susceptible to aspiration, hypoxemia, IVH? during CPT procedures.

Children do not have an effective cough until 4 yrs. of age.

Flexion of hip and knees will reduce abdominal muscle tension and allow greater diaphragm descent.

Diaphramatic breathing is diminished in neonates because of the high position of their abdominal organs.

Special efforts should be taken to relax the infant or child, before and during CPT. Holding & cuddling are often of tremendous benefit.

Maintain special thermal and O_2 environments.

Watch for bronchospasm if the child gets emotionally stressed.

All therapy should be adjusted based on the patient's clinical condition & tolerance.

Procedures	Indications	Contraindications	Precautions/Hazards	Techniques
Postural Drainage (PD) (see also AARC CPG in Appendix)	**Bronchial Hygiene:** Excessive secretions Retained secretions Remove as aspirates (meconium, milk, foreign body, etc.)	**Absolute:** Severe hypoxemia (PPHN, CHD, RDS < 48 hrs, lack of patient tolerance to procedures) Pulmonary hemorrhage with hemoptysis Head down position or: Increased ICP intracranial hemorrhage or surgery Burns < 1250 gm Severe resp. failure Acute CHF Status asthmaticus Untreated hydrocephalus Untreated tension pneumothorax	Avoid head down position after eating or feedings Provide head support for infants Do not dislodge chest or ET tubes Watch for ↑ICP Watch for resp. compromise: ↓ Diaphragmatic excursion in head down position Airway obstruction (secretions or collapse) Hypoxemia Watch for overmobilization of secretions (esp. in infants)	**Technique:** Positioning Place the lung segment to be drained so its main bronchus is pointing downward See following pages Some positions may need to be modified or deleted depending on pt. tolerance & condition **Timing** Positional changes for drainage purposes (esp. head down) are done before or > 1 hr. after meals or feedings. They should follow aerosol therapy

Procedures

Procedures

8-17

Procedures	Indications	Precautions/Hazards	Techniques
	Prophylactic: Prevent accumulation of secretions (post op, post-extubation) Prevent $\dot{V}/\dot{Q}$ inequally from immobility	**Relative:** Patient tolerance Apnea & bradycardia T-E fistula Undrained empyema Unstable cardiac status Surgery Recent meal or tube feeding Pulmonary embolism Pulmonary edema Orthopedic procedures Increased BP Head trauma Flail chest/fractures Aneurism Seizures Abdominal position for: Post abdominal surgery Chest/abdomen malformation Abdominal distention	Use extreme caution when performing procedure in any condition that is relatively contraindicated	Complete sessions up to q2 hrs. Duration Any one position (drainage purposes); Infant-5-10 minutes Child-15-20 minutes Total for head down positions per session: Infant -10 min. max.

Procedures	Indications	Contraindications	Precautions/Hazards	Techniques

Percussion	Same as PD
	
	Used primarily to loosen thick secretions or aspirate in the upper airways
		Same as PD plus:
		Relative
		PEEP impending pneumothorax)
		Clotting problems
		(↑ ICP any position)
		Intracranial hemorrhage any position
		Pain
		Flail chest fractures
		Metastatic cancer
		Sub Q emphysema
		TB
		Obesity (older child)
		Lung contusion
		Osteoporosis
		Infant <1500 g and/or <2 wks of age (↑ IVH)
			Same as PD plus:
			Use caution around chest tubes, incisions, wounds & fractures
			Avoid excessive pressure on chest wall. (esp. infants)
			Insure soft edges on percussor
			Do not percuss over bones, wounds, incisions, abdominal organs or drain tubes
			Stop percussion therapy if pt's clinical condition deteriorates
			(↓ TcO2 or SaO2, apnea, bradycardia, tachycardia, <> BP, resp. distress, etc.)
				Commonly used in conjunction with PD
				Position - same as PD
				Timing - same as PD
				Duration -
				 Infant: 1-2 min per position
				 Child: 3-5 min per position
				Percussor-
				 Infant -
				  cupped fingers
				  rubber nursing nipple
				  medicine cup
				  face mask
				  commercial neonatal percussor
				 Child -
				  cupped hands
				  commercial percussor

	Procedure - Percuss affected segments first then prophylactically (if indicated) over the remaining segments Always work from lower segments (lobes) to upper segments (lobes)			

8-19

Procedures	Indications	Contraindications	Precautions/Hazards	Techniques
Vibration	Same as PD or primarily to thin and mobilize secretions in the lower airways	Same as PD & percussion (may sometimes be tried with caution when percussion is contraindicated)	Same as PD & percussion Use only battery-operated (elect safe) vibrators Do not directly vibrate immature or damaged skin Ineffective if vibrating only the skin (& not below) *Procedure* - Apply vibration only during exhalation (if possible) Perform after percussion of each segment	Commonly used in conjunction with PD Position - same as PD Timing - same as PD Duration - same as percussion Vibrator - therapists' hands or fingertips padded electric toothbrush commercial vibrator (the "massage type" may be used on infants but is not powerful enough for children)

Diaphragmatic breathing, side bending, segmental breathing, thoracic squeezing, etc., are essentially the same for children as for adults.

Cough stimulation or cough reinforcing is accomplished by compressing the chest rather than abdomen as in adults.

Postural Drainage Positions

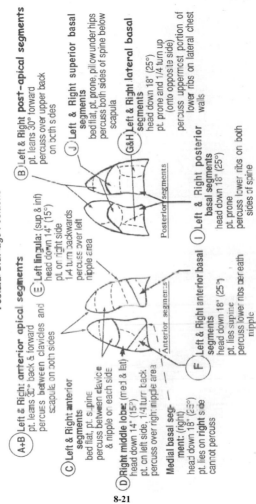

(A+B) Left & Right anterior apical segments
pt. leans 30° back & forward
percuss between clavicles and
scapula on both sides

(B) Left & Right post-apical segments
pt. leans 30° forward
percuss over upper back
on both sides

(C) Left & Right anterior segments
bed flat, pt. supine
percuss between clavicle
& nipple on each side

(J) Left & Right superior basal segments
bed flat, pt. prone, pillow under hips
percuss both sides of spine below
scapula

(D) Right middle lobe: (med & lat)
head down 14" (15°)
pt. on left side, 1/4 turn back
percuss over right nipple area

Medial basal segment: (right)
head down 18" (25°)
pt. lies on right side
cannot percuss

(E) Left lingula: (sup & inf)
head down 14" (15°)
pt. or right side
1/4 turn backwards
percuss over left
nipple area

(G&H) Left & Right lateral basal segments
head down 18" (25°)
pt. prone and 1/4 turn up
(onto opposite side)
percuss uppermost portion of
lower ribs on lateral chest
walls

Anterior segments

Posterior segments

(F) Left & Right anterior basal segments
head down 18" (25°)
pt. lies supine
percuss lower ribs beneath
nipple

(I) Left & Right posterior basal segments
head down 18" (25°)
pt. prone
percuss lower ribs on both
sides of spine

Procedures

8-21

Drainage Positions for the Neonate

Drainage of the apical segment of the upper lobe. The infant is leaned backward about 30° from the sitting position, and the clinician claps or vibrates above the clavicle on both sides.

Drainage of the posterior basal segments of the lower lobe. The clinician places the infant on the stomach with the hips at a level 8 inches above that of the head. He or she claps and vibrates over the lower ribs close to the spine on both sides.

For drainage of the right middle lobe, the caregiver elevates the hips to about 5 inches above the head. He or she rolls the infant backward one-quarter turn and then claps and vibrates over the right nipple. For drainage of the lingular segments of the left upper lobe, the caregiver places the infant in the same position but with the left side lifted upward; he or she then claps and vibrates over the left nipple.

Drainage of the anterior basal segment of the lower lobes. The caregiver places the infant on the left side with the hips at a level about 8 inches above that of the head. He or she then claps and vibrates just beneath the axilla. Note that for drainage of the opposite anterior basal segment, the infant is turned on the right side.

Drainage Positions for the Neonate (con't)

Drainage of the lateral basal segments of the lower lobes. The caregiver places the infant on the left side with the hips elevated to a level about 8 inches above that of the head. The caregiver rolls the infant forward one-quarter turn and then claps or vibrates over the lower ribs. Note that the position shown is for draining the right side. For draining the left side, the same procedure is followed, except that the infant is placed on his or her right side.

Drainage of the posterior segments of the upper lobe. The infant is seated over at a 30° angle from the sitting position. The clinician claps and vibrates over the upper back or both sides.

Drainage of the anterior segments of the upper lobe. While the infant is lying flat on his or her back, the clinician claps and vibrates between the nipple and the clavicle on both sides.

Drainage of the superior segments of the lower lobe. The clinician places the infant flat on the stomach and then claps or vibrates at top of the scapula on the back side of the spine.

Used with permission from, Goldsmith, J.P., & Karotkin, E.H. *Assisted Ventilation of the Neonate*, 4th Edition, W.B. Saunders, 2003.

Procedures

Drainage positions for the infant *

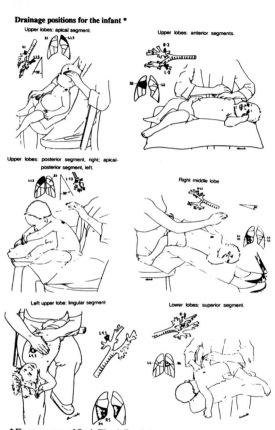

Upper lobes: apical segment.

Upper lobes: anterior segments.

Upper lobes: posterior segment, right; apical-posterior segment, left.

Right middle lobe

Left upper lobe: lingular segment

Lower lobes: superior segment.

* Figures courtesy of Cystic Fibrosis Foundation.

Procedures

Lower lobes: anterior basal segments.

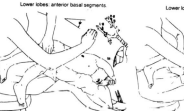

Lower lobes: lateral basal segments.

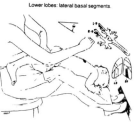

Lower lobes: posterior basal segments.

L & R ANTERIOR APICAL

A

Right Left

L & R POSTERIOR APICAL

Left Right

B

L & R ANTERIOR SEGMENTS

C

Right Left

RIGHT MIDDLE LOBE

D

Right Left

Raise 12 inches

LEFT LINGULAR

E

Right Left

Raise 12 inches

L & R ANTERIOR BASAL

F

Right
Left

Raise 18 inches

RIGHT LATERAL BASAL

G

Right Left

Raise 18 inches

LEFT LATERAL BASAL

H

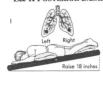

Right Left

Raise 18 inches

L & R POSTERIOR BASAL

I

Left Right

Raise 18 inches

L & R SUPERIOR BASAL

J

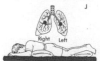

Right Left

Adapted from Hirsch, J. and Hannock, L. *Mosby's Manual of Clinical Nursing Practice.* Copyright 1985 by Mosby.

9   CPAP

Neonatal CPAP

See also AARC CPG, *Application of Continuous Positive Airway Pressure to Neonates via Nasal Prongs (NCPAP) or Nasopharyngeal Tube (NP-CPAP),* in Appendix.

Indications

Diseases causing a $PaO_2 < 50$ mmHg on $FiO_2 \geq 0.6$	*Apnea of prematurity* (early for prevention?) *Delivery room resuscitation?*
Disease examples: Atelectatic disease (RDS, pneumonia)	*Differential diagnosis* of cardiac vs. pulmonary cyanosis in newborn – Give CPAP trial:
Meconium aspiration syndrome*	If $PaO_2 \uparrow > 20$ mmHg and $\downarrow$ or no change in $PaCO_2$ = pulmonary disease
Patent ductus arteriosus (PDA)	If $PaO_2 \downarrow$ and $PaCO_2 \uparrow$ = congenital heart disease or PPHN
Persistent pulmonary hypertension (PPHN)**	*Post-extubation management*
Pneumonitis (inhalation or chemical)	*Sleep apnea* *Tracheobronchomalacia*
Post-op thoracotomy or major bowel procedure Pulmonary edema (fluid overload)**	*Weaning from MV* (Use when ABG's are acceptable, $FiO_2 \geq 0.4$ and machine rate ≤ 8-10 bpm).
TTN	Note: May use nasal CPAP and apply machine rate (nasal ventilation).

* *Use with caution in these diseases.*

Clinical Notes

Some clinicians do not recommend ET-CPAP for infants < 1500 gm, except during weaning from ventilator support, due to the ↑ WOB and high O_2 consumption. They proceed directly to low rate SIMV, then to extubation.

Other clinicians prefer "early CPAP" (PaO_2 < 50 mm Hg on FIO_2 ≥ 0.4) in premature infants (esp. < 1500 gm).

Hazards of CPAP

Abdominal distention	Over-distension and ↓ C_L
CV impairment	↑ Risk of air leaks
CO_2 retention	May ↑ PVR

Contraindications

See *AARC Clinical Practice Guideline in Appendix.*

PHYSIOLOGICAL EFFECTS OF CPAP

↑ FRC → ↓R→L Shunt

↓ Alveolar Collapse

↑ Surface Area → ↓ Alv. Deadspace

↑ Regular breathing ↓ RAW
pattern by:
 ↓ thoracic distortion
 stabilizing chest wall
 splinting airway and
 diaphragm
 ↓ obstructive apnea
 ↑ surfactant release

↑ Compliance → ↑ Alv. Ventilation

↓ WOB ← ↑ Surfactant → ↑ Gas Exchange

↓ Rate

↑ PaO_2

↓ V̇E

Methods of Administration

Method	Advantages	Disadvantages
Nasal Prongs (NCPAP) or Nasopharyngeal Prongs (NPCPAP)	Ease of application Avoids complications of endotracheal intubation Good accessibility to the patient Mouth leak provides pressure pop off Minimal cost	Irritating and ↑ WOB Remove and clean q 2 hr to reduce nasal irritation and erosion During the periods of crying, the infant loses pressure and inhales room air (may need chin strap).
Endotracheal Tube (ETCPAP)	Most efficient method of delivering CPAP Low gas flows can be used High CPAP Pressures obtained with low flows Can easily switch to MV Access to the infant is greatest No problem with leaks, fixation of tube easy	Invasive, acute airway trauma and/or infection ET tube may become kinked, malpositioned, or blocked during or following insertion Tracheal stenosis, scarring, and irritation are possible May increase WOB Eliminates infants ability to grunt
Face Mask	Simple, easy to use Less WOB than prongs	Severe gastric distention Pressure necrosis, cerebral hemorrhage, gastric rupture Hypercapnia due to increase dead space
Nasal Masks	Recent innovation, less dead space then face mask	Limited data available

Clinical Notes:

CPAP in pediatric patients follow closely the same guidelines as adults. It is used primarily during weaning to evaluate the patient's ability to adequately ventilate and oxygenate before extubation and its use in acute lung disease has been primarily replaced by forms of NPPV (BiLevel, BiPAP, or APRV).

It is usually less well tolerated then in adults, especially toddlers between 1-3 years of age.

Initiating and Management of CPAP

> *Clinical Note.* The following are only general guidelines and must be applied with flexibility for each patient.

Initiation:

Initial CPAP 4 - 6 cmH$_2$O (when PaO$_2$ < 50 mm Hg on FiO$_2$ > 0.6 and stable PaCO$_2$ and pH). **See also Page 10-3.**

Adjusting:

Adjust CPAP by the following steps for continued hypoxemia (PaO$_2$ < 50 mmHg):

1) ↑ CPAP by 2 cmH$_2$O increments up to 10 - 12 cmH$_2$O
2) ↑ FiO$_2$ by 0.05 - 0.1 increments up to 1.0
3) Insert ET tube (if not already used)
4) Mechanical ventilation if CPAP failure (see below)

CPAP Levels (Advantages and Adverse Effects), see Page 10-13.

Management Strategies

Appropriate CPAP level	Optimal CPAP level
↑ PaO$_2$ / SpO$_2$, ↓ RR towards normal (RR may ↑), ↓ WOB, and CXR: improved aeration (diaphragm @ 8-9th thoracic vertebrae)	Highest PaO$_2$ / SpO$_2$ without significant change in PaCO$_2$, pH, or CV status (or) Point of initial rise in esophageal pressure (3 - 6 cmH$_2$O)

Attempt to maintain PaO_2 50 - 80 mm Hg ($SpO_2 > 90\%$) ($SpO_2 \geq$
  85% is sometimes acceptable).
Assess patient after each change: BS, BP, RR, WOB, SpO_2.
Obtain ABG 10 - 15 min after Δ or use continuous SpO_2.
Worsening hypoxemia, hypercapnia, respiratory distress, $\downarrow$ BP,
  and/or active abdominal expiratory effort may indicate excessive
  CPAP or CPAP failure. $\downarrow$ CPAP and consider MV.

Rule of Thumb

$\uparrow$ CPAP if oxygenation is main problem.	$\downarrow$ CPAP if CO_2 retention is not improving at 6 - 8 cm H_2O.

Parameters To Monitor During CPAP Administration

Patient	CPAP setup
Abdominal distention	CPAP pressure / popoff
ABGs	Gas temperature, humidity
SpO_2	$\dot{V}_I$ (2-3 x $\dot{V}_E$)
CXR	
Skin color	
CNS (lethargy or unresponsive)	
Vital signs (HR, RR, BP)	
WOB (RR, pattern, grunting, retractions)	

CPAP failure (Any one of the below)

$PaO_2 < 50$ mm Hg on FIO_2 1.0 and CPAP 10 - 12 cm H_2O $PaCO2 > 55-60$ mm Hg or rising, pH < 7.20 (resp) or 7.30 if decreasing	Apnea and bradycardia Patient becomes lethargic and unresponsive

When CPAP fails, move on to MV.

Common Causes of CPAP Failure

Apnea Atelectasis not overcome $\uparrow$ V_D and $\uparrow$ $PaCO_2$ before $\uparrow$ PaO_2 IVH Subglottic stenosis (NCPAP)	Muscle fatigue (inadequate nutrition, severe prematurity) Metabolic acidosis Pulmonary edema

Complications To Watch For

Air leaks (esp. during weaning phase)	Infection (esp. ET tube)	Renal dysfunction
Aspiration	Muscle fatigue (esp. small infants)	Respiratory failure
Excessive CPAP (esp. during weaning phase) ($\uparrow$ $PaCO_2$, $\downarrow$ PaO_2, $\downarrow$ BP or CO, $\uparrow$ WOB, $\uparrow$ PVR)	Necrotizing enterocolitis	Sepsis
	PDA	Tube/prong obstruction, dislodgment, irritation, necrosis of nose
	PPHN	
Gastric distention/ rupture	Pulmonary edema	
Hypothermia	Recurrent apnea	
Increased ICP (IVH)		Under or over hydration or gas temperature

---

Initiation

ABG's improving ($SpO_2 \geq 90\%$ or $PaO_2 \geq 70$ mm Hg) and/or $\uparrow$ esophageal pressure	CXR improving No apnea or respiratory distress Vital signs stable

Adjustments

1) $\downarrow$ FiO_2 by 0.03 - 0.05 increments, down to 0.4

2) $\downarrow$ CPAP by 1 - 2 increments, down to 3 - 4 cm H_2O

3) Remove CPAP when $FiO_2 \leq 0.4$, CPAP 3 - 4 cm H_2O, and no respiratory distress for several hours (several days for BPD patients)

   Note: In babies with apnea of prematurity; keep CPAP at 4 cm H_2O and lower FiO_2 to 0.21 - 0.3 before removing CPAP.

4) Extubate ET tube when discontinuing CPAP, due to the high resistance of small ET tubes.

5) Place patient in slightly higher FiO_2 then was on with CPAP.

CPAP

Clinical Notes:

Maintain $SpO_2 \geq 90\%$, PaO_2 50 - 70 mm Hg, $PaCO_2 < 55$ mm Hg, and pH > 7.25.

Move to next step as $SpO_2 > 90\%$ or $PaO_2 > 70$ mm Hg.

Incremental changes may be made as often as q 2 hrs.

Obtain CXR to assess for adequate lung inflation.

Stop wean if $PaO_2 < 50$ mm Hg or retractions increase.

10 Mechanical Ventilation

Mech. Ventilation

Neonatal Physiology Affecting Ventilation
- Compliant chest wall (excessive inspiratory efforts will collapse upper airway and lungs, decreasing V_T)
- Horizontal ribs and flatness of diaphragm reduce potential lung expansion and V_T
- Possible R-L shunting (PDA and/or foramen ovale) (L-R shunt through PDA increases the risk of pulmonary edema)
- Increased risk of atelectasis and airway closure due to paucity of collateral ventilation between alveoli.
- Surfactant deficiency ($\downarrow C_L$, $\downarrow$, FRC; may grunt and/or shorten T_E to maintain FRC)
- Postnatal clearance of lung liquid and $\uparrow$ pulmonary interstitial fluid
- High metabolic rate
- $\downarrow$ Muscle mass, $\downarrow$ oxidative capacity, $\downarrow$ Type 1 (slow twitch) muscle fibers

Indications for Mechanical Ventilation

1) **Apnea:**
   Prolonged unresponsive apnea associated with bradycardia or cyanosis
2) **Respiratory failure in newborns:**
   $PaO_2 < 50$ mm Hg on $FiO_2 \geq 0.6$
   $PaCO_2 > 60 - 65$ mm Hg (> 55 in infants < 1500 gm)
   pH < 7.20
3) **Impending ventilatory failure:**
   Worsening oxygenation and/or respiratory distress ($\uparrow$ RR [> 60 infants; > 40 children], retractions, grunting, nasal flaring) even when ABG values are within acceptable ranges.

There are no well-defined criteria for when to initiate MV in infants and children. Many clinical factors come into play and must be individualized for each patient's problem.

Early intubation and MV is recommended in many situations including:

- Congenital anomalies affecting ventilatory function (CDH)

Mech. Ventilation

- Infants with low Apgar scores and responding poorly to resuscitation efforts
- Infants with severe sepsis or PPHN
- Extremely premature babies < 1000 gm
- Progressive atelectatic disease

Contraindications to MV
- < 23 week gestation
- Congenital anomalies incompatible with survival
- Severe prolonged HIE with no reasonable chance of survival

Blood Gas Scoring System For Assisted Ventilation
Points

	0	1	2	3
PaO$_2$ (mm Hg)	< 60	50 - 60	< 50 **	< 50 **
PaCO$_2$ (mm Hg)	< 50	50 - 60	61 - 70	> 70
pH	> 7.30	7.20 - 7.29	7.10 - 7.19	< 7.10

A score of 3 or more indicates the need for CPAP or IMV.
   Ambient O$_2$ failure: go to CPAP
   CPAP failure (10 cm H$_2$O & FIO$_2$ 1.0): go to IMV
** May indicate the need for CPAP or IMV by itself, if cyanotic heart disease not present.

----

* Adapted from Goldsmith, J. and Karotkin, E. *Assisted Ventilation of the Neonate*, 4th Ed., Copyright 2003 by W.B. Saunders Co.
Clinical Note: Newborns tolerate hypoxemia and acidosis better than children and adults.

Types of Ventilation

Pressure Ventilation (PV)

> The actual practice of MV of infants varies widely among centers. The vast majority of neonatal ventilation is PV, however VV is gaining in popularity due to improved ventilators. No clinical evidence supports the superiority of one over the other.

See Oakes' *Ventilator Management: A Bedside Reference Guide* for a detailed comparison of Pressure versus Volume ventilation (including advantages/disadvantages of PV)

Volume Ventilation (VV)

Conventional Indications
- ♦ Infants > 1.5 kg without significant lung disease
- ♦ BPD patients requiring long term ventilation
- ♦ Post-cardiothoracic or abdominal surgery

Clinical Notes:

VV is becoming widely used on smaller and smaller infants as ventilator technology improves. Some of the newer ventilators are now capable of ventilating babies as small as 500 - 600 gms.

A consistent V_T may be beneficial in diseases with constantly changing C_L (e.g. BPD).

Cautions: The consistent V_T of VV may over-distend normal lung units and volume loss around uncuffed ET tubes must be accounted for, as well as compressible volume loss in the circuit,.

Neonatal Pressure Support

PS for the neonate is gaining in clinical use and popularity and is now commonly used in combination with V-SIMV and P-SIMV. It is used primarily as a weaning mode or in patients with CLD.

Clinical Notes: PS levels < 10 cmH$_2$O are not recommended due to the high resistance of the small diameter neonatal ET tube. Extra care must be taken to observe triggering, synchrony, T_I, and V_T.

Combination Modes

Generally pressure ventilation with a volume guarantee. Various combinations of volume and pressure ventilation are becoming common (e.g., PRVC, VAPS).

See *Oakes' Ventilator Management: A Bedside Reference Guide* for detailed descriptions of over **30 Modes** and the comparison of **Pressure vs. Volume** ventilation.

Patient-Triggered Ventilation (PTV)

Newer ventilators have improved abilities to detect and respond to infant ventilatory demands, making possible newer modes *of assisted* and **synchronized** ventilation.

Assist/control ventilation (A/C) is becoming the preferred choice as the initial mode of ventilation in acute respiratory failure of the neonate, as it requires the least amount of patient effort.

As the patient shows signs of improvement, the mode is commonly switched to SIMV in order to prevent muscle atrophy from prolonged use of A/C.

Slow rate SIMV with pressure support ventilation (PSV) is becoming the preferred method of weaning in volume ventilation.

Note: Unsupported SIMV rates < 20 are not recommended due to ↑ WOB through the ET tube.

Hazards and Complications to Watch for

Airleak (barotrauma or overinflation):
PIE, pneumo-mediastinum/ pericardium/peritoneum/ thorax, subcutaneous emphysema

Airway complications (intubation):
Airway damage or necrosis, ET tube airleak/ kinking/ malposition/obstruction, Extubation (unplanned), LTB malacia Subglottic stenosis, ↑ WOB

Cardio or cerebrovascular complications:
↓ CO, ↑ ICP, ↓ venous return,

Chronic lung disease (MV and O_2 toxicity) (e.g., BPD),

ET suctioning complications

Infection (nosocomial) (e.g., pneumonia),

Oxygen (↑ risk of ROP)

Patient-ventilator asynchrony

Technical complications:
Failure of alarms, gas supply, circuit, humidifier, or ventilator

Ventilator settings inappropriate (leading to):
Auto-PEEP, hyper/hypoventilation, hyper/hypoxemia, ↑ WOB

Monitoring of Mechanical Ventilation

Cardiac activity

CO_2 ($TcCO_2$ or $ETCO_2$) (unstable infants)

O_2 (TcO_2 or SaO_2) (unstable infants)

Proximal airway pressures (PIP, PEEP, $\overline{Paw}$)

Note: ↑ $\overline{Paw}$ may result in ↑ PaO_2. $\overline{Paw}$ > 12 cm H_2O may result in barotrauma

V_T varies with ΔP (PIP – PEEP)

Initial PIP is adjusted to achieve adequate V_T (reflected by chest excursion and adequate BS and/or V_T measurement)

PEEP increases FRC and may improve oxygenation and V/Q

PEEP > 4 - 7 cm H_2O may result in hyperinflation

Respiratory rate

V_T (proximal airway flow sensor)

Ventilator *f*, T_I, and/or I:E

Note: ↑ T_I → ↑ $\overline{Paw}$ and may ↑ PaO_2

I:E > 1:1 may result in auto-PEEP and hyperinflation

f of 30 – 60 with short T_I are commonly used in RDS

Periodic monitoring:

ABG's (arterial, capillary or venous):

Keep PaO_2 < 80 mm Hg in preterm infants

Blood pressure (a-line or cuff)

Chest radiographs

Expiratory resistance leading to ↑ WOB and ↑ PEEP

Physical assessment (chest excursion, BS, ↑ WOB, cyanosis)

Patient-vent checks (q 2 - 4 hrs)

Initial Management Plan for the Neonate with Pulmonary Disease*

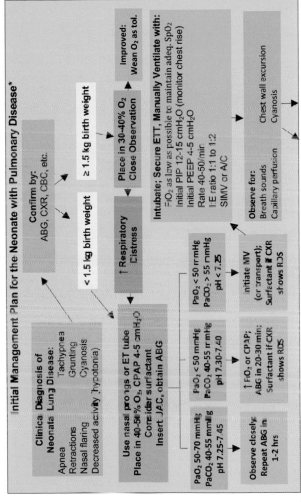

Clinical Diagnosis of Neonatal Lung Disease:
Apnea
Retractions
Nasal flaring
Tachypnea
Grunting
Cyanosis
Decreased activity (hypotonia)

Confirm by:
ABG, CXR, CBC, etc.

≥ 1.5 kg birth weight

< 1.5 kg birth weight

↑ Respiratory Distress

Place in 30-40% O₂
Close Observation

Improved: Wean O₂ as tol.

Use nasal prongs or ET tube
Place in 40-50% O₂, CPAP 4-5 cmH₂O
Consider surfactant
Insert UAC, obtain ABG

Intubate; Secure ETT, Manually Ventilate with:
FiO₂ as low as possible to maintain adeq. SpO₂
Initial PIP 12-15 cmH₂O
Initial PEEP 4-5 cmH₂O
Rate 40-50/min
I:E ratio 1:1 to 1:2
SIMV or A/C

PaO₂ 50-70 mmHg
PaCO₂ 40-55 mmHg
pH 7.25-7.45

PaO₂ < 50 mmHg
PaCO₂ 40-55 mmHg
pH 7.30-7.40

PaO₂ < 50 mmHg
PaCO₂ > 55 mmHg
pH < 7.25

Observe closely;
Repeat ABG in 1-2 hrs

↑ FiO₂ or CPAP;
ABG in 20-30 min;
Surfactant if CXR shows RDS

Initiate MV
(or transport);
Surfactant if CXR shows RDS

Observe for:
Breath sounds
Capillary perfusion

Chest wall excursion
Cyanosis

10-7

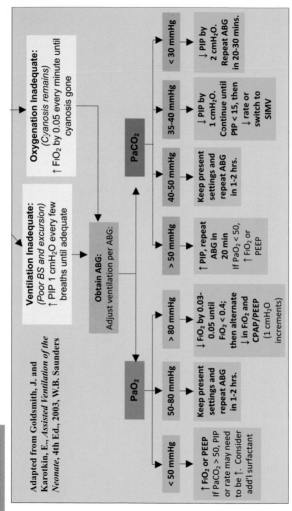

Adapted from Goldsmith, J. and Karotkin, E., *Assisted Ventilation of the Neonate*, 4th Ed., 2003, W.B. Saunders

Ventilation Inadequate:
(Poor BS and excursion)
↑ PIP 1 cmH₂O every few breaths until adequate

Oxygenation Inadequate:
(Cyanosis remains)
↑ FiO₂ by 0.05 every minute until cyanosis gone

Obtain ABG:
Adjust ventilation per ABG:

PaO₂

< 50 mmHg → ↑ FiO₂ or PEEP If PaCO₂ > 50, PIP or rate may need to be ↑. Consider add'l surfactant

50-80 mmHg → Keep present settings and repeat ABG in 1-2 hrs.

> 80 mmHg → ↓ FiO₂ by 0.03-0.05 until FiO₂ < 0.4; then alternate ↓ in FiO₂ and CPAP/PEEP (1 cmH₂O increments)

PaCO₂

> 50 mmHg → ↑ PIP, repeat ABG in 20 min. If PaO₂ < 50, ↑ FiO₂ or PEEP

40-50 mmHg → Keep present settings and repeat ABG in 1-2 hrs.

35-40 mmHg → ↓ PIP by 1 cmH₂O. Continue until PIP < 15, then ↓ rate or switch to SIMV

< 30 mmHg → ↓ PIP by 2 cmH₂O. Repeat ABG in 20-30 mins.

10-8

Ventilator Parameters

Parameter	Clinical Notes	Cautions
V_T 4 - 6 mL/kg (low-birth weight infants) 4 - 8 mL/kg (term infants) 6 - 10 mL/kg (children)	V_T can be measured or estimated by BS, chest excursion, ABG's, and respiratory reflexes (e.g., Hering-Breuer). *Measured* V_T monitor (V_T should be measured at ET tube) *Note:* V_T monitor can measure % leak % leak = V_T delivered − V_T expired × 10) / V_T delivered Up to a 20% leak is common, acceptable, and desired around cuffless ET tubes used in neonates. The presence of a leak assures tracheal inflammation is minimal.	Use lowest V_T possible to ↓ lung over-expansion (volutrauma).
PIP 15 - 25 cm H_2O	The lowest PIP that adequately ventilates the patient is usually appropriate. PIP should remain < 30 cm H_2O in infants and children and higher PIP's should be avoided if possible, but may be necessary in some patients with ↓CL or intentional hyperventilation. It is a misconception that PIP should be proportional to gestational age or weight. Appropriate PIP can usually be assessed by BS, chest movement, and ABG's and adjusted for ventilating open or partially open alveoli. *When high PIP's are used to open closed alveoli, the open alveoli may over-distend, resulting in volutrauma.*	*In PV, PIP and $\overline{P}aw$ must often be decreased quickly when surfactant is administered.* Rapidly changing (increasing) C_L and FRC places the patient at high risk for lung over-distension and resultant air leaks. V_T should be continuously monitored.

Mech. Ventilation

Selecting Initial PIP:

1) Initial PIP may be determined by manual ventilation with a pressure gauge by taking the average PIP required to obtain bilateral chest movement, good BS, color, and SpO_2.

2) When a V_T monitor can be placed in line, the PIP may be adjusted to obtain the desired V_T.

   Note: $V_T = PIP - PEEP$ (approx). Hence, V_T will vary when changing PEEP as well as PIP ($\downarrow$ PIP and/or $\uparrow$ PEEP results in $\downarrow V_T$).

3) Volume – Pressure Loop: Adjust PIP to point where there is little or no flattening of loop.

Low PIP $\leq$ 20 cm H_2O		High PIP $\geq$ 20 cm H_2O	
Advantages	*Side Effects*	*Advantages*	*Side Effects*
Fewer side effects (esp. BPD, PAL)	Insufficient ventilation (may not control $PaCO_2$) $\downarrow PaO_2$ if too low	May help re-expand atelectasis $\uparrow PaO_2$ $\downarrow PaCO_2$ $\downarrow PVR$	Associated with $\uparrow$ PAL, BPD May impede venous return.
Normal lung development may occur more rapidly.	Generalized atelectasis may occur (may be desirable in air leaks)		May $\downarrow$ CO

Adapted from Goldsmith, J, and Karotkin, E. *Assisted Ventilation of the Neonate,* 4th Ed., Copyright 2003 by W. B. Saunders Co.

Parameter	Clinical Notes	Cautions
Paw 5 - 15 cm H_2O	$\overline{Paw}$ is often the most critical factor in determining optimal gas exchange (oxygenation) as it correlates with lung volume. Generally, there is a linear rise in P_aO_2 with $\uparrow$ $\overline{Paw}$ until over-distension occurs, then a $\downarrow$ P_aO_2 (and $\uparrow$ P_aCO_2) occurs. Best correlation occurs with RDS. *Factors affecting* $\overline{Paw}$ (in probable order of magnitude): PEEP, T, PIP, $f/(\downarrow T_E)$, $\dot{V}_I$, and pressure waveform. *Optimal level*: The lowest level at which exchange is most efficient and beyond which alveolar over-distension occurs.	*In PV, PIP and* $\overline{Paw}$ *must often be decreased quickly when surfactant is administered.* Rapidly changing (increasing) C_L and FRC places the patient at high risk for lung over-distension and resultant air leaks (VILI).

Methods to Increase Mean Airway Pressure (MAP)

INTERVENTIONS
1. ↑ PEEP
2. ↑ PIP
3. ↑ T_I
4. ↑ Rate
5. ↑ Flow

How to calculate

1. Equation (if square wave and press limited)
   MAP = (PIP)$\left(\dfrac{T_I + \uparrow PEEP}{T_{TOT}}\right)\left(\dfrac{T_E}{T_{TOT}}\right)$

2. Electronic devices (eg, BP transducer and monitor)

3. Homemade devices (Chatburn, RC 27:276, 1982)

Parameter	Clinical Notes	Cautions

PEEP
4 - 7 cm H2O
	PEEP is used to prevent airway and alveolar collapse and establish FRC, but is not usually used to recruit atelectatic lung units in newborns.
	
	A PEEP titration study may be performed to determine appropriate PEEP level: Start low and ↑ PEEP in 1 - 5 cm H_2O increments q 20 min, until achieve best SpO_2, C_L and hemodynamics.
	  Optimal Level = Lowest level producing the best gas exchange and the largest end-expiratory volume without over-distension.
	  Minimum PEEP (3 - 4 cm H_2O) is usually employed to help overcome ET tube resistance and prevent lung collapse, esp. in newborns. < 3 cm H_2O <u>**should**</u>
	  <u>**not**</u> be used unless indicated.
	
	Infants with surfactant deficiency require low to moderate PEEP.
	Infants with abdominal distension may require high PEEP.
	PEEP > 5 - 6 cm H_2O may begin to worsen C_L and > 10 cm H_2O is rarely used in newborns.
	PEEP > 7 cm H_2O should be used with caution in infants with airway obstruction, such as meconium aspiration or bronchiolitis
		Excessive PEEP may cause ↓ VR and CO, ↓ O_2 transport, ↓ C_L, ↑ V_T and $PaCO_2$ (by ↓ PIP - PEEP difference), ↑ PVR, and air-leak syndromes (e.g., PIE).
		Always maintain PEEP level while hand bagging.

Rule of Thumb

Infant on O_2%:	Requires a PEEP:
100	6-8
90	5-7
80	5-7
70	5

Infant on O_2%:	Requires a PEEP:
60	5
50	4
40	3-4
30	2-3

Monitoring PEEP Effects

1) Increased PaO_2
2) CXR is commonly employed to monitor effect of PEEP by determining lung under/over inflation.
3) Volume – Pressure Loop: Beneficial effects of PEEP = shift of loop to left (↑ V_T at same PIP)

CPAP or PEEP Levels

Low (2-3 cm H$_2$O)		Medium (4-7 cm H$_2$O)		High (8 cm H$_2$O)	
Advantages	Adverse Effects	Advantages	Adverse Effects	Advantages	Adverse Effects
Used during late phases of weaning. Maintenance of lung volume in very premature infants with low FRC. Useful in some ELBW infants or A-C ventil.	May be too low to maintain adequate lung volume. CO$_2$ retention from $\dot{V}/\dot{Q}$ mismatch, as alveolar volume is inadequate.	Recruit lung volume with surfactant deficiency states (e.g., RDS). Stabilizes lung volume once recruited. Improve $\dot{V}/\dot{Q}$ matching.	May over distend lungs with normal compliance.	Prevents alveolar collapse in surfactant deficiency states with severely ↓ CL. Improves distribution of ventilation.	Pulmonary air leaks. Decreases CL if lung overdistends. May impede venous return to the heart. May ↑ PVR. CO$_2$ retention

Adapted from Goldsmith, J. and Karotkin, E., *Assisted Ventilation of the Neonate.* 4th Ed. Copyright 2003, WB Saunders Co.

Parameter	Clinical Notes	Cautions
f (Rate) 20 - 40 breaths/min	Rate is the parameter used most commonly to adjust PaCO$_2$ and pH (i.e., $\dot{V}_E$). Best rate is highly variable depending on the disease state, complications, infant size, ventilator capabilities, and clinical response. *General rule of thumb:* The worse the CL (↓ TCL), the faster the rate. High rates are commonly used in PPHN to induce respiratory alkalosis and ↓ PVR; and in PIE and barotrauma - to reduce EIP and ↓ VT. Also, permissive hypercapnia is well tolerated in infants and children.	High rates (↓Te) may lead to air-trapping, inadvertent PEEP, and ↓VR and CO.

Neonatal Mechanical Ventilatory Rates (f)

Slow (≤ 40 bpm)		Medium (40 – 60 bpm)		High (≥ 60 bpm)	
Advantages	Adverse Effects	Advantages	Adverse Effects	Advantages	Adverse Effects
↑PaO₂ with ↑MAP Useful in weaning Used with square wave ventilation Needed when I/E ratio is inverted	Must ↑PIP to maintain VE ↑PIP may cause barotrauma Patient may require paralysis	Mimics normal ventilatory rate Will effectively treat most neonatal lung diseases Usually does not exceed TC of lung, so air trapping is unlikely	May not provide adequate ventilation in some cases ↑PIP may still be needed to maintain VE	Higher PaO₂ (may be the result of air trapping) May allow ↓PIP and VT Hyperventilation may be useful in PPHN May reduce atelectasis (? air trapping)	May exceed TC and produce air trapping May cause inadvertent PEEP May result in change in compliance (frequency dependence of compliance) Inadequate VT and VE if only deadspace is ventilated

Adapted from Goldsmith, J. and Karotkin, E., *Assisted Ventilation of the Neonate*, 4th Ed., Copyright 2003, WB Saunders Co.

Parameter	Clinical Notes	Cautions
TI 0.25 - 0.5 sec (LBW) 0.4 - 0.5 sec (term infants) 0.5 - 0.75 sec (toddlers) 0.5 - 1.5 sec (child)	Select TI for patient comfort and synchronous breathing. Considerations include lung TC, patient age, and breathing pattern. Infants with ↓CL (e.g., surfactant deficiency) have a short TC (use short TI = 0.3 sec. initially). Infants with ↑Raw (e.g., chronic lung disease; BPD) have a long TC (use long TI = 0.5 - 0.7 sec. May lead to air-trapping.	The longer the TI (esp. > 1.0 sec), the greater the risk of barotrauma, CV effects, and ↓TE.

Parameter	Clinical Notes	Cautions
$\dot{V}_I$ 5 – 8 L/m (low birth weight infants) 6 – 10 L/m (term infants)	In $\dot{V}_I$ set to lowest value that will generate the desired PIP and pressure waveform. Minimum flow should be 2 × $\dot{V}_E$ (normal neonatal $\dot{V}_E$spont = 0.2 - 1.0 L/m). Ideal $\dot{V}_I$ = 3 × $\dot{V}_E$. High flows may be needed to maintain V_T when Ti is shortened. However, flows > 10 L/m may result in ↓ V_T due to ↑ turbulence in small ET tubes and are associated with an ↑ risk of air-leaks. Slower $\dot{V}_I$'s are used for patients with ↑ Raw and/or poor gas distribution. In ↓ $\dot{V}_I$ the flow will be patient determined.	*Signs of Insufficient Flow* Desired PIP not reached with mandatory breaths. ↑ WOB (retractions, etc.). Pressure fluctuations on pressure manometer around baseline PEEP setting. Ventilator asynchrony

Flow Rate Adjustment in Neonatal Ventilation

Low Rate (0.5 – 3 L/min)		High Rate (4 – 10 L/min or more)	
Advantages	Adverse Effects	Advantages	Adverse Effects
Slower Ti, more sine wave Less barotrauma to airways	Hypercarbia if flow rate is not adequate to remove CO_2 from the system Adjusting ventilator rate, low flow may not enable the machine to reach PIP ↓ PaO₂ in some cases	Produces more sine wave ventilatory pattern ↑PaO₂ Needed to deliver high PIP with rapid ventilator rates Prevents CO_2 retention	↑ barotrauma in moderate to severe RDS, may precuce more airway injury ↑ turbulence, ↓ V_T in small ET tubes

Adapted from Goldsmith, J. and Karotkin, E., *Assisted Ventilation of the Neonate*, 4th Ed., Copyright 2003, W. B. Saunders Co.

Waveforms in Neonatal Ventilation

Sine Wave		Square Wave	
Advantages	**Adverse Effects**	**Advantages**	**Adverse Effects**
Smoother ↑ of pressure More like normal respiratory pattern	Lower MAP	Higher MAP for equivalent PIP Longer time at PIP may open atelectatic areas of lung and improve distribution of ventilation	With high flow, the ventilation may be applying higher pressure to normal airways and alveoli Impede venous return if longer Ti is used or I/E ratio is reversed

Adapted from Goldsmith, J, and Karotkin, E. *Assisted Ventilation of the Neonate*, 4th Ed., Copyright 2003, W. B. Saunders Co.

Parameter	Clinical Notes	Cautions
TE 0.5-1.5 sec	TE is most commonly the result of a desired rate and Ti.	0.2-0.3 sec is commonly the lower limit. Shorter TE's may result in auto-PEEP, ↓ VT, and worsening oxygenation.
I:E 1:1 to 1:3	Today, more emphasis is on selecting appropriate Ti and TE than a specific I:E ratio. I:E ratio is not as effective as PIP or PEEP in altering PaO₂, and PaCO₂ is usually not altered by changes in I:E. Waveform monitoring is preferred for setting Ti and TE. *See Ti.*	Inverse ratios carry a high risk of auto-PEEP and the potential of hyperinflation, barotrauma, ↓ CO, and cerebral injury. Other methods are now preferred.

I/E Ratio Control in Neonatal Mechanical Ventilation

	Normal (1:1 to 1:3)			Prolonged TE (< 1:3)	
Advantages	Adverse Effects	Advantages	Adverse Effects	Advantages	Adverse Effects
↑ Paw ↑ PaO₂ in RDS May enhance alveolar recruitment when atelectasis is present	May have insufficient emptying time and air trapping may result May impede VR to heart ↑ PVR and worsen diseases such as PPHN and CHD Worsen PAL	Mimics natural breathing pattern May impede best ratio at higher rates	Insufficient emptying at highest rates	Useful during weaning, when oxygenation is less of a problem May be more useful in diseases such as MAS, when air trapping is a part of the disease process	Low TI may decrease the VT May have to use higher flow rates, which may not be optimal for distribution of ventilation May ventilate more dead space

Adapted from Goldsmith, J. and Karotkin, E., *Assisted Ventilation of the Neonate*, 4th Ed., Copyright 2003, WB Saunders Co.

Parameter	Clinical Notes	Cautions
FiO₂ 0.4 - 0.5 (or as previously established)	**PaO₂ known** – use same FiO₂ as adequate for spontaneous ventilation or bagging. Caution initial MV may dramatically ↑ PaO₂, monitor closely and ↓ FiO₂ accordingly. **PaO₂ unknown** – use minimum dosage necessary to keep neonate or infant pink until ABG can be obtained. See target PaO₂ values below.	Inadequate FiO₂ may lead to hypoxemia and severe neurologic injury. Excessive FiO₂ may lead to ROP in infants <1500 gms (≈ PaO₂ > 100 mm Hg) or BPD in infants (≈ FiO₂ > 0.4 for prolonged periods).

Mech. Ventilation

Ventilator Management Strategies

* The most important aspect of proper ventilatory management is the continuous presence of skilled personnel.

Oxygenation	*Ventilation*
The primary controls for oxygenation are FIO_2 and $\overline{Paw}$ (PIP, I:E, PEEP, $\dot{V}_I$, and waveform).	Primary controls for ventilation are PIP/V_T and f.
Aggressive efforts should be employed to keep FIO_2 and $\overline{Paw}$ as low as possible (esp. $FIO_2 < 0.5$ and $PaO_2 < 90$ mmHg in premature infants)	1) Adjust PIP/V_T to achieve appropriate lung inflation (assess by BS, chest excursion, exhaled V_T, and CXR).
	2) Adjust f to achieve target $PaCO_2$ and pH values (see below).
During increasing MV, FIO_2 is first ↑ to 0.6 before additional increases in $\overline{Paw}$.	***PaCO_2*:**
See target PaO_2 values below.	Aggressive conventional MV to reduce $PaCO_2$ is discouraged.
	Permissive hypercapnia is well-tolerated in infants and children.

Initial Settings

* There are no absolute rules or definitive guidelines – only suggestions. All settings are variable and must be modified based on the disease state, ventilation type, gestational age, postnatal age, and weight.

Parameters associated with optimal tissue oxygenation and ventilation are often associated with detrimental side effects (pulmonary toxicity, BPD, barotrauma, IVH, CV instability, etc.). The benefits of any type or mode of MV must be carefully weighed against the risks.

One general rule is to employ values and modes which minimize complications and risks.

Over the last decade, neonatologists have moved more towards "gentle ventilation" and permissive hypercapnia.

Initial V_T, PIP, T_I, and f "may be estimated by observing response to manual bagging.

Summary Overview of Initial Settings (See guidelines below)

Parameter	Infant Setting
V$_T$	4 - 6 mL/kg
PIP (P/L)	15 - 20 cm H$_2$O
$\overline{\text{Paw}}$	5 - 15 cm H$_2$O
PEEP	4 - 7 cm H$_2$O
f	20 - 40 breaths/min

Parameter	Infant Setting
T$_I$	0.3 - 0.5 sec
V$_I$	8 - 12 L/m
TE	0.5 - 1.5 sec
I:E	1:1 to 1.3
FiO$_2$	0.4 - 0.5

Arterial Blood Gases (ABGs)

Target Values

Peripheral artery puncture or peripheral/UAC	Heel or finger stick (appropriately done)	Pulse Oximeter
PaO$_2$ 50 - 80 mm Hg (infants) 70 - 100 mm Hg (children) SaO$_2$ 05 - 93% PaCO$_2$ 35 - 55 mm Hg pH 7.25 - 7.45	PaO$_2$ usually not accurate (measurement of blood oxygenation should be with pulse oximeter) PaCO$_2$ 35 - 55 mm Hg pH 7.25 - 7.45	SpO$_2$ ≥ 90% (with an upper limit of 94% for very low birthweight)

Exceptions*

Infants < 28 wk gestation	Infants 28-40 wk gestation
PaO$_2$ 45-65 PaCO$_2$ 40-55 (60) pH ≥ 7.25 (7.20)	PaO$_2$ 50-70 PaCO$_2$ 45-55 (60) pH ≥ 7.25 (7.20)

Term infant with PPHN	Infant with BPD
PaO$_2$ 80-120 PaCO$_2$ 30-40 pH 7.30-7.50	PaO$_2$ 30-80 PaCO$_2$ 55-65 (70) pH 7.35-7.45

* Adapted from Goldsmith, J, and Karotkin, E. *Assisted Ventilation of the Neonate*, 4th Ed., Copyright 2003 by WB Saunders Co. ( ) values may be accepted in certain strategies.

Mech. Ventilator

Clinical Notes:

Permissive hypercapnia is gaining in popularity in newborns, as well as adults, in order to minimize lung injury.

The pulmonary circulation of infants and children is highly sensitive to changes in oxygenation. PVR increases due to hypoxemia can become life threatening.

O_2 delivery to tissues is highly dependent on hematocrit level. Maintain $\geq 35\%$ in infants and children.

O_2 delivery and tissue perfusion may be assessed by capillary refill. Tissue oxygenation may be assessed by observing skin and mucous membrane color.

Two Main Types of Neonatal Pulmonary Disorders*

Atelectatic	Obstructive
Physiology: ↓ Lung volumes (↓ FRC, ↓ CL) Normal airway resistance Normal time constant	*Physiology:* ↑ Lung volumes (↑ FRC, ↓ CL) ↑ Airway resistance ↑ Time constant
Clinical appearance: Prematurity- common Severe retractions	*Clinical appearance:* Term or post term – common ↑ A-P diameter
Management: Early PPV to stabilize alveoli, ↑ FRC, and ↓ WOB Correct hypoventilation PPHN rare	*Management:* Avoid PPV Avoid overventilation PPHN common
Examples: RDS, pneumonia	*Examples:* MAS, BPD

* Adapted from Goldsmith, J, and Karotkin, E. *Assisted Ventilation of the Neonate*, 4th Ed., Copyright 2003 by WB Saunders Co

Mech. Ventilation

One Approach To Ventilator Management

Note: This is only one of many approaches available. Numerous other strategies have been successfully employed by experienced clinicians. An <u>overall plan or strategy</u> is better than just making individual changes based upon a single blood gas.

Overall Balance Of Ventilatory Support Parameters*

O_2 %	PIP (< 1500 gm)	PIP (> 1500 gm)	PEEP	Rate
100	25-30 cmH$_2$0	25-30 cmH$_2$O	6-8 cmH$_2$0	40-60
80-90	25-30	25 30	5-7	40-60
60-70	20-25	22-30	5	35-50
50	20-25	22-30	4	30-45
40	15-20	18-25	3-4	20-35
30	10-18	15-22	2-3	< 30

Notes:

These values are only guidelines that may not be appropriate in all clinical situations. If a patient's vent settings differ significantly from the overall pattern across any one row, then a ventilation strategy should be incorporated to return the settings to a more appropriate combination.

An I:E ratio of 1:1 to 1:3 and an initial rate of 40-60 breaths/minute is assumed.

Normal ABG values for this table are:

PaO$_2$ 50-80 mmHg

PaCO$_2$ 40-55 mmHg

pH   7.25-7.45

* Adapted from Goldsmith, J, and Karotkin, E. *Assisted Ventilation of the Neonate*, Copyright 2003 by W. B. Saunders Co.

Various Approaches to Neonatal Mechanical Ventilation

Approach	Rationale	Technique
Slow Rate Ventilation	↑ oxygenation by ↑ MAP. *Caution:* ↑ risk of air trapping and ↑ $PaCO_2$, and IVH; rarely used today	f 20-30 bpm, long Ti or inverse I/E ratio
Gentle Ventilation or Permissive Hypercapnia	Accept higher $PaCO_2$ (up to 60) and lower pH (down to 7.15-7.20) to reduce VILI; maintain adequate oxygenation and minimize the atelectasis; may ↓ need for ECMO in PPHN	f 20-30 bpm, but ↑ f rather than PIP, keep PIP low
Rapid-Rate Ventilation	Higher rates and hand ventilation to achieve oxygenation at lower PIP, ↓ barotrauma, accept some inadvertent PEEP	f 60-80 bpm or up to 150 bpm, keep low PIP, use ↓ Ti
Hyperventilation	Used to treat PPHN Use high rate and PIP as necessary to ↓ $PaCO_2$ to the *highest* level (critical $PaCO_2$) at which oxygenation occurs. ↓ R-L shunting by ↓ PVR Use cautiously: ↑ risk of neurologic injury and air leak. NO therapy, ECMO or HFV commonly preferred.	f 60-150 bpm and sufficient PIP to ↓ $PaCO_2$ to ≤ 35 Periodically, *cautiously* challenge infant by ↓ support to see if PPHN has resolved or transition phase has begun. Watch for "flip-flop".
High Frequency Ventilation	High rates at very low Vt and PIP for severe lung disease or pulmonary air leak.	*See page 10-30*
Nitric Oxide Therapy	NO is a direct pulmonary vasodilator approved for use in PPHN	*See page 10-31*

*Adapted from Goldsmith, J, and Karotkin, E. *Assisted Ventilation of the Neonate*, 4th Ed., Copyright 20C3 by WB Saunders Co.

**Suggested Ventilatory Strategies for
Common Neonatal Respiratory Disorders**

Apnea of Prematurity	f 10-15 bpm PIP 7-15 cmH_2O PEEP 3 cmH_2O FiO_2 < 25 (usually)	pH 7.25-7.30 PaO_2 50-70 mmHg $PaCO_2$ 55+ mmHg
Bronchopulmonary Dysplasia	f 20-40 bpm PIP 20-30 cmH_2O PEEP 5-6 cmH_2O T_I 0.4-0.7 sec V_T 5-8 mL/kg	pH 7.25-7.30 PaO_2 50-70 mmHg $PaCO_2$ 55+ mmHg
Congenital Diaphragmatic Hernia	f 40-80 bpm PIP 20-24 cmH_2O PEEP 4-5 cmH_2O T_I 0.3-0.5 sec	pH > 7.25 PaO_2 80-100 mmHg* $PaCO_2$ 40-65 mmHg
Meconium Aspiration Syndrome (without PPHN)	f 40-60 bpm PEEP 4-5 cmH_2O T_E 0.5-0.7 sec **	pH 7.30-7.40 PaO_2 60-80 mHg* $PaCO_2$ 40-50 mmHg
PPHN	f 50-70 bpm PIP 15-25 cmH_2O PEEP 3-4 cmH_2O T_I 0.3-0.4 sec FiO_2 0.8-1.0	pH 7.40-7.60 PaO_2 70-100 mmHg* $PaCO_2$ 30-40 mmHg
Respiratory Distress Syndrome	f > 60 bpm PIP 10-20 cmH_2O PEEP 4-5 cmH_2O T_I 0.3-0.4 sec V_T 4-6 mL/kg	pH 7.25-7.35 PaO_2 50-70 mmHg $PaCO_2$ 45-55 mmHg

* Sicker neonates may need less aggressive goals for oxygenation, as
  long as preductal SpO_2 is > 85%.
** If gas trapping occurs, ↑ T_E to 0.7-1.0 sec and ↓ PEEP to
   3-4 cmH_2O.
Adapted from Goldsmith, J, and Karotkin, E. *Assisted Ventilation of
the Neonate*, 4th Ed., Copyright 2003 by WB Saunders Co.

Mech. Ventilation

Making Parameter Changes

Non-Acute Situations	Acute Deterioration
Make only one change at a time so the result may be appropriately assessed.	May make several simultaneous changes as needed when time does not allow.

How Parameter Changes Generally Affect ABGs *

	PaO_2	$PaCO_2$
↑ FiO_2	↑	
↑ PIP	↑	↓
↑ V_T	↑	↓
↑ PEEP**	↑	↓
↑ f	↑	↓
↑ T_I	↑	↓
↑ V_I	↑	↓
↑ MAP	↑	↓

* *Exception:* When manipulation of one or more of these parameters cause alveolar overdistention, ↓ pulmonary perfusion, CV instability, air leaks, and/or IVH, then just the opposite effects are likely to occur.

** $PaCO_2$ will ↑ if ↓ delivered V_T.

Reversing the parameters should result in the opposite change.

To:	PIP	V_T	f	T_I	$\dot{V}_I$	PEEP	FiO_2	MAP
↑ $PaCO_2$	↓	↓	↓	↓	↓	↓		↓
↓ $PaCO_2$	↑	↑	↑	↑	↑	↑		↑
↑ PaO_2	↑	↑	↑	↑	↑	↑	↑	↑
↓ PaO_2	↓	↓	↓	↓	↓	↓	↓	↓

Clinical Notes:

There are few controlled studies indicating which methods or modes
of ventilation are superior in pediatric patients.

After the first few months of life, the pediatric ventilatory strategy
and techniques more closely resembles that of adult patients, than
the newborn population.

Historically, because of the limitations of ventilators that were
available, patients < 10 kg were ventilated with PV, whereas those
> 10 kg were ventilated with VV. Modern ventilators make this
distinction unnecessary, although there may be reasons to consider
one method over another, as noted below.

The most common mistakes made in iatrogenic causes of inadequate
oxygenation or ventilation are:

1) *Inadequate Ti* – for *significant* lung disease, start with a Ti of
   0.8 sec.

2) *Inadequate distending pressure* – for *significant* lung disease,
   PIP may need to reach 30 - 35 cmH₂O to adequately recruit
   alveoli for adequate ventilation and/or oxygenation. This should
   be evaluated by chest rise, BS, chest x-ray, and ABGs.

Note: This may also be applicable upon weaning. As pediatric
patients in the first few years of life may have airways that close
in the V_T range (closing volumes), it is not infrequent that during
weaning lowering the PIP < 30 cmH₂O, may lead to atelectasis in
those patients with the most severe disease.

Indications for Mechanical Ventilation

The same as for adults, see Oakes' *Ventilator Management: A
Bedside Reference Guide.*

Initial Settings

Parameter	Child Setting	Parameter	Child Setting
V_T	6 - 10 mL/kg	Ti	0.5 - 1.5 sec
PIP (P/L)	25 - 30 cm H₂O	Vi	2 - 3 x MV
$\bar{P}$aw	5 - 15 cm H₂O	Te	0.5 - 1.5 sec
PEEP	4 - 10 cm H₂0	I:E	1:1 to 1:4
f	12 - 25 bpm	FiO₂	0.4 - 0.5

Target ABG Values *

| PaO$_2$ | 70 – 100 mm Hg | PaCO$_2$ | 35 - 45 mm Hg |
| SaO$_2$ | > 92 % | pH | 7.3 - 7.45 |

* Excluding permissive hypercapnia or permissive hypoxemia

Pressure Ventilation (PV)

Indication

PV is considered, as in adults, when the patient is at ↑ risk for ventilator-induced lung injury. Criteria used by some clinicians for children who are difficult to oxygenate: *i.e., when PIP > 35 cm H$_2$O, PEEP > 8 cm H$_2$O, PaO$_2$/FiO$_2$ < 100*

Advantage

Immediate rise to PIP permitting extended time for gas distribution within the lung. (Note: this is also true for decelerating wave pattern in general, even in volume ventilation, also this would be true for pressure limited ventilation).

The decelerating flow wave pattern favors this method as a lung protective strategy (↓ PIP, ↑ $\overline{Paw}$) compared to VV with a constant flow.

PV may also compensate better than VV for leaks around uncuffed ET / trach tubes used in small children.

Common Problems In Pediatric PSV

Small ET tube:

1) Premature Pressure Support Termination (PPST) – is common when small ET tubes (esp. < 4.5 mm) offer excessive resistance. The ventilator circuit pressurizes before sufficient flow enters the airway causing a premature termination of the inspiratory phase with a resultant ↓ in delivered V$_T$.

2) Failure of flow-cycle due to ET tube leaks.

See Oakes' ***Ventilator Management: A Bedside Reference Guide*** for an excellent and detailed explanation of:

> **Improving Ventilation**
> **Improving Oxygenation**
> **Improving Patient-Ventilator Interaction**

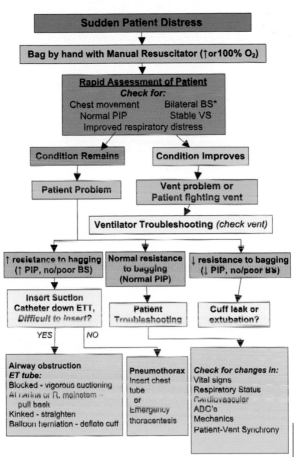

Sudden Patient Distress

↓

Bag by hand with Manual Resuscitator (↑or100% O₂)

↓

Rapid Assessment of Patient
Check for:

Chest movement	Bilateral BS*
Normal PIP	Stable VS
Improved respiratory distress	

Condition Remains → **Patient Problem**

Condition Improves → **Vent problem or Patient fighting vent**

↓

Ventilator Troubleshooting *(check vent)*

↑ resistance to bagging (↑ PIP, no/poor BS)

Insert Suction Catheter down ETT, *Difficult to Insert?*
- YES
- NO

Normal resistance to bagging (Normal PIP)

Patient Troubleshooting

↓ resistance to bagging (↓ PIP, no/poor BS)

Cuff leak or extubation?

Airway obstruction
ET tube:
Blocked - vigorous suctioning
At carina or R. mainstem –
pull back
Kinked - straighten
Balloon herniation - deflate cuff

Pneumothorax
Insert chest tube
or
Emergency thoracentesis

Check for changes in:
Vital signs
Respiratory Status
Cardiovascular
ABG's
Mechanics
Patient-Vent Synchrony

* Note: BS in small infants may sound OK due to transmittal – proceed as though not OK.

10-27

Mech. Ventilation

See Oakes' ***Ventilator Management: A Bedside Reference Guide***
for a detailed analysis and differential diagnosis of Patient – Ventilator Trouble-Shooting, including causes of changes in:

Vital Signs	*Mechanics*	*Patient - Ventilator Asynchrony ("Fighting the Vent")*
Respiratory	*Patient Comfort / Psychology*	
ABG's		
Cardiovascular	*Ventilator Parameters*	

Neonatal Discontinuation/Weaning

See Page 10-7 for a suggested approach.

Clinical Notes:

Weaning should initiate it as soon as possible after the patient is stable for at least 4 to 8 hrs and ABGs suggest that ventilatory needs are ↓.

Obtain baseline CXR before initiating wean.

↓ FiO_2 and PIP first, then Ti and PEEP if excessive. Gradual and frequent small changes are preferred to infrequent larger decreases. Change only one parameter at a time. When ↓ PIP keep V_T 4-8 ml/kg.

Monitor SpO_2 and $ETCO_2$ (ABG if needed) and clinical status with each parameter change.

If mode is A/C, switch to SIMV when FiO_2 is < 0.4 and PIP is < 12 cmH_2O, then begin to ↓ *f.*

When *f* is ↓ to 5-10 bpm, proceed to extubation (consider extubation when *f* reaches 20 bpm if ET tube < 3.5 cm)

Note: ETCPAP with ≤ 2 distending pressure or low *f* usually results in ↑ WOB and not recommended, esp. in smaller infants.

Extubation
Extubation Readiness Criteria

Ability to protect airways (cough, cry)	No apnea or periodic breathing
Appropriate respiratory parameters	Minimal WOB
Appropriate vital signs	No sedation

Stop feeding 4 hrs before or empty stomach with nasogastric tube.

Obtain CXR before extubation and again at 2 and 24 hrs after extubation.

Attach manual resuscitator and give a prolonged sigh of 15–20 cm H_2O to prevent the negative pressure of tube removal from causing atelectasis.

Place patient on nasal SIMV, nasal CPAP (5-6 cmH$_2$O), or just O_2 (oxyhood or nasal cannula). Give FiO$_2$ 5% above what patient was on.

Prone positioning may be beneficial.

Watch closely for deterioration for several minutes.

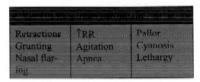

Retractions	↑R.R.	Pallor
Grunting	Agitation	Cyanosis
Nasal flaring	Apnea	Lethargy

Monitor SpO$_2$. Reintubate if distress is significant or recurrent, severe apnea.

For stridor, racemic epinephrine may ↓ Raw.

Methylxanthines may ↓ Raw and ↑ respiratory drive.

Withhold feeding for 4-6 hrs or until patient can make an audible cry (i.e., ability to protect airway).

Pediatric discontinuation is more similar to adults than neonates.

See the ACCP/AARC/SCCM Evidence-Based Guidelines for Weaning and Discontinuing Ventilatory Support algorithm in Oakes' *Ventilator Management: A Bedside Reference Guide.*

Failure To Wean
See Oakes' *Ventilator Management: A Bedside Reference Guide* for an excellent summary.

Mech. Ventilation

High Frequency Ventilation

Types	Frequency	V_T	Expiration
High Frequency Positive Pressure Ventilation (HFPPV)	60-150/min	$> V_D$	Passive
High Frequency Jet Ventilation (HFJV)	150-660	$>$ or $< V_D$	Passive
High Frequency Oscillatory Ventilation (HFOV)	180-900	$< V_D$	Active
High Frequency Flow Interruption Ventilation (HFFIV)	300-3000	$>$ or $< V_D$	Passive

Indications
Early Rescue-
1) VLBW infants with RDS
2) Air leak syndromes (PIE, pneumothorax, T_E or BP fistula)

Late Rescue-
1) Failure of conventional MV (ARDS, CDH, MAS, PPHN, pneumonia, pulm hemorrhage)
2) Decrease risk of VILI (when conventional MV settings are high) (e.g., $\overline{Paw} > 15$ cmH$_2$O)

Two Common Strategies

Low-volume Strategy	High-volume Strategy
Low PIPs to minimize air leaks	Lung recruitment with optimal lung volume
Used to treat: Air leak syndromes (BP fistula, PIE, pneumothorax) MAS, PPHN Pulmonary hypoplasia (CDH)	*Used to treat:* RDS or similar atelectatic conditions

Potential Benefits

↓ PIP and $\overline{Paw}$ ↓ risk of CLD/VILI ↓ O$_2$ requirements Improved gas exchange Improved hemodynamics	More uniform lung inflation Rapid resolutin of air leaks Recruitment/maintenance of lung volume Bridge or alternative to ECMO.

Mech. Ventilation

Potential Hazards

Air trapping (esp. HFPPV)	Inadequate pressure monitoring
Tracheal injury (high flow velocity)	Complex to operate
Inadequate humidification	Increased IVH rates
Limited alarms	

Inhaled Nitric Oxide (INO)

Indications

Hypoxic respiratory failure (HRF) with pulmonary hypertension (PPHN) and failure of conventional therapies.

- 34 week gestation, < 14 days old
- Oxygen Index ≥ 25
- Pre-ductal/post-ductal SpO_2 gradient

$$OI = \frac{\overline{P}aw \times FIO2 \times 100}{PaO2}$$

Contraindications

CHD with dependent R to L shunting
High baseline methemoglobinemia (follow metHb levels)

Pre-Treatment Strategies

Stabilize with FiO_2 1.0, moderate alkalosis (induced pharmacologically and/or hyperventilation), stable BP (vasoactive agents/fluids), and sedation and/or muscle relaxation.

Surfactant therapy to stabilize lung volume (caution: therapy may worsen PPHN if patient becomes hypoxic during instillation).

MV strategies to optimize alveolar recruitment.

Studies indicate a combination of HFOV and iNO results in best improvement in oxygenation

Procedure

Use an FDA approved delivery device.

Dose: recommended starting dose is 20 ppm.

Response: Immediate improvement in PaO_2 (≥ 20 mmHg) and a decrease in pre/post-ductal SpO_2 is a positive response.

If no brisk improvement, may try 40 ppm (up to max of 80 ppm)

Mech. Ventilation

Weaning and Discontinuation:

After a period of sustained improvement (4 hrs?) on 20 ppm, begin a weaning process.

FIO_2 should be weaned first to ≤ 0.60. Maintain PaO_2 60-80 mmHg and $SpO_2 > 90\%$ during the weaning process.

MV is weaned concomitantly to maintain acceptable $pH/PaCO_2$.

Incrementally reduce iNO dose by 50% (10, 5, 2 and 1 ppm). If oxygenation is not maintained, return to previous dose. Retry 4-8 hrs later.

At 1 ppm, increase FIO_2 20% above current, and discontinue iNO. (Note: Withdrawal of iNO can be associated with life-threatening elevation in PVR and profound O_2 desaturation).

Re-institute at 1 ppm, if there is a rebound effect of PPHN.

Notes:

Continuously monitor O_2, NO and NO_2 concentrations. (Keep NO_2 < 2 ppm).

Periodically evaluate metHb level. (Decrease iNO dose if > 5%).

iNO effectiveness for CDH is questionable, but is commonly employed for stabilization, during transport, and transitioning as ECMO is discontinued.

Centers without capability for ECMO must establish treatment failure criteria and mechanisms for timely transfer to an ECMO center for non-responders. iNO must not be interrupted during transport.

Use of iNO in preterm infants (<34 wks) is still controversial and investigational.

Potential Patient Complications

Alteration of surfactant proteins

Decreased lung host defenses

Lung injury

Methemoglobinemia

NO_2

Nitric acid (HNO_3) (NO and H_2O in vent circuit – minimize circuit rainout)

Platelet dysfunction, bleeding

Potentiation of O_2 lung toxicity and/or airway injury

Extracorporeal Membrane Oxygenation (ECMO; ECLS)

Purpose: Circulation and gas exchange for temporary life support for reversible heart or lung failure, which is failing maximal conventional medical, pharmacological, and ventilator therapies, and/or when the dangers of convent. MV outweigh the risk of ECMO.

Goal is to rest the lungs and heart.

Diseases Treated

Air leak syndromes	CHD (periop support)	PPHN
Asphyxia	Diaphragmatic hernia	RDS
Cardiogenic shock	MAS	Septic shock
	Postop cardiac surgery	

Indications	*Contraindications*
$AaDO_2 > 610$ x 8 hrs or > 605 x 4hrs, if PIP > 38 cmH_2O	*Relative:* Prolonged severe hypoxia
$OI > 40$	Prolonged MV > 7 days
$$OI = \frac{Paw}{postductal \ PaO_2} \times FiO_2 \times 100$$	Structural cardiac disease (preop)
Acute deterioration with $PaO_2 < 40$ x 2 hrs and/or pH < 7.15 x 2 hrs	History or evidence of ischemic neurological damage
Barotrauma (any 4 concurrently): pneumothorax, pneumopericardium, pneumoperitoneum, PIE, persistent air leak > 24 hrs, MAP > 15 cmH_2O and subQ emphysema	*Absolute:* Lack of parental consent Inadequate conventional therapy Weight < 2000 g Gestational age < 35 wks
Postoperative cardiac dysfunction	Contraindication to anticoagulation: severe pulmonary hemorrhage, IVH grade II or
Bridge to cardiac transplantation	4, GI hernia, head trauma Prolonged MV > 7-14 days
Adapted from Goldsmith, J, and Karotkin, E. ***Assisted Ventilation of the Neonate***, 4th Ed., Copyright 2003 by WB Saunders Co.	History of severe asphyxia or global cerebral ischemia Lethal genetic condition Untreatable nonpulmonary disease

11 Respiratory Diseases/Disorders

Chapter Contents

Explanation of Key Used throughout this Chapter

NAME - MOST COMMONLY ACCEPTED MEDICAL TERM LISTED IN ALPHABETICAL ORDER (OTHER NAMES OR ABBREVIATIONS)

Def	Definition
Etiology	Origin of disease or disease-causing organisms.
CM	Clinical Manifestations Listings indicate the most commonly found pulmonary manifestations (not all-inclusive). Manifestations of other body systems are generally not included.
CXR	Chest X-Ray - common findings
Tx	Treatment (generalized) "?" denotes therapy is questionable. It may be controversial, under research, or highly dependent on the individual's clinical status or circumstances. Investigate further before using.

AIR LEAK SYNDROME (BAROTRAUMA)
(Volutrauma, Pulmonary Air Leak, Extrapulmonary Air, Pneumothorax, Pneumomediastinum, Pneumopericardium, Pulmonary Interstitial Emphysema [PIE], Pneumoperitoneum, or Subcutaneous Emphysema)

Def

Alveolar or airway rupture with the dissection of air into the lung interstitium and then pleural rupture allowing the air to escape into the pleural, mediastinum, pericardium, or abdominal cavity, or under the skin.

Etiology

Uneven ventilation
Lung overdistention
Chemical injury
Trauma - see page 11-80
Surgery or iatrogenic (needle puncture or tracheal intubation)
Valsalva maneuvers
Spontaneous (e.g. TTN)

***Predisposing factors*:**
Lung disease and immaturity (esp. RDS)
Positive pressure ventilation (esp during recovery stages of lung disease):

↑ V_T	Inverse I:E ratio
↑ MAP	Trauma of air flow
↑ PEEP/CPAP	Fighting the vent
↑ T_I	
↓ T_E	

Fetal distress/asphyxia	Resuscitation
Intubation (malpositioning)	Suctioning (tracheal)
Atelectasis	Pneumonia
Renal malfunction	Aspiration

CM

See table on next page

CXR

See table on next page

Tx

See table on next page

Manifestations and Treatment by Disorder

	Clinical Manifestations	CXR	Treatment
Pulmonary Interstitial Emphysema (PIE)	Sudden clinical and ABG deterioration Usually occurs in first few days of life Often associated with pneumothorax	Multiple small linear streaks and/or cysts or blebs	↓ vent volumes (↓ MAP) (if possible) Minimize ET sx and hand-bagging Place involved lung down Selective intubation? HFJV or HFOV Lobectomy
Pneumo-mediastinum	±symptomatic or variable resp. distress Distant crunching heart sounds	air in mediastinum "sail" sign	↓ vent MAP (if possible) Observe closely No drainage is usually necessary
Pneumo-pericardium	asymptomatic or muffled distant heart sounds ↓ BP ↑ or ↓ HR Cyanosis ↑ RR Weak pulses ↓ pulse pressure	radiolucent area (darker = air) encircling heart	*Asymptomatic:* ↓ vent MAP (if possible) Observe closely *Symptomatic:* immediate needle aspiration (see Fig 6-34) Pericardial tube? Pericardectomy

	Clinical Manifestations	CXR	Treatment
Pneumothorax (Simple)	↑ RR ↑ HR Dyspnea Cyanosis Chest pain Nasal Flaring Retractions	Partially collapsed lung (rare in RDS) with free air outlining lung (radiolucent) and absent pulmonary markings beyond border	Transilluminate/CXR for extent Observe closely ↓ vent MAP (if possible) 100% O_2 to absorb air (caution!) Sedatives/paralysis if on MV? No drainage if ↓ BP or HR not in distress, not a cont. leak, or not on MV Perform thoracentesis (pg 6-29) Insert Chest Tube (pg 6-30) Drainage required if patient in distress, continuous leak, or receiving MV)
Pneumothorax (Tension)	Same as simple, plus: PMI/tracheal shift ↑ or ↓ HR ↑ or ↓ BP ↑ respiratory distress/apnea Sudden ABG deterioration ↓ Chest movement Chest asymmetry Pallor, dusky ↓ or absent BS (may be normal in sm. infants)	Tension is simple, plus atelectasis of opposite side of pneumothorax, depressed diaphragm Hyperresonance to percussion (ipsilateral) JVD (↑ CVP) ↓ pulse pressure Pulsus Paradoxus Restlessness	Treat immediately - do not wait for CXR confirmation Perform thoracentesis (pg 6-29) or insert chest tube (choice) (pg 6-30) Agitation Fighting the vent ↑ Raw to vent Abdominal distention Subcutaneous emphysema Cardiac arrythmias

AIRWAY OBSTRUCTION (UPPER)

Def

Decreased or difficult ventilation due to airway obstruction above the small bronchi

Etiology

Nose	Trachea & Bronchi	Larnyx
Choanal Atresia URI Burns Iatrogenic (tubes/tapes)	Malacia Stenosis Croup Lobar Emphysema	Epiglottitis Floppy epiglottis Subglottic stenosis Laryngospasm Laryngeal Web Cord Paralysis

Mouth & Pharynx	Extrinsic	Other
Hypoplastic Mandible Tongue Enlargement (Down Syndrome) Pierre-Robin Syndrome Diptheria Tonsillitis Cysts	Goiter Vascular Ring Mediastinal Mass T-E Fistula T-O Fistula	Foreign Body Aspiration

Variable, depending on cause/location (see disease specific examples in Treatment box)

CM

Differential Diagnosis of Airway Obstruction			
	Extrathoracic Airway Obstruction	Intrathoracic Extrapulmonary Airway Obstruction	Intrapulmonary Airway Obstruction
Tachypnea	↑	+	++
Retraction	++++	++	++
Stridor	++++	++	–
Grunting	±	±	++
Wheezing	±	+++	++++

Reprinted with permission from Vidyasagar: *Neonatal and Pediatric Intensive Care*. Copyright 1985 by PSG.

Other Signs —

Nasal flaring, agitation, ↑ HR, diaphoresis ↓ air movement

Late Signs —
      Hypoxemia and/or hypercarbia
      Bradycardia
      Bradypnea
      Altered LOC

Sequence of Events in Progressive Upper Airway Obstruction
Cough
Stridor
Dyspnea   }   ↓ PaO_2 and normal $PaCO_2$
Restlessness
Air hunger
Cyanosis
Fatigue   }   ↓ PaO_2 and ↑ $PaCO_2$
Coma
Death

Reprinted with permission from Lough, M. etal: ***Pediatric Respiratory Therapy***, 3rd Ed. Copyright 1985 by Yearbook Medical Pub. Inc.

General (see also specific examples below):
    O_2 therapy (as needed)
    Rule out epiglottitis (see Pg. 11-48)
    Secure airway (oral or trach as needed)
    Treat cause (see examples below)

Foreign Body Aspiration

CM —

Asymptomatic to acute asphyxia	Wheezing	Apnea
History (gagging, choking)	Dysphonia	Stridor
Sudden onset of dyspnea	↓BS	
Hyperresonance	Cyanosis	
Paroxysmal cough		

TX —
Remove obstruction (see CPR, Ch 13)
Laryngoscopy
Bronchoscopy

Choanal Atresia (membraneous or bony obstruction between nose and pharynx)

    CM —

        Unilateral — asymptomatic, apnea or mild resp. distress

        Bilateral — acute signs at birth

            gasping   apnea   stridor
            retractions   cyanosis   wheezing
            flaring   hypoxemia

        CM subside and infant becomes pink upon crying.

        Diag — unable to pass catheter through one/both nares.

    TX —

        Unilateral & asymptomatic — no immediate care needed

        Bilateral —

            Emergency oral airway;

                McGovern nipple — old-fashioned rubber nipple with tip cut off

            Oropharyngeal or ET tube

            Secure airway so can't fall or be pushed out

            Surgery

            Laser?

            May have many associated anomalies

Subglottis stenosis (intrinsic narrowing of airway, most commonly due to prolonged intubation)

    CM —

        Post-extubation   Apnea   ↓ PaO_2
        Resp. distress   Stridor   ↑ $PaCO_2$
        Cyanosis

    TX — Cool mist

            Dexamethasone

            Heliox therapy?

            Racemic epinephrine

            Intubation

            Trach or plasty?

Pierre-Robin Syndrome (micrognathia, cleft palate and large tongue)

    CM — Stertorous (snoring-like) and raspy breathing

            Choking and gagging with feeding

    TX — Prone position

            Nasopharyngeal or ET intubation?

            Surgery

APNEA OF PREMATURITY

Apnea of Infancy (AI), Infantile Apnea, Sleep Apnea, Acute (apparent) Life Threatening Event (ALTE)

Def

Cessation of breathing for > 20 sec. or < 20 sec. when associated with bradycardia (< 80-100), cyanosis, pallor, and/or ↓ muscle tone in preterm infants (< 37 wks)

Central apnea — simultaneous cessation of breathing and airflow (most often in newborns)

Obstructive apnea — breathing movements but no airflow (most often > 1 mo. age)

Note: Most infants with apnea do not die of SIDS and most SIDS victims had no identifiable apnea.

Etiology

Not a disease but a symptom of an underlying cause:

Prematurity (all other causes should first be excluded, ceases by 43-44 weeks post-conceptual age)

Sepsis (suspect 1st)

Cardiorespiratory		
Hypoxia/acidosis	*Pulm disease:*	*Airway obstruction:*
Asphyxia	RDS	Anatomical
Anemia	BPD	Head flexion/extension
Shock	Pneumonia	Choanal atresia
PDA	Diaphragm fatigue	Tonsillitis or hypertro-
CHF	Pneumothorax	phy (most common
	Polycythemia	cause in older
	Pulm. edema	children)
		Eye mask (bilirubin
		therapy)
		Secretions

Vagal Stimulation	Drugs
Hyperinflation with bagging	Maternal
Suction	Neonatal
Gastric detention	
Rapid feeding	**Temp. Instability**
N-G tube	Infant
GE reflux	Environment

CNS Dysfunction	Other
Trauma	Necrotizing enterocolitis
Hemorrhage (IVH)	Sleep
Seizures	Idiopathic
Infection (TORCH, menningitis)	Hypoglycemia

CM

Cessation of breathing and/or airflow.
Cyanosis, ↓ HR, ↓ Muscle tone

Tx

Treat cause (see Previous Page)
Prevent further episodes
General
    Maintain airway/prevent obstruction
        Sx oropharynx gently, PRN
        Do not flex or hyperextend neck
    Maintain normal PaO_2
        Monitor continuously (SpO_2 88-92%) to prevent
          hypoxemia
        Prevent hyperoxemia (↓ resp. drive)
    Minimize vagal stimulation
        Do not hyperinflate while bagging
        Do not give cold O_2 to face
        Gentle Sx
        Feed slowly / do not overfeed
        Remove NG tube if possible
        ↓ handling
    Maintain norm electrolytes & temp (may try to lower
        range of NTE)
    Monitor HR & resp. continuously (all pts. < 34 wks)
        until no apnea 5-7 days
Specific —
    Tactile stimulation (flick sole, rub legs, chest or back)
    Do not inflict pain
    Apnea mattress or waterbed
    O_2 < 35% (avoid hyperoxia), high flow nasal cannula
        (1-2.5 LPM) > CPAP
    Xanthines

PHARMACOLOGIC MANAGEMENT OF APNEA			
Drug	Route	Dose	Therapeutic Level
Aminophylline	IV	8 mg/kg loading dose then 1.5-3 mg/kg q 8-12 hr.	7-12 mcg/mL
Theophylline	oral	same as aminophylline	7-12 mcg/mL
Caffeine (base)	oral	10-20 mg/kg loading dose, then 2.5-4 mg/kg q 24 hr.	5-25 mcg/mL

Caution: Do not use initially at birth. Apnea may be due to asphyxia and xanthines may ↓ CBF.

Xanthines - Watch for:
↑ HR
Abdominal distention
Diuresis
Jitteriness
Vomiting
Hyperglycemia
Seizures
Wean over 3-7 days (if no apnea for 7-14 days)

CPAP + IMV or NIPPV
Provide "physiologic" ventilation:
Normal rates 30-40 (12-15 if intermittent apnea),
PEEP 3-4 cm,
PIP 10-18 cm,
Normal $T_I + \dot{V}_I$.

When apnea occurs: gently, but firmly, stimulate infant, then if needed, briefly bag and mask ventilate until HR, cyanosis and tone improve.
Use same FIO_2 as infant was receiving.
100% O_2 is **contraindicated**.
Air/O_2 should be warmed (cold air on face may stimulate apnea)
Avoid hyperinflation.

Do not discharge from hospital if:
Apnea without treatable cause
Apnea without response to therapy
Abnormal sleep study or pneumogram
Family history of SIDS
Potential chronic hypoxemia
Potential airway obstruction
Unable to be appropriately monitored

Discontinue Home Monitoring:
When apnea of prematurity > 43 weeks PMA
No clinical apnea > 2 mo.
No apnea requiring stim. > 3 mo.
Ability to handle URI or immunization

ASPHYXIA
Perinatal asphyxia, hypoxic-ischemic encephalopathy (HIE)

Def

An hypoxic and/or acidotic insult to the fetus or newborn due to lack of O_2 and/or perfusion of body organs

Etiology

Maternal Factors	Intrapartum Factors	Fetal Factors
Maternal disease	Prolonged labor	Multiple births
Maternal drugs	Precipitious labor	Polyhydramnios
Inadequate prenatal care	Difficult delivery	Oligohydramnios
	Cord compression	Immature L/S ratio
Prolonged rupture of membranes	Prolapsed umbilical cord	Premature delivery
Abruptio placentae, placenta previa	Cesarean section	Post-term delivery
		SGA/LGA
Blood type isoimmunization		Meconium-stained
Toxemia of pregnancy, hypertension		

CM

Depends on severity of insult to each organ

Pulmonary	Heart
Respiratory Distress	*CHF:*
↑ RR or apnea	↑ HR
Cyanosis	↑ RR
Grunting	Hepatomegaly
Flaring	Gallop
	Murmur
	↓ BP

Cerebral	Renal
HIE:	Oliguria
↑ LOC	Anuria
↓ Reflexes	
↓ Tone	
Posturing	
↓ HR	
Seizures	
Temp instability	
↑ICP	

11-13

Clinical Stages of HIE			
	Stage 1	**Stage 2**	**Stage 3**
Stage	Hyperalert	Lethargic	Stuporous
Tone	+/− Hypotonic	Hypotonic	Flaccid
Stretch reflexes	Exaggerated	Diminished	Absent
Suck	Normal	Weak	Weak./Absent
Moro	Normal/ Exaggerated	Incomplete	Absent
Seizure activity	None	None/ Intermittent	Repetitive/ Status
Oculoves-tibular response	Present	Present	+/− Present
Spontaneous respirations	Present	Present	Apnea/None

Reprinted with permission from *Pediatric Annals* 17:8. Copyright 1988. (Modified from Sarnot, 1976.)

Delivery Room Management: (see Ch 1)

Post Delivery Management: Maintain norm ABG's - Caution:

↑ PaO_2	May ↓ CBF → ischemia
↓ PaO_2	May worsen ischemia + IVH
↑ $PaCO_2$	May ↑ CBF → IVH
↓ $PaCO_2$	May ↓ CBF → ischemia

O_2 as needed, avoid hypoxemia or hyperoxemia

MV as needed, avoid hypoventilation or hyperventilation.
(Method depends on underlying pulm. disease, if any).

Maintain normal BP and CPP. Monitor BP, CVP, and ICP continuously, if possible. Avoid abrupt changes. Infuse blood, volume expanders and $NaHCO_3$ very slowly. Avoid fluid overload (cerebreal edema).

↑ BP may ↑ CPP → IVH
↓ BP may ↓ CPP → ischemia

Treat complications: Aspiration, CHF, DIC, RDS, MAS, NEC, pneumothorax, PPHN, pulmonary edema, renal tubular necrosis, shock

ASTHMA

Definition

A chronic inflammatory disorder of the airways.
Airway hyperresponsive, resulting in reversible or partially reversible airway obstruction, that leads to recurrent episodes of wheezing, breathlessness, chest tightness, and coughing.

Types

Extrinsic (allergic) asthma: 90% of all asthma; typically develops in childhood

Intrinsic (non-allergic) asthma: 10% of all asthma; develops after age of 30 to 40

Etiology

Inhalation	Other Factors Inflencing Severity
Genetic?	Cold air, exercise
Allergens:	Drugs, food
Animal (dander, urine, etc)	Emotional stress
	Gastroesophageal reflux
Cockroach feces	Rhinitis/sinusitis
House dust mites	Sensitivity to drugs (aspirin,
Indoor fungi (mold)	beta-blockers, nonsteroidal
Outdoor (pollen, spores)	anti-inflammatory, sulfites)
Occupational exposure:	Viral respiratory infections
Dust, gases, fumes, chemicals	
Irritants: Air pollution, odors, sprays, stove fumes, tobacco smoke	

CM

Agitation/restless	↑RR, ↑HR	Wheezing*
Anxiety	↑Te, ↑WOB	
Chest tightness	Hyperinflation	Late signs:
Cough	Hyperresonance	↓PaCO₂ (initial)* →
Diaphoresis	Hypoxemia	↑PaCO₂ (late)
Dyspnea/SOB	Pulsus paradoxus	↓ BS
Flaring	Retractions	Cyanosis

* DANGER – (also see next page)
Respiratory distress without wheezing and/or with normal PaCO₂ is indicative of impending respiratory failure!

Is it Asthma? *

The presence of any of these signs and symptoms should increase the suspicion of asthma:

- Wheezing
- History of:
  - Cough, worse at night
  - Recurrent wheeze, difficult breathing, or chest tightness
- Symptoms occur or worsen at night, awakening the patient
- Patient also has eczema, hayfever, or family history of asthma
- Symptoms occur or worsen in the presence of: (see etiology previous page)
- Symptoms respond to anti-asthma therapy
- Patient's colds "go to the chest" or take more than 10 days to clear

* Adapted from Global Initiative for Asthma (GINA), 2007.

PFTs: Obstructive Pattern
↓FVC, ↓FEV & FEV₁%, ↓PEF   ----   ↑FRC, ↑RV, ↑TLC

CXR Hyperinflation, ↑bronchial markings, flat diaphragm, ↑rib spaces, more radiolucent, narrow heart shadow.

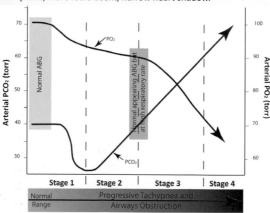

Arterial blood gas, ABG, during various stages of asthma.
11-16

Asthma Severity, Control, and Treatment

Classifying Severity of Asthma Exacerbations *

ASTHMA Tx

Parameter[1]	Mild	Moderate	Severe	Respiratory Arrest Imminent
Breathless	Walking, can lie down	Talking, prefers sitting	At rest, hunched forward	
Talks in	Sentences	Phrases	Words	
Alertness	May be agitated	Usually agitated	Usually agitated	Drowsy or confused
RR[2]	↑	↑	Often > 30/min	
Accessory Muscle Use	None	Usually	Usually	Paradoxical Breathing
Wheeze	Moderate, end-explr	Loud	Usually loud	Absent
Pulse[3]	<100	100-120	> 120	< 60
Pulsus paradoxus	Absent, < 10mmHg	May be present, 10-25 mmHg	Often present, > 25 mmHg[7]	Absent? – respiratory fatigue?
PEF[4]	> 80%	60-80%	< 60% [5]	
PaO2 (on RA)	Normal	> 60mmHg	< 60 mmHg	
PaCO2 [6]	< 45mmHg	< 45 mmHg	> 45 mmHg	
SaO2 (on RA)	> 95%	91-95%	< 90%	

1) The presence of several parameters, but not necessarily all, indicates the general classification of the attack.

2) Normal RR for children: < 2 mo, < 60/min; 2-12 mo, < 50/min; 1-5 yrs, < 40/min; 6-8 yrs, < 30/min.

3) Normal pulse for children: infants (2-12 mo), < 160/min; pre-school (1-2 yrs), < 120/min; school age (2-8 yrs), < 110/min.

4) After initial bronchodilator, % pred or % personal best.

5) < 100 L/min adults or response lasts < 2 hrs.

6) Hypercapnia develops more readily in young children than in adults and adolescents.

7) 20-40 mm Hg in children

11-17

Levels of Asthma Control*

Characteristic	Controlled (all of the following)	Partly con-trolled (any measure present in any week)	
Daytime symptoms	None (≤ 2/week)	> 2/week	3+ features of partly controlled asthma present in any week
Limitations of Activities	None	Any	
Nocturnal symptoms/ awakening	None	Any	
Need for re-liever/rescue treatment	None (≤ 2/week)	> 2/week	
Lung Function (PEF or FEV₁)	Normal	< 80% pred or personal best	
Exacerbations	None	≥ 1 /year	1 in any week

* Adapted from Global Initiative for Asthma (GINA), 2007. See below.

For more information on asthma see:

1. National Asthma Education and Prevention Program Expert Panel Report 3 (EPR3): *Guidelines for the Diagnosis and Management of Asthma,* National Heart, Lung, and Blood Institute (NHLBI), NIH. Available from www.nhlbi.nih.gov/guidelines/asthma/index.htm.

2. *Global Strategy for Asthma Management and Prevention: 2007 Update.* Global Initiative for Asthma (GINA). Available from www.ginasthma.org.

And Oakes' *Ventilator Management: A Bedside Reference Guide* for further details and strategies for mechanical ventilation of the asthma patient.

Key Indicators for Considering a Diagnosis of Asthma

Consider asthma and performing spirometry if any of these indicators are present.* These indicators are not diagnostic by themselves, but the presence of multiple key indicators increases the probablyility of a diagnosis of asthma. Spirometry is needed to establishy a diagnosis of asthma.

Wheezing: high pitched whistling sounds when breathing out (especially in children). Lack of wheezing and a normal chest examination do not exclude asthma.

History of any of the following: cough, worst particularly at night; recurrent wheeze; recurrent difficulty in breathing; recurrent chest tightness.

Reversible airflow limitation and diurnal variation as measured by using a peak flow meter for example:

Peak expiratory flow (PEF) varies 20% or more from PEF measurement on arising in the morning (before taking an inhaled short-acting beta 2 agonist) to PEF measurement in the early afternoon (after taking an inhaled short-acting beta 2 agonist).

PFT's: Airway obstruction ($\uparrow$ FVC, $\downarrow$FEV/FVC)

Reversibility of obstruction ($\uparrow \geq 12\%$ and 200 mL in FEV_1 after bronchodilator)

Symptoms occur or worsen in the presence of: airborne chemicals or dust, animals with fur or feathers, changes in weather, exercise, house dust mites, menses, mold, pollen, smoke (tobacco, wood), strong emotional expression, viral infection.

Symptoms occur or worsen at night, awakening a patient

* Eczema, hay fever, or a family history of asthma or atopic diseases are often associated with asthma, but they are not key indicators

Final diagnosis is made by the exclusion of other possible diagnoses (see next table)

Differential Diagnostic Possibilities for Asthma in Infants and Children

Upper Airway Disease	Allergic rhinitis and sinusitis
Obstruction involving large airways	Foreign body in trachea or bronchus, vocal cord dysfunction, vascular rings or laryngeal webs, laryngotracheomalacia, trachea stenosis, bronchostenosis, enlarged lymph nodes or tumor
Obstruction involving small airways	Viral bronchiolitis or obliterative bronchiolitis, cystic fibrosis, bronchopulmonary dysplasia, heart disease
Other Causes	Recurrent cough not due to asthma, aspiration from swallowing mechanism dysfunction or GERD

Monitoring

Signs and symptoms Quality of life/functional status
PFT's - spirometry and PEF Patient satisfaction
History of exacerbations Pharmacotherapy

Note: Recommended for moderate to severe persistent asthma or history of exacerbations:
1) A written plan of action.
2) Daily peak flow monitoring. PEF upon waking in morning (before taking bronchodilator):
   < 80% indicates need for additional medication
   < 50% indicates acute exacerbation

Prevention

Patient education: including self-management plan
Pharmacotherapy: Quick relief meds, long-term control medications
Environmental control: Reduce exposure to: tobacco smoke, air pollution (ozone, SO_2 and NO_2), URI (rhinitis, sinusitis), gastroesophageal reflux, certain medications

General Therapy

O_2 therapy should be given to all patients in respiratory distress.

Follow oxygenation with pulse oximeter or A-line.

Maintain $SaO_2 > 90\%$

HOB elevated per patient comfort.

Hydration: aggressive hydration may be indicated for infants and small children, but it is *not recommended* for older children.

CPT, mucolytics, and sedation *are not* generally recommended.

Pharmacotherapy

Treat Impending Respiratory Failure.

Signs:

Decreased mental clarity

Worsening fatigue

$PaCO_2 \geq 42$ mmHg

Intubation. Do not delay once it is deemed necessary

Guidelines for Intubation and Initial Ventilation

Note: All modalities of therapy should be maximized during the initial phases of minimize the need for intubation

Perform Rapid Sequence Intubation (RSI)

Hyperoxygenate with bag and mask (ensure enough pressure to ventilate, but not too high to cause increased air trapping and ensure adequate T_E).

Monitor patient with pulse oximetry and cardiorespiratory monitor.

Initial Ventilator Settings:

V_T 6-10 mL/kg (if VV)

Decrease V_T to keep PIP < 35 cmH$_2$O or use pressure control at 30-35 cmH$_2$O

Rate 12-25 bpm

PEEP 4-10 cmH$_2$O

F$_I$O$_2$ 1.0

T$_I$ short enough to ensure expiration ends before next inspiration.

Immediately assess for chest rise, BS, airflow and T$_E$

Watch for induced additional air-trapping and pulmonary barotrauma.

Monitor with end-tidal CO$_2$.

Note: Permissive hypercapnia (controlled hypoventilation) is the recommended strategy, but it is not uniformly successful. Minimize high airway pressures and barotrauma.

Heliox therapy?

See Oakes' *Ventilator Management: A Bedside Reference Guide* for further details and strategies.

BRONCHIOLITIS

Def

Acute lower airway respiratory infection in the infant causing inflammation, edema, increased mucous production, and bronchoconstriction of the small airways.

Etiology

RSV (90%) and other viruses.
Usually < 2 years or age (peak @ 6 months)

CM

Mild:	RR < 50,	no or mild retractions
Mod:	RR 50-70,	mild-to-moderate retractions
Severe:	RR > 70,	moderate-to-severe retractions

Preceding URI	Hypoxemia	Hyperresonant to
Marked ↑ RR or	Cyanosis/	percussion
Apnea	pallor	Low-grade fever
Diffuse wheezing	↑ or ↓ HR	Vomiting
Retractions	↑ TE	Cough (maybe)
Flaring	↓ BS	Restless or listless
Hyperinflated chest		

For comparison with asthma, see Asthma

CXR

Hyperinflation
Diffuse patchy infiltrates (moderate to severe cases)

Tx

Supportive:
General supportive measures are the mainstay of therapy.
Allow patients to be as comfortable as possible (sitting in the position of comfort or held in a parent's arms).
Ensure adeq. airway and air movement (nasopharyngeal sx).
Do not use high humidity mist.

General Management (see table next page)

Treat Complications:
Apnea, respiratory failure (exhaustion), dehydration, air leak, pneumonia.
Ribavirin (SPAG therapy) – controversial and generally no longer recommended
CPAP/MV for expiratory airway obstruction.
Heliox therapy?, ECMO? - rare

Diagnosis and Management of Bronchiolitis*

	Recommendation
Prophylaxis	
Breastfeeding	Recommended to decrease a child's risk of having LRTD
Palivizumab	Clinicians may administer palivizumab prophylaxis for selected infants and children with CLD or a history of prematurity ($<$ 35 weeks) or with CHD.
Smoke	Infants should not be exposed to passive smoking.
Diagnosis	
	Clinicians should diagnose bronchiolitis and assess disease severity on the basis of Hx and PE and should not routinely order lab and x-ray studies for diagnosis.
Management	
	Should not be used routinely in the management of bronchiolitis.
Bronchodilators	A carefully monitored trial of _-adrenergic or _-adrenergic medication is an option. Inhaled bronchodilators should be continued only if there is a documented positive clinical response to the trial using an objective means of evaluation.
Chest PT	Should not be used routinely in the management of bronchiolitis
Hydration	Clinicians should assess hydration and ability to take fluids orally.
Infection	Antibacterial medications should only be used in children with bronchiolitis who have specific indications of the coexistence of a bacterial infection. When present, bacterial infection should be treated in the same manner as in the absence of bronchiolitis.

Continued next page

	Recommendation
Infection Control	Hand decontamination is the most important step in preventing nosocomial spread of RSV. Hands should be decontaminated before and after direct contact with patients, after contact with inanimate objects in the direct vicinity of the patient, and after removing gloves. Alcohol-based rubs are preferred for hand decontamination. An alternative is hand-washing with antimicrobial soap.
Oxygen	Supplemental O_2 is indicated if SpO_2 falls persistently below 90% in previously healthy infants. If $SpO_2 < 90\%$, adequate supplemental oxygen should be used to maintain an $SpO_2 \geq 90\%$. O_2 may be discontinued if SpO_2 is $\geq 90\%$ and the infant is feeding well and has minimal respiratory distress. As the child's clinical course improves, continuous measurement of SpO_2 is not routinely needed. Infants with a known history of hemodynamically significant heart or lung disease and premature infants require close monitoring as oxygen is being weaned.
Ribavirin	Should not be used routinely in children with bronchiolitis.
Risk Factors	Clinicians should assess risk factors for severe disease such as age less than 12 weeks, a history of prematurity, underlying cardiopulmonary disease, or immunodeficiency when making decisions about evaluation and management of children with bronchiolitis.
Steroids	Should not be used routinely in the management of bronchiolitis.

* Clinical Practice Guideline recommendations on the diagnosis and management of bronchiolitis in infants less than 2 years of age by the *American Academy of Pediatrics*, 2006.

BRONCHOPULMONARY DYSPLASIA
(BPD, Chronic Lung Disease [CLD])

Def

Chronic lung disease with respiratory failure (the need for supplemental O_2 at 36 weeks postmenstrual age), presumably due to oxygen and positive pressure therapies on the immature newborn lung

NIH Classification

Mild BPD: On RA @ 36 wks*

Moderate BPD: < 30% FiO_2 @ 36 wks

Severe BPD: > 30% FiO_2 +/- MV or CPAP @ 36 wks

* For < 32 wks GA, or 56 days PMA for > 32 wks

Etiology

Unknown

Primary?	Secondary?	
O_2 (FIO2 and duration)	PDA	Intubation
	Fluid overload	Malnutrition
PPV	Air leaks	Genetics?
Volutrauma?	Infections	Fetal inflammatory
Immaturity?	Cytokines	response

Pulmonary Disease (CDH, CHD, MAS, RDS, Pneumonia)

CM

Highly variable, depending on degree of lung compromise.
Characterized by:

Hypercarbia	↑RR (↓VT)	Expir. wheeze
Hypoxemia	Retractions	Irritability
Cyanosis	Diffuse fine crackles	
Failure to thrive		
Episodic bronchospasm		

CXR

Northways Radiologic Staging of BPD		
Radiologic stage	Patient age (days)	Radiologic description
I	2-3	Granular pattern
II	4-10	Opacification
III	10-20	Fine sponge
IV	Beyond 30 days	Coarse sponge

The above staging is still used, but the x-ray appearances are less dramatic and lag considerably behind the actual stage of pathology due to better management of O_2 and PPV.

Prevent/Treat:

O2 therapy: Use lowest FiO_2 possible (SaO_2 target 88-92%)

Avoid MV as much as possible using NCPAP.

If MV is unavoidable: ↓ O_2 toxicity and volutrauma. Maintain PaO_2 50-70 mmHg (SpO_2 88-92%). $PaCO_2$ allow up to 60, pH allow down to 7.20.

V_T 3-5 mL/kg

T_I 0.3-0.4 sec (some allow up to 0.6 for ↑ alveolar ventilation)

$\dot{V}_I$ 5-7 Lpm

PEEP variable (4-6 cmH_2O)

Extubate ASAP

Weaning from O_2 and MV often requires prolonged period (1 mo - 2 years)

Although the goal is to wean ASAP, weaning should proceed very slowly and cautiously to prevent clinical deterioration (e.g., ↓f 1/day or ↓PIP 1/day). ↓ PIP ≤ 12 and ↓FiO_2 ≤ 0.6 before ↓f.

O_2 weaning should be done by < 2% at a time (oftentimes < 1/2% at a time)

CPAP may be used after weaning from MV

CPT as needed

Bronchodilators PRN for acute bronchospastic episodes.

NOTE: Frequently, a temporary increase of PIP by 2-3 cmH_2O + ↑ FiO_2 to 1.0 may totally relieve the bronchospasms. If the changes are not effective within 2 minutes, then use bronchodilator.

Surfactant (early)?

Methylxanthines?

Diuretics?

Steroids? (Short term — limited/long term — no) (The routine use in VLBW infants is not recommended.)

Vitamin A < 1000 gm

Nitric Oxide?

HFV?

Superoxide dismutase?

Treat/Correct:

Air leaks, Fluid overload, PDA, RHF, Pneumonia

Tx

BURNS (PULMONARY)

Def Tissue injury due to heat or toxins

Etiology

Hot water	Smoke inhalation	Chemicals
Open flames	Electricity	Caustic agents

CM

S + S of CO poison (see next section)

Stage I — Acute resp. distress
May occur within a few hours
Resembles upper airway obstruction
Resp. distress: hoarseness, cough, ↑ RR,
Wheezing and/or stridor
↑ T$_E$

Stage II — Pulmonary edema
8-36 hrs.

Stage III — Bacterial pneumonia
2-day — 3 weeks after injury

S & S OF RESPIRATORY TRACT INJURY

Central cyanosis
Singed nasal hairs
Facial burns
Reddened pharynx
Soot deposits
Sooty sputum
Adventitious BS (crackles, wheezing, and stridor)

NOTE: SpO$_2$ can be very inaccurate in the presence of ↑ HbCO levels, e.g., smoke inhalation.

CXR May be normal initially

Tx

Ensure patent airway (burns to face, neck &/or oropharynx are indicative of early intubation)
O$_2$ as needed (100% if CO poison is a possibility)
Correct acidosis, electrolyte & fluid loss
Intrapulmonary percussive ventilation
Monitor VS & I+O closely
Medicate for pain (Demerol)
Bronchodilators (esp. Racemic epi)
Treat shock, resp. failure, pulm edema, pneumonia, and burn sites

Indications for Airway Support After Smoke Inhalation:

Tx

1. Altered mental status and loss of airway reflexes.
2. Evidence of increased ICP
3. Facial burns associated with circumferential full thickness burns of the neck and/or chest.
4. Full thickness facial burns, including those of the nose and lips.
5. Hypoventilation or apnea.
6. Severe pulmonary edema necessitating use of PEEP therapy.
7. Symptomatic upper airway obstruction.

CARBON MONOXIDE POISONING (CO POISON)

Def
Inhalation of carbon monoxide causing an inhibition of transport (COHb & $\downarrow O_2$ sat), delivery (L shift of oxyheme curve), and utilization (inhibits cytochrome oxidase) of oxygen

Etiol
Auto exhaust, home exhaust, space heaters, obstructed chimney, other (incomplete combustion of organic materials)

CM

Saturation of Blood (COHb%)	Symptoms **See Note Next Page**	FiCO
0-10%	None	
10-20%	Tightness across forehead; slight headache; dilation of cutaneous vessels.	0.007-0.012
20-30%	Headache; throbbing in temples	0.012-0.022
30-40%	Severe headache; weakness and dizziness; dimness of vision; nausea and vomiting; collapse and syncope; increased pulse and respiratory rate.	0.022-0.035
40-50%	As above, plus increased tendency to collapse and syncope; increased pulse and respiratory rate.	0.035-0.052
50-60%	Increased pulse and respiratory rate, syncope; Cheyne-Stokes respiration; coma with intermittent convulsions.	0.052-0.080
60-70%	Coma with intermittent convulsions; depressed heart action and respiration; death possible.	0.080-0.120
70-80%	Weak pulse, depressed respiration; respiratory failure and death.	0.120-0.195

Patients do not typically appear "**cherry red**"!

There also may be significant overlap of symptoms.

Some patients may not exhibit symptoms until 40% (SpO_2 may be very inaccurate in the presence of ↑ HbCO levels)

Clinical symptoms and COHb level may not coincide; treat whichever is the most severe (symptoms or COHb level)

> **10% COHb:** 100% O_2

Use tight fitting nonrebreather mask, ET tube or other (insure as close to 100% as possible)

Continue until < 10%

> **15% COHb:** 100% O_2 plus admit to hospital if history of heart disease

> **25% COHb:** 100% O_2 plus admit to hospital to observe.

Monitor heart, ABG's and COHb level

Hyperbaric chamber? (2-2.5 ATA for 1-2 hrs.)

* 1/2 life of COHb	Time
In Air	≈ 300 min
In 100% O_2	≈ 90 min
At 2.5 to 3 ATA	≈ 30 min

Intubate and ventilate if unconscious or uncooperative

Avoid hyperventilation & $NaHCO_3$ (shifts oxyheme curve further to L)

Steroids?

Hypothermia?

> **40% or alternations of mental status, neuro signs, circulatory collapse, pulmonary edema, ischemia on EKG, severe acidosis:**

100% O_2 plus transport to hyperbaric chamber is highly recommended

Watch for latent deterioration (usually 4-9 days later)

Pulmonary edema

MI or CHF

CONGENITAL HEART DISEASE (CHD)

Def Cardiovascular malformations

Etiology

Unknown or associated with:

Congenital syndromes	IDM
Congenital infection	Incest
Maternal drug ingestion	Chromosomal anomalies

CM

General.	Heart murmur	Poor wt. gain
	Hypoxemia	Tachypnea
	Poor feeding	S & S of CHF

Signs and Symptoms of Cardiac Disease in Infants

1. Cry: weak and muffled, loud and breathless
2. Color
   a. Cyanotic: usually generalized; increases in supine position; often unrelieved by oxygen, usually deepens with crying; gray, dusky; mild, moderate, severe
   b. Acyanotic: pale, with or without mottling on exertion
3. Activity level
   a. Restless
   b. Lethargic
   c. Unresponsive except to pain
   d. Lack of movement of arms and legs when crying (severe distress)
   e. Arms become flaccid when eating
4. Posturing
   a. Hypotonic: flaccid even when sleeping
   b. Hyperextension of neck
   c. Opisthotonos
   d. Dyspnea when supine
   e. Favors knee-chest position
5. Persistent bradycardia — 120 beats/min — or persistent tachycardia — 160 beats/min
6. Respirations: counted when neonate is sleeping to identify problem early
   a. Tachypnea: 60 breaths/minute
   b. Retractions with nasal flaring or tachypnea

    c. Dyspnea with diaphoresis or grunting

    d. Gasping followed in 2 or 3 minutes by respiratory arrest if not treated promptly

    e. Chronic cough (not often seen)

    f. Grunting with exertion such as crying or feeding by nipple

7. Feeding behavior

    a. Anorexic

    b. Poor suck: from lack of energy or when unable to close mouth around nipple because of dyspnea

    c. Difficulty in coordinating sucking, swallowing, breathing; pulls away from nipple to take breath

    d. Slow, with pauses to rest

    e. Unable to feed by nipple

From Jensen, M.D., Benson, R.D., and Bobak, I.M.: **Maternity care: the nurse and the family**, St. Louis, 1977. The C.V. Mosby Co.

CXR ↑ or ↓ pulmonary vasculature

Tx O2? PGE1?
Digitalis/diuretics? Palliative or corrective surgery?

Congenital Heart Defect	Definition	Clinical Manifestations	Management + Treatment	
Acyanotic (Left to Right Shunt)				
Atrial Septal Defects (ASD)	Hole in atrial septum - not usual cause of morbidity and mortality in infancy.	CHF (later in life)	Surgical closure using patch	
Atrioventricular Septal Defects	Hole in atrial and ventricular septa. Trisomy 21.	mild cyanosis CHF if severe, systolic murmur CXR: cardiomegaly with atrial dilation, dilated PA	Diuretics Digoxin (for CHF) Surgical patch	
Ventricular Septal Defect (VSD)	most common congenital heart abnormality; hole in ventricular septum, often assoc. with other CHDs	CHF (4 wol, earlier for premies) murmur occurs between dol 3 and 3 wol	50% spon. close Surgical closure when symptom.	

Congenital Heart Defect	Definition	Clinical Manifestations	Management + Treatment	
Aortic Stenosis	Obstruction of blood flow from LV to aorta aortic valve with 2 leaflets thickened, less pliable, commisures fused	LVH murmur with assoc. clicking	Balloon dilation of valve Ross procedure	
Pulmonary Stenosis	Obstruction of blood flow from RV to PA; valve leaflets fused and thickened along commisures	murmur with assoc. click cyanosis (if severe) RV failure SOB	Balloon dilation of valve Surgical correction	
Coarctation of the Aorta	narrowing of aorta near ductus arteriosus attachment	CHF LVH lack of palpable pulses in legs, groin	PGE Mechanical Vent. Surgical repair (resection, reanastamosis, patching)	

Congenital Heart Defect	Definition	Clinical Manifestations	Management + Treatment	
Patent Ductus Arteriosus (PDA)	Failure of ductus to close after birth; increased incidence in prematurity; may be part of other CHD; final functional closure normally occurs within 24 hours in newborns (90% by 48-hr, 100% by 96-hr)	Systolic murmur Pulmonary edema Bounding peripheral pulses Hypotension	Oxygen (term) Indomethacin (premie) Surgical repair (if severe)	
Double Aortic Arch	Persistency of fetal aortic growth; aorta wrapped around trachea and esophagus	Stridor Difficulty swallowing Weak pulses in an arm or legs	Surgical removal of left portion of ring Treat tracheomalacia Gradual improvement in swallowing	

Congenital Heart Defect	Definition	Clinical Manifestations	Management + Treatment		
Cyanotic (Right to Left Shunt)					
Ebstein Anomaly	Abnormal tricuspid valve; Leakage into RA with each RV contraction; enlarged RA; PFO	Heart murmur CHF Cyanosis Cardiomegaly	Surgical repair of tricuspid valve Closure of PFO		
Hypoplastic Left Heart Syndrome	Accounts for 25% of cardiac deaths during 1st WOL; underdeveloped LV; mitral and aortic valve stenosis; small aorta	Pallor Cyanosis Poor Perfusion Poor/absent peripheral pulses Hetapomegaly	Nitrogen PGE 3-Stage surgery (Norwood, Glenn, Fontan)		
Single Ventricle	Includes many defects, including: tricuspid atresia, double outlet right ventricle, double inlet right ventricle	Cyanosis Symptoms vary	2-Stage surgery (Glenn, Fontan)		

Congenital Heart Defect	Definition	Clinical Manifestations	Management + Treatment	
Tetralogy of Fallot	4 anomalies: Pulmonary stenosis, VSD, Overriding aorta, RV hypertrophy	Cyanosis Systolic Ejection murmur Boot-shaped heart on CXR	PGE Surgery (patch VSD, resection, enlarge RV outlet path patch)	
Total Anomalous Pulmonary-Venous Return	All 4 pulmonary veins drain to RA by way of abnormal connection, ASD necessary for survival	Severe cyanosis Low BP Pulmonary edema PPHN Respiratory distress Murmur	Surgery Pulmonary confluence connected to back of LA ASD patch Tie off pulmonary drainage units	

Congenital Heart Defect	Definition	Clinical Manifestations	Management + Treatment	
Transposition of the Great Arteries	Most common cardiac cause of cyanosis in 1st year of life; aorta comes from RV, PA from LV, VSD necessary for survival	Large, vigorous infant with cyanosis without resp distress Murmur possible "egg on a stick" on CXR	Creation of VSD via emergent balloon septostomy Surgery (repair ASD/VSD, cut off great vessels and switch, move coronary arteries)	
Truncus Arteriosus	one great blood vessel leaving ventricles; 2-5 leaflets on one valve; VSD present	Cyanosis CHF Hepatomegaly Cardiomegaly on CXR	Surgery (Separate PA from truncus, close VSD, create connection for RV and PA via valved conduit)	

Figures courtesy of Ross Labs and AHA

CONGESTIVE HEART FAILURE (CHF)

Def

Decreased cardiac output with inadequate systemic perfusion and failure to meet metabolic demands of the body

Etiology

Many and various:

CHD	Hypertension
Infection/sepsis	Ischemia
Myocarditis/opathy	Shock
Acquired heart disease	Anemia
PDA	Cardiac tamponade
Arrhythmias	Metabolic disorders

CM

Cardiac	Respiratory	Other
↑HR	(Mostly when assoc.	Poor feeding
Muffled heart sounds	with pulm edema)	Poor wght gain
Murmurs, gallops	↑ RR	Failure to thrive
↓ BP	Dyspnea	Sweating
Pulsus paradoxicus	Orthopnea (older child)	Fatigue
Pulsus alternans	Crackles/wheezes	Irritable
(Pulses vary with cause)	Cough	
Peripheral edema	Hypoxia	
↓ Peripheral perfusion	Cyanosis (maybe)	
Hepatomegaly/JVD	Resp. & metab. acidosis	

CXR

Cardiomegaly
↑ Pulmonary vasculature?

Tx

Treat cause & complications (eg. Pulmonary edema)
Prevent hypoxemia (O₂, PEEP?)
Mech. vent to ↓ work of breathing & unload Ⓛ ventricle
Keep HOB elevated 10° - 45°
Restrict intake
Correct anemia & electrolytes
Diuretics
Increase Cardiac Output
    Digoxin
    Inotropic agents are drug of choice if in shock
    Vasodilators?
    Surgery?
Decrease afterload (diuretics, afterload-reducing agents)

CROUP
Laryngotracheitis (LT),
Spasmodic croup (spasmodic laryngitis)

Def

Acute inflammation of larynx and trachea

Etiology

Viral infection:
> Parainfluenza
> RSV
> Influenza

Allergy or psychogenic (spasmodic croup)

CM

See Scoring below
See Page 11-48

Tx

Rules out Epiglottitis (see page 11-48)
If stridor at rest — See page 11-48
No stridor at rest:
Send home if parents can observe closely and provide:
> Humidity (cool or warm shower or room vaporizer,
> walk in cool night air)?
> Hydration — push fluids

Consider steroids
Instruct parents to return to hospital if stridor is persistent
> 5 min at rest
Call ambulance if: Stridor worsens, severe resp. distress,
turns blue, drooling, agitated

CROUP SCORE			
Indicator	*0 Score*	*+ 1 Score*	*+ 2 Score*
Retractions	0	Suprasubsternal	Intercostal and nasal flaring
Color	Normal	Peripheral cyanosis	Generalized cyanosis
Cough	0	Mild "barking"	Severe paroxysms
Mental status	Normal	Anxious, restless, obtunded	Delirious or comatose
Stridor	0	Audible when excited	Audible with stethoscope when quiet
Air entry	Normal	Decreased	Minimal with stethoscope
0 = no distress; 12 = severe distress			

Reprinted with permission from Pierog, J. and Pierog, L., **Pediatric Critical Illness and Injury**. Copyright 1984 by Aspen Systems Corp.

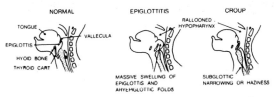

NORMAL   EPIGLOTTITIS   CROUP

TONGUE
VALLECULA
EPIGLOTTIS
HYOID BONE
THYROID CART.

BALLOONED
HYPOPHARYNX

MASSIVE SWELLING OF
EPIGLOTTIS AND
AHYEPIGLOTTIC FOLDS

SUBGLOTTIC
NARROWING OR HAZINESS

Reprinted with permission from Burgess, W. and Chesnick, V., *Respiratory Therapy in Newborn Infants and Children*, 2nd Ed. Copyright 1986 by Thieme Inc.

CYSTIC FIBROSIS (CF)

Def

Generalized disease of the exocrine glands, primarily affecting the lungs, pancreas, sweat glands and liver

Etiology

Genetic malfunction of the cystic fibrosis transmembrane conductance regulator protein leading to thickened mucous, infection, and inflammation leading eventually to bronchiectasis, permanent lung damage, and death

CM

Early
   ↑ Sweat Chloride > 60 mEq/l.
   + Immunoreactive trypsinogen test (IRT) / Genetic Testing
   Dry, hacking, non-productive cough
   Increased respiratory rate
   Prolonged expiratory phase of respiration
   Decreased activity

Moderate
   Increased cough with sputum production
   Crackles, scattered or localized wheezes
   Repeated episodes of respiratory infection
   Signs of obstructive lung disease:
      increased A-P diameter
      diminished area of cardiac dullness
      depressed diaphragms
      palpable liver border
   Decreased appetite — may still be good but not voracious
   Failure to gain or grow, or weight loss
   Decreased exercise tolerance

CM (Cystic Fibrosis) cont.

Advanced

Chronic, paroxysmal, prod. cough, often assoc. w/ vomiting

↑ RR, shortness of breath on exertion, orthopnea, dyspnea

Diffused and localized crackles and wheezes

Signs of marked obstructive lung disease

    marked increase in A-P diameter — barrel chest,
                                            pigeon breast

    limited respiratory excursion of thoracic cage

    depressed diaphragms

    hyper-resonance over entire chest

    decreased exchange

Noisy respiration — wheezing, bubbling, audible rales

Marked decrease in appetite associated with weight loss

Growth failure — stunting

Muscular weakness — flabby

Cyanosis

Digital clubbing

Rounded shoulders, forward position of head, poor posture

Fever, tachycardia, toxicity

Hemoptysis

Atelectasis

Pneumothorax

Lung abscess

Signs of cardiac failure (edema, elarged/tender liver,
    venous distention)

CXR

Variable with stage

Early	Later
Hyperinflation	Cystic changes
↑ Bronchovascular markings	(Atelect & emphysema)

Indications for Hospitalization of Children with CF

1. Weight loss or failure to gain weight
2. Increased cough
3. Increased sputum production, purulence and/or thickness
4. Increased fatigability
5. Increased respiratory rate and/or dyspnea
6. Overt respiratory distress with or without heart failure
7. CXR evidence of new infiltrates, atelectasis, or pneumothorax
8. Hemoptysis

Reprinted with permission from Gregory, G. *Respiratory Failure in the Child.* Copyright 1981 by Churchill Livingstone.

Treat pulmonary complications (airway obstruction, atelectasis, hemoptysis, pneumothorax, respiratory failure)

Hydration

Airway clearance (PD, percussion & vibration in all positions except head down) 2–4 × per day

Active cycle of breathing, autogenic drainage, oscillating PEP, high-frequency chest wall oscillation, intrapulmonary percussive ventilation.

> Caution: Hemoptysis and pneumothorax are frequent CF complications; discontinue CPT until resolved

Tx

O_2 therapy for hypoxemia (esp. at night)

Bronchodilators ⎫
Mucolytics? ⎪
DNA ase? ⎬ PRN
Decongestants ⎪
Expectorants ⎭

Inhaled hypertonic saline?

Anti-inflammatory therapy (ibuprofen)?

Antibiotics (aerosol & systemic) and ↑ airway clearance for infection (Tobramycin, Colistin)

Inhaled corticosteroids?

Nutrition —— High protein, carbohydrate & salt diet
Pancreatic enzyme & fat-soluble vitamin supplements

Exercise

Bronchoscopy & lavage?

Nocturnal BiPAP

Intubation and ventilation? (can resp. failure be reversed?)

Treat COR pulmonale

Lung transplantation

Gene therapy (research)

See page 8-14, ACCP Guidelines on Bronchial Hygiene

Cystic Fibrosis Pulmonary Guidelines (1)

"A" Grade Recommendations*:

Inhaled tobramycin - for CF patients with moderate-to-severe disease

Doranse alfa - for CF patients with moderate-to-severe disease

"B" Grade Recommendations*:

Azithromycin - for patients with *P aeruginosa* persistently present in cultures of the airways

Beta 2-adrenergic receptor agonists

Dornase alfa - for CF patients with mild disease who are asymptomatic (with *P aeruginosa* persistently present in cultures of the airways)

Ibuprofen - for patients with $FEV_1 > 60\%$ predicted

Inhaled hypertonic saline

Inhaled tobramycin – for patients with mild disease or who are asymptomatic (with *P aeruginosa* persistently present in cultures of the airways)

The guidelines recommend against:

Inhaled or systemic corticosteroids (> 6 yrs) - excluding patients with concomitant asthma

Prophylactic anti-Staphylococcal antibiotics

Evidence is insufficient to recommend for, or against:

Inhaled or oral N-acetylcysteine

Long-term use of inhaled anti-cholinergic bronchodilators

Long-term use of leukotriene modifiers or cromolyn

Other long-term inhaled antibiotics (ie, colistin, gentamicin, ceftazidime) (for those with *P aeruginosa* persistently present in cultures of the airways)

* For patients 6 years and older with CF

1) By CF Foundation, published in ***Am J Respir Crit Care Med***. 2007;176:957-969.
2) See article for more precise details.

DIAPHRAGMATIC HERNIA

Def
The herniation of abdominal viscera into the thoracic cavity through a congenital defect in the diaphragm resulting in lung compression, hypoplasia and often respiratory failure

Etiology
Congenital (unknown)

CM
Usually presents within a few hours of birth
85% are Ⓛ sided
Asymptomatic to severe cardiorespiratory distress (proportional to degree of herniation)
Severe respiratory distress (may become worse with bag and mask ventilation)
PMI shift (to contralateral side)
↓ BS or absent (ipsilateral side)
Abdomen is scaphoid
May hear bowel sounds above diaphragm (ipsilateral side)
Often associated with severe PPHN leading to hypoxemia.

CXR
Air filled bowel seen in thorax, displaced mediastinum (may see opaque chest early, before air has filled bowel loops.)

Tx
Bag & mask ventilation is contra-indicated!
(Pushes air into stomach & further compresses lungs)
If no distress:
  Keep in semi-fowler's position
  Prevent crying
  Observe closely
  Prepare for surgery
If distressed:
  Intubate immediately
  MV — Low PIP as possible to provide adequate chest rise, ↑ RR, zero to minimum PEEP; keep affected side down & HOB elevated. (Often high PIPs are required.) (Gentle ventilation now preferred.) PaCO$_2$ 40-60 mmHg unless PPHN is present then treat as such, see PPHN).
  See Caution, Next Page

Caution: often only one lung is being ventilated resulting in a high risk of pneumothorax (Keep PIP < 15 cmH$_2$O if possible) **Do not** attempt to expand the ipsilateral lung beyond its state of maturation.

Place NG tube and decompress GI tract with low Sx

Oxygen as needed (keep PaO$_2$ 50-60 mmHg)

  Not enough oxygen causes PPHN (wean very gradually)

  Enough O$_2$ causes closure of PDA, increasing PVR, which may result in ® ventricular failure.

Muscle paralysis to prevent "fighting the vent" and air swallowing.

Prostaglandins to keep PDA open?

Surgery?

HFV?

Nitric Oxide?

ECMO?

DROWNING (NEAR)

Definition

Aspiration of water during submersion causing hypoxia and acidosis with survival for ≥ 24 hrs after submersion.

Drowning = death by asphyxia < 24 hrs following submersion.

Types

Differences between fresh and salt water near drowning are theoretical, and have no clinical significance concerning patient mgmt. Water temperature and the presence of contaminants in the water are greater considerations than the salinity.

Etiology

Leaving small children unattended, trauma (head/neck), exhaustion, intoxication (alcohol, drugs), seizures.

CM

Variable with minimal findings to cardiorespiratory arrest (often a delay of 2-6 hrs).

Pulmonary: cyanosis, pallor, crackles, frothy sputum, wheezing, cough, apnea.

Cerebral: changed mental status, seizures, stupor, coma.

Other: arrhythmias, evidence of trauma, metabolic acidosis, shock.

CXR

May be normal; atelectasis, pulmonary edema (alveolar & interstitial infiltrates)

CPR if needed, O_2 therapy ASAP, treat bronchospasm, treat hypothermia if present, treat respiratory failure with O_2, MV with PEEP, and HCO_3. Use PEEP early (especially if O_2 > 40%).

Treat cerebral edema with diuretics and hyperventilation. Treat pulmonary edema ("secondary drowning") with diuretics and PEEP/CPAP. Watch for arrhythmias, inotropic drugs to improve tissue and cerebral perfusion? Antibiotics? (If infected source).

EPIGLOTTITIS

Def

Acute infection of the supraglottic structures (epiglottis and surrounding) resulting in edema & swelling causing upper airway obstruction.

Etiology

Hemophilus influenza, type B
Occasionally other bacteria & maybe a virus

Differential Diagnosis of Epiglottitis vs. Croup

	Epiglottitis	Croup	Spasmotic Croup
Age	> 3 (usually 3-7 yrs)	< 3 yrs	1-5 yrs
Season	**Not seasonable**	**Fall & winter**	
Onset &			
Progression	**Rapid** (4-12 hrs)	Gradual (> 24 hrs) (usually preceded by URI for several days)	**Abrupt** (few minutes)
Signs & Symptoms	**Sitting up, leaning forward** Mouth open, chin forward, neck extended **Sore throat, drooling** Muffled voice **Anxious (appears extremely ill) Resp distress:** Marked inspir stridor, no cough, ↓ BS, retractions (maybe) Cyanosis/ pallor (maybe) Fever/chills (> 103°F)(↑ WBC) **Throat red, inflamed** * Epiglottis — cherry red 8 very large	**Any position** No drooling (able to swallow) **Hoarse voice** Not especially anxious **Resp distress** Mild inspir (& expir) stridor **Barking, brassy cough** ↓ BS Retractions (maybe) Cyanosis/ pallor (maybe) Prolonged TE (maybe) Mild fever (< 103° F) Throat (maybe mildly red 8/or swollen)	**Suddenly awakens at night** Hoarseness **Anxious/frightened Resp distress** (minimal but aggravated with excitement) Inspir stridor **Barking cough** Retractions? Cyanosis? ↓ BS **No fever** Throat-minimal inflammation

Continued Next Page

	Epiglottitis	Croup	Spasmotic Croup
X-ray[1]	**Supraglottic swelling** **Enlarged epiglottis** Thumb sign (lateral neck)	Normal to sub-glottic — swelling (hazy) "Church Roof" sign (A-P)	**Not indicated**
TX	Do not agitate the child during examination **Immediate intubation[2]** **Oxygen (as needed)** High Humidity **Hydration** Antibiotic therapy	**If no stridor at rest** (see Page 11-40) **If stridor at rest —** Hospitalize O₂ (as needed) High humidity therapy? Room vaporizer?	Not hospitalized if improved within few hours **Cool or warm mist** Hydration Racemic epi? Steroids (May return to hospital the next night for another episode).
	Treat resp failure (as needed) Minimize anxiety & manipulation **Prevent self-extubation** Be ready to reintubate at all times (See also next 2 pages)	Hydration **Racemic epine-phrine** (Watch for rebound) Steroids Heliox therapy? Observe closely: be ready to intubate **Minimize anxiety & manipulation (Do not sedate)**	

1) Time is allotted for an x-ray *only* if patient is *not* in severe distress and there is *no* evidence of airway obstruction. Otherwise, do not delay intubation. A clinician experienced in intubation must *always* accompany the patient to x-ray, along with all the intubation equipment needed.

2) *Do not* attempt to visualize epiglottis (do not use tongue depressor) until totally prepared to intubate or trach the patient. Ideally, an anesthesiologist and otolaryngologist or surgeon should accompany the patient to the O.R. where the patient is anesthetized and intubated by an expert in airway management. Allow patient to "sit up" enroute to O.R. It has been reported that "looking" at the epiglottis with a tongue depressor or laryngoscope blade has caused epiglottic constriction and total airway obstruction. A trach may need to be performed in this case. Most deaths from epiglottitis occur in the first few hours after arrival at a hospital (presumably due to inadequate airway).

ALGORITHM FOR THE TREATMENT OF EPIGLOTTITIS AND SEVERE CROUP

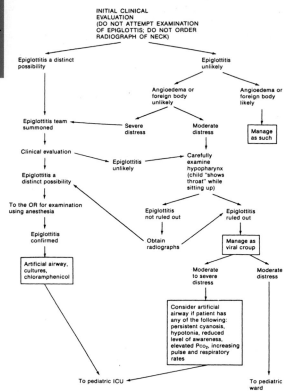

Reprinted with permission from Dickeman, J.D. eial, *Smith's The Critically Ill Child*, 3rd Ed. Copyright 1985 by W. B. Saunders Co.

PROTOCOL FOR MANAGEMENT OF EPIGLOTTITIS

I. *Once the diagnosis of epiglottitis is suspected,* the following steps are to be followed without exception:

   A. Begin continuous observation of the patient. Allow the parents to remain with the patient. Do not place the child in a supine position.

   B. Contact the team designated to secure the airway — anesthesiologist, intensivist, otolaryngologist.

   C. Place equipment for bag/face mask ventilation, intubation, oxygen, suction, tracheostomy, and cardiopulmonary resuscitation at bedside.

   D. Do not agitate the child with noxious procedures such as oral examination, blood drawing, or IV catheter placement.

   E. Begin continuous ECG, respiratory, and pulse oximetry monitoring.

   F. Obtain lateral neck roentgenogram only if the child is stable and the diagnosis is uncertain. A physician capable of intubation must accompany the child to the radiology department.

   G. Administer oxygen at 1 to 2 L/min or at a rate sufficient to maintain oxygen saturation > 90% by pulse oximetry.

   H. Consider administering nebulized racemic epinephrine (2.25%) at 0.2 mL in 2 mL 0.9% sodium chloride solution for worsening airway obstruction.

   I. If complete airway obstruction occurs before the arrival of the airway team, begin assisted ventilation with bag and face mask.

II. *Once the airway team has arrived,* perform the following:

   A. Transport the child to the operating room or PICU.

   B. Ask the otolaryngologist to be prepared for fiberoptic examination, rigid bronchoscopy, or tracheostomy and to remain in the room.

   C. Induce anesthesia with the patient in a sitting position using an inhalation agent and oxygen. Confirm the diagnosis of epiglottitis. Intubate the child through the oral route with an endotracheal tube one size smaller than recommended for that age patient.

   D. Hyperoxygenate the child for 2 minutes. Replace the oral endotracheal tube with a nasotracheal tube.

   E. Obtain a chest roentgenogram to ensure proper palcement of the endotracheal tube and to evaluate for pulmonary abnormalities.

F. Place an IV catheter; obtain blood and pharyngeal cultures.

G. Begin antibiotic therapy.

H. Transfer to the PICU after administering a sedative (e.g., midazolam) and placing arm restraints.

Reprinted with permission from Levin, D. and Morris, F., ***Essentials of Pediatric Intensive Care***. Copyright 1990 by Quality Medical Publishers.

INTRACRANIAL HYPERTENSION

Def Increased intracranial pressure (↑ICP > 20 mmHg) from an increase in volume of substances within the cranial cavity

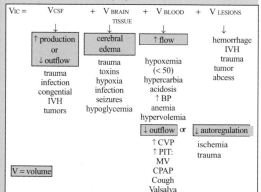

Etiology

$$\uparrow ICP = \uparrow \text{ intracranial volume } (V_{IC})$$

$V_{IC} =$	V_{CSF}	+	$V_{BRAIN\ TISSUE}$	+	V_{BLOOD}	+	$V_{LESIONS}$

↑ production or ↓ outflow

trauma
infection
congential
IVH
tumors

cerebral edema

trauma
toxins
hypoxia
infection
seizures
hypoglycemia

↑ flow

hypoxemia (< 50)
hypercarbia
acidosis
↑ BP
anemia
hypervolemia

hemorrhage
IVH
trauma
tumor
abcess

↓ outflow or ↓ autoregulation

↑ CVP
↑ PIT:
MV
CPAP
Cough
Valsalva

ischemia
trauma

V = volume

FACTORS AFFECTING CEREBRAL BLOOD FLOW

Factors resulting in increased cerebral blood flow	Factors resulting in decreased cerebral blood flow
Increased carbon dioxide tension	Increased intracranial pressure
Hypoxia (PaO_2 < 50)	Profound hypocapnia (max ≈ 20 mmHg)
Increased systemic arterial pressure (severe)	Severe hypotension
Anemia	Increased cerebral venous pressure
Hyperthyroidism	Polycythemia
Reduced cerebral venous pressure	Hypothyroidism
Seizures	Administration of vasoconstrictor drugs
Administration of vasodilator drugs	

Infant		Child	
Apnea	Anorexia	Headache	Blurred vision
Bradycardia	Vomiting	Nausea	Lethargy
Lethargy	Full fontanelles	Vomiting	Irritable
Irritability	Papilledema	Papilledema	Confusion
↓ Eye Contact			

Late signs: (medical emergency)

Cushing reflex (best sign)	Abnormal resp pattern
↑BP	Apnea
↑PP	Apneustic
Bradycardia	Cheyne-Stokes
↓ RR or apnea	Hyperventilation

CM

Pupil dilation & ↓ reaction to light

↓BP

Seizures

Posturing

↓ Reflexes & response to pain

↓ LOC (see Pgs 5-2,3)

Neurogenic pulm edema

    Resp failure

    Dyspnea

    ↓ Lung compliance

    Coma

General/Preventive:

Keep HOB elevated 30°

Keep head in neutral position (flexion or rotation may obstruct venous drainage from head & ↑ ICP)

Avoid rapid changes in head position

May turn body side to side q 2 hrs for PD if monitored (stop if ↑ ICP, keep head neutral)

Ensure ET tube is stabilized (do not dislodge when turning!)

Maintain PaO$_2$ 80-100 (60-80 premie)

Sx only as necessary

    Ensure preoxygenation & hyperventilation

    Consider barbituate therapy or IV lidocaine

Prevent coughing (use muscle paralysis if needed)

Prevent Valsalva maneuver (use stool softener and avoid pressure on abdomen)

Tx

Keep anxiety and stress to a minimum

Watch for signs of ↑ HR or ↑ BP

Sedate if necessary before turning, Sx, or fighting the vent

Maintain BP (mean BP should be > 40 mmHg more than ICP)
and monitor continuously

Ensure adequate cerebral blood flow (CBF = CPP / CVR)

(CPP = cerebral perfusion pressure,

CVR = cerebral vascular resistance)

When autoregulation of CVR stops, then CBF ≈ CPP

> CPP = BP — ICP
> Normal = > 40-60

Keep CVP < 5-8 mmHg (if CO is adequate)

Restrict fluid intake (2/3 maintenance) & monitor
output (↑ if necessary)

Avoid fever or shivering

Maintain blood glucose

Treat cause (etiology)

Treat ↑ ICP:

↑ ICP = > 20 mmHg

Monitor continuously (see Pg 5-5)

When to treat:

1) If ICP is 16-20 mmHg for > 30 min

2) If ICP is > 20 mmHg for > 3 min

3) If ↑ ICP is associated with ↓ HR, pupil dilation, ↑ BP
or Δ in responsiveness

How to treat:

↓ CSF —

Withdraw fluid if possible (> 50 mmHg)?

Surgical shunt? (chronic increases)

↓ Brain volume —

Fluid restrictions

Diuretics

Osmotic therapy (mannitol, glycerol)?

Steroids? (for tumor or abcess)

↓ Blood volume —

Hyperventilation *

Manual — for acute rises or Sx (use ↑ rate <u>not</u>
volume) Use pressure manometer

Mechanical — for chronic ↑ ICP
Keep $PaCO_2$ 30-35 (acute decreases may
cause ↓ cerebral perfusion
Keep intrathoracic pressure minimal:
Use ↑ rate to achieve ↓ $PaCO_2$
Use lowest V_T + PIP possible
Use no or minimal PEEP + ↓ T_I
Place N-G tube to keep stomach decompressed
Weaning from MV — (usually after ICP < 20 for
24 hrs)
Adjust only one parameter at a time
Allow $PaCO_2$ to rise ≤ 5 mmHg
Wait 4-12 hrs before next change
Observe ICP closely
Barbiturate coma?
Muscle paralysis? (only if ICP is monitored)
Hypothermia? (34-36°C especially in head trauma)

---

* Intubation procedure may be very hazardous (↑ BP → ↑ ICP).
It is imperative that pt. be anesthetized & hypocarbic during
procedure.

INTRAVENTRICULAR HEMORRHAGE
Periventricular or subependymal — intraventricular hemorrhage (PVH/ IVH or SEH/IVH)

Def

Intracranial bleeding in the newborn of unknown cause associated with prematurity and assisted ventilation.

Etiology

Usually occurs in first few days of life (90% before 72 hrs.
of age)
Prematurity (may occur in full term infants) (usually < 1500 gm)
Impaired autoregulation of cerebral blood flow
Asphyxia (hypoxemia, hypercarbia, acidosis):
Severe pulm disease (RDS, etc.)
Apnea
Seizures
CHF

11-55

Blood pressure fluctuations:
Hyper/Hypotension
↑ mean intrathoracic press (pneumothorax, ↑ PIP, PEEP/CPAP)
Infusions (rapid vol expansion, hyperosmolar solns, exchange transfusion)
PDA ("cerebral steal" syndrome)
Hypernatremia
↑ CVP
Physical manipulations

Asymptomatic to severe neuro & cardiorespiratory dysfunction
Silent — asymptomatic (maybe mild ↓ HCT, hypotonia &/or mild metabolic acidosis
Stuttering — ↓ tone & activity (& perhaps other signs) then subsequent stabilization or improvement. This sequence repeats with worsening clinical signs.
Catastrophic (rapid/severe deterioration within min to hours)

CM

Neuro	↓ BP Irritable Staring Temp instability Bulging ant. fontanelle	Pupils fixed Seizures Decerebrate posturing ↑ ICP Coma
Cardio-respiratory	Apnea/Bradycardia Resp failure (↓ PO_2 + ↑ PCO_2) Shock Respiratory Acidosis ↓ HCT (pallor)	
Metabolic	Metabolic acidosis ↓ Na ↑ glucose	

CXR

CT Scan or ultrasonography (choice)
Classification of bleed (Papile et al)

Grade I	SEH
Grade II	IVH without ventricular dilation
Grade III	IVH with ventricular dilation
Grade IV	IVH with parenchymal bleed

Prevention:

Prevent premature births

Exogenous surfactant?

Maintain normal: BP, temp, glucose, ABG's

Correct apnea & bradycardia

Avoid rapid swings in PaO_2 and $PaCO_2$

Avoid: rapid or hyperosmolor infusions, pneumothorax
(minimal bagging & vent press), unnecessary physical
manipulation (esp. Sx)

Phenobarbital, indomethicin?

Avoid further damage (once bleed has occurred)

Minimize hypoxia, hypercarbia and acidosis with O_2, MV

$NaHCO_3$ (give slowly)

Use SaO_2 monitor

Sx & CPT only if necessary (insure preoxygenation)

Avoid prolonged intubation attempts

Maintain BP —

Use caution with infusions/transfusions

Avoid: head down position, rapid changes in head position or neck flexion (↓ venous return)

Do not place IV's in head

Monitor ICP (noninvasively, see Pg 5-5)

Serial lumbar puncture?

Ventriculoperitoneal shunt?

(margin label: **Tx**)

MECONIUM ASPIRATION SYNDROME (MAS)

Def

Aspiration of meconium, in utero or during first breaths at birth,
resulting in airway obstruction, chemical pneumonitis and pos-
sibly PPHN

> Note: PPHN must be present before birth and be
> mostly responsible for respiratory distress

Etiology

Fetal asphyxia

Predisposing factors:

Postmaturity	Prolapsed cord	Maternal hypo/hypertension
Prolonged labor	SGA	Maternal hemorrhage
Breech presentation	Abruptio placenta	Fetal distress or acidosis

CM

Meconium stain	Adventitious	Cyanosis or pallor
Gasping at birth	breath sounds	Hypercarbia
Tachypnea	↑ T_E	Metabolic acidosis
Chest hyperinflation	Profound hypoxia	Signs of barotrauma
	Resp failure	

Yellow or "old" meconium indicates prolonged hypoxia
(ominous sign)

CXR

areas of consolidation (atelectasis) &/or hyperinflation,
air leaks

Tx

Prevent in utero asphyxia:
>   Prevent postmaturity
>   If evidence of fetal distress (see Pg 1-3 thru 1-8):
>   Give O_2 to mother, turn to side, tocolytics?
>   Immediate delivery?

Clearing the Airway of Meconium

If meconium is present upon delivery:
Do not perform intrapartum suctioning. After full delivery,
    suction nose, mouth & posterior pharynx with bulb syringe
    or 12-14 FR suction catheter.

A. If baby is vigorous: (strong respiratory efforts, HR > 100,
and good muscle tone)
Do not perform tracheal suctioning.

B. If baby is not vigorous: (depressed respiratory efforts, HR
< 100, poor muscle tone)
Perform tracheal suctioning. (Do not ventilate without
clearing airway).

Procedure:
Provide warm, humidified 100% O_2 across face during
    suctioning
Insert appropriate size ETT into trachea (3.0 – 3.5 mm ID)
Attach ETT to suction source using a meconium aspirator
    (100 mmHg)
Apply suction and withdraw ETT slowly over 3-5 seconds

Repeat as necessary (usually 1-4 x) until:

1. Little/no meconium is recovered
2. Baby becomes vigorous
3. Baby has significant bradycardia requiring manual resuscitation. Attach bag to ETT during last suction attempt and begin ventilation. (Subsequent suctioning may be performed down the ETT).

The instillation of saline is controversial.

Extubate as soon as adequate spontaneous respirations.

Post delivery care:

Aspirate meconium from stomach after vital signs are stable

Provide high humidity O_2 as needed

Maintenance of PaO_2 is crucial (60-80 mmHg) (see PPHN)

Provide SaO_2 or SpO_2 monitoring (Pre & post ductal)

Correct acidosis

Watch for airway obstruction (ball-valving, air-trapping, and pneumothorax), atelectasis from surfactant inactivation, pneumonitis, and increased PVR.

Surfactant for severe cases?

CPT?

Antibiotics

CPAP if $FiO_2 > 0.4$

  Caution: May aggravate air-trapping &/or ↓ CO

  Observe for hyperinflation & monitor BP

MV — as indicated

  Use SIMV, (PIP to keep V_T 4-8 mL/kg)

  Allow adequate T_E if air-trapping

  Use PEEP <u>cautiously</u> (4-5 cmH$_2$O may help to splint open partially obstructed airways. Higher levels may cause hyperinflation).

  Note: Ball-valving during MV may result in sig. air leaks.

  Maintain $PaCO_2$ 40-50? (If no PPHN)

  Sedation or muscle relaxants may help minimize air leaks if patient is fighting the ventilator.

Treat complications: Air leaks (HFV?) - have thoracentesis setup ready; PPHN - ECMO?, Nitric oxide therapy?

NECROTIZING ENTEROCOLITIS (NEC)

Def

Acute intestinal necrosis

Etiology

Unknown (Predisposing Factors:)		
Prematurity	PDA	↓ BP
Hypoxia/asphyxia	Polycythemia/	Hypothermia
RDS	anemia	CHD
Infection (bact or	Exchange transfu-	Umbilical
viral?)	sions	catheters
Early feeding or	Cold stress	
hypertonic solns	Ischemia	

CM

Abdominal distention
Vomiting
Poor feeding (gastric residuals)
Bloody or mucoid stools
Temperature instability
Lethargy
Hyponatremia
Apnea
Hypotension
Metabolic acidosis
Thrombocytopenia

CXR

Abdomina Free Air (ominous sign)
Abnormal gas pattern (Ileus)
Portal or hepatic air

Tx

Support with O_2 & vent needs
NPO
NG tube, TPN
Remove umbilical catheters
Antibiotics
Surgery for perforation or persistent acidosis or resection
Volume replacement

PATENT DUCTUS ARTERIOSUS (PDA)

Def

Persistence of an open ductus arteriosus after birth resulting in L-R shunting (acyanotic)

Courtesy Ross Labs

Etiology

Immaturity &/or hypoxia/acidosis
Predisposing factors:
RDS (esp. recovery stage)
Fluid overload
Hypocalcemia

CM

Small PDA	Med-Large PDA	General Signs
Asymptomatic or systolic murmur	Continuous murmur	Feeding intolerance
Full pulses	Bounding pulses	Failure to wean from MV
	↑ PP	Poor physical growth
	Active precordium	Freq, resp infections
	Tachycardia	$PaO_2 > 15$ mmHg diff between radial and umbilical
	Apnea/bradycardia	
	Hypoxia	
	Hypercarbia	Sig. PDA may have no heart murmur
	↓ Lung compliance	
	CHF	

CXR

cardiomegaly
↑ Pulm vasculature
Hepatomegaly

Tx

Asymptomatic or small PDA
No TX needed
Ductus normally closes within 72 hrs of birth or spontaneously close at anytime in first year 20% shunt is normal for first few days of life

"Clinically significant" or large PDA:

Medical management:
Fluid restriction/diuretics
Prevent hypoxia/hypercarbia/acidosis/hypocalcemia
CPAP or MV depending on underlying process
Caution: As PDA closes, lung compliance may increase and barotrauma from MV may occur
Digitalis (for CHF)?

If unresponsive to medical management:

Indomethacin —

Indications:

Premies < 2 wks old

Failure to wean +/or CHF

AGE AT FIRST DOSE	DOSE (mg/kg)		
	1st	2nd	3rd
< 48 hours	0.2	0.1	0.1
2-7 days	0.2	0.2	0.2
>7 days	0.2	0.25	0.25

Longer treatment courses may be used:

   0.2 mg/kg Q24 hours for a total of 5-7 days

Contraindications —

Renal or hepatic failure

   NEC or GI bleed or intracranial bleed

   Thrombocytopenia

   Hyperbilirubinemia

   Dehydration

Surgical ligation —

   Indication: When indomethacin fails (3 trials) or is contraindicated

PDA Complications			
Shunt	Probable Cause	S&S	Treatment
L → R	Dilated PDA &/or Fluid overload	Bounding pulse Systolic murmur Widened pulse press ↑PaCO$_2$	Fluid restriction Lasix Indomethacin Ligation
R → L	Pulm Vasoconstriction (↑ PVR)	↓ BP (esp. diastolic) Apnea Abdominal distention Failure to wean Hypoxemia	Dopamine? Inhaled Nitric Oxide?

PERSISTENT PULMONARY HYPERTENSION OF THE NEWBORN (PPHN)
formerly PERSISTENT FETAL CIRCULATION (PFC)

Def

Pulmonary hypertension ($\uparrow$ PVR), in term or near-term infants, without lung disease and at any gestational age as a complication of pulmonary disease, resulting in severe hypoxemia secondary to R-L shunting through persistent fetal channels (FO & PDA) (in the absence of CHD).

Etiology

Primary pulmonary vasoconstriction (chronic intrauterine hypoxia or idiopathic) and/or secondary to:

Perinatal hypoxia/ asphyxia/acidosis	Hypoglycemia	Septicemia
Aspiration (meconium, blood, fluid)	Hypothermia	CHD (TAPVR)
	Hypotension	Maternal ingestion of aspirin or indomethicin
Diaphragmatic hernia	Hypocalcemia	
	Polycythemia	
RDS (severe)	Pulmonary hypoplasia	IDM
Pneumonia (Group B Strep)		

CV

S&S usually appear in first 24 hrs after birth:

Severe hypoxia/cyanosis in $\geq$ 60% O_2

PaO_2 < 100 mmHg in 100%

Sudden changes in color from pink to cyanosis in a few seconds

Mild to moderate respiratory distress.

Hypoxia & resp. distress: worsens with crying, stress or agitation

Metabolic acidosis

Systolic heart murmur

$\uparrow$ PAP and labile (PAP > BP)

Heart failure or shock

CXR

Normal or $\downarrow$ pulm vasculature (1° disease only)

Possible hyperinflation

Cardiomegaly

First establish diagnosis (2D Echo of heart often necessary
to establish diagnosis and guide daily management.)

1) R-L shunting
2) Rule out parenchymal lung disease (RDS, MAS)
3) Rule out CHD

1. **Pre & postductal PaO_2** (to show R-L shunting)
   ® Radial or temporal PaO_2 > 15-20 mmHg more
   than umbilical or lower extremity PaO2.
   Note: Must be simultaneous and pt. at rest. Neg. test
   does not rule out PPHN. (Shunting may only be
   occurring via F.O.)

2. **Hyperoxia test** (to distinguish PPHN & CHD from
   parenchymal disease)
   Give 100% O_2 x 10-15 min.
   PPHN or CHD = PaO_2 < 100 mmHg
   Parenchymal = PaO_2 >100 mmHg
   This test is controversial for premies

3. **Hyperoxia—hyperventilation test** (to distinguish
   PPHN from CHD)
   Administer 100% O_2
   Hyperventilate (face mask or ET tube) to "criti-
   cal" $PaCO_2$ level (see below)
   PPHN = PaO_2 > 100 mmHg
   CHD = PaO_2 little change (< 100 mmHg)
   Caution: Should be performed by skilled person-
   nel only
   Pt. should be requiring $FIO_2 \geq 0.7$
   This test is controversial in premies

NOTE

↓ $PaCO_2$ to 20-30 mmHg
When the "critical" level is reached ($TcCO_2$), there
will be a sudden ↑ in PaO_2 (SpO_2) and/or patient
will turn from cyanotic to pink.
RR of 100-150 are recommended.
PIP minimal for adequate chest expansion (use
manometer)
The ventilating parameters used may then be used as
initial ventilator settings. Caution — manual and
ventilator manometers often differ.

Treat/correct secondary cause (see etiology):

**Promote normal neonatal circulation
(↓ PVR & reverse R-L shunt):**

Minimal to "no" handling

Agitation, stress, crying, etc., worsen vasoconstriction

No heelsticks or punctures (use a-line or SaO_2)

Delay routine weighing

Minimal auscultation

Minimal Chemstrips® and temp taking

CPT & sx <u>only</u> if absolutely necessary (use 2 people to Sx)

O2 Therapy

Administer 100% O_2, in at or near term infants, <u>as soon as</u>
PPHN is suspected (use more judiciously with premies)

The ensuing effects of hypoxia can be far more detrimental
than the risks of high O_2

Then wean FiO_2 + maintain PaO_2 > 100-120 mmHg (at or
near term; premie level is controv. - 80-100 mmHg?)

Prone position is often beneficial

Use two SpO_2 monitors — one on rt. upper extremity and
one lower extremity

Weaning O_2 — <u>Do not</u> decrease FiO_2 unless PaO_2 > 120
mmHg (100 mmHg in premie?)

Then decrease cautiously and <u>observe closely</u>

Maintaining PaO_2 > 100 mmHg and minimal decreases
in FiO_2 helps prevent the "flip flop" mechanism, where
dramatic changes in PaO_2 (often > 50 torr) occur with
slight or no changes in FiO_2.

Nasal CPAP is **not** recommended. (It often will worsen
pulmonary perfusion and agitate the infant.)

Mechanical Ventilation

Indication —

$PaCO_2$ > 50-60 mmHg

PaO_2 < 70 mmHg on $FiO_2 \geq 0.7$

Some clinicians will not wait for these parameters to
develop, but institute MV as soon as PPHN is
diagnosed.

Two Management Approaches

1) *Hyperventilation* —

Indication — PaO_2 < 60-80 mmHg on 100% O_2 plus being mechanically ventilated

Goal — ↓ $PaCO_2$ to "critical level" where PaO_2 ↑ 80-100

"Critical level" is different for each pt.:

Usually $PaCO_2$ 20-30 mmHg (pH > 7.45-7.60)

Use continuous SaO_2 monitoring (keep SaO_2 > 95%)

$PaCO_2$ < 20-25 mmHg may decrease cerebral blood flow and is controversial

HFV or high rates (100-150), short T_I (0.2),

High flows (10-15 LPM), and high PIPs (whatever it takes for adequate chest expansion) are often required

Caution: High PaO_2 and barotrauma increases risks for premies

Watch for inadvertent PEEP (keep PEEP to minimum < 5 cmH_2O)

Continue hyperventilation for 1-2 days until FiO_2 has been ↓ ≤ 0.6

2) *Gentle Ventilation* — (accepting mild hypercarbia)

pH ≥ 7.25, $PaCO_2$ 40-60, PaO_2 50-70, *f* (match patient's rate), PIP minimum needed to make chest rise, T_I approx. 0.6 sec.

Sedation/Paralysis — (often employed to facilitate hyperventilation)

Indications — Labile ABGs (flip-flopping)

Fighting the vent

↑ O_2 consumption (↑ WOB)

↑ Risk of barotrauma (premies with parenchymal disease)

Note: When paralysis is instituted, mechanical ventilation may need to be increased due to absent spontaneous ventilation. Watch for clinical or ABG deterioration.

Weaning — (usually after 72 hours of age)
   First ↓ PIP to ≤ 35
      Reduce 1 cm <u>only</u> at a time
      Keep PaO_2 > 100-120 mmHg and $PaCO_2$ at critical level
      Watch for barotrauma during recovery phase
   Then ↓ FiO_2 to ≤ 0.6 - 0.7
      Reduce 1-2% <u>only</u> at a time
      Keep PaO_2 > 100-120 mmHg

Common error: Weaning too rapidly and allowing $PaCO_2$ > "critical level" or PaO_2 < 100mmHg, may result in "flip-flop" (vasoconstriction and sudden hypoxia)

If this occurs, it is hard to get it reversed and often one has to employ much higher MV parameters and high FiO_2 to reverse it.

Often 4 hrs should elapse between vent change.

Goal: FiO_2 ≤ 0.5, PIP < 25 within 48 hrs.

(>PHN Tx continued)

Once FiO_2 is ≤ 0.5, the patient is probably no longer labile. At this point one can rapidly revert to conventional MV with $PaCO_2$ 35-50 mmHg and PaO_2 50-80 mmHg.

Additional Therapies

If PaO_2 remains < 50 mmHg despite the above therapies, then the following therapies may be trialed: (see MV Chapter)
   1) *Nitric Oxide Therapy*
   2) *HFV*
   3) *ECMO*

RESPIRATORY DISTRESS SYNDROME (RDS)

Def

A disease primarily of premature infants with a decreased surfactant production and/or release resulting in pulmonary hyaline membranes, atelectasis and decreased lung compliance.

Etiology

Decreased surfactant

Predisposing Factors:		
Immaturity (↑ risk with ↓ gestational age)		
Perinatal asphyxia	Hypovolemia	Maternal hypotension
Hypoxia	Hypercapnia	Rh incompatibility
Acidosis	IDM	Second born twin
Hypothermia	C-section	Male

CM

Respiratory distress within 2-3 hrs of birth:

Tachypnea	Nasal flaring
Apnea (tiring from ↑ WOB)	Expiratory grunt
Cyanosis	↓ BS or Bronchial BS
Retractions	↑ $PaCO_2$
↓ PaO_2	Resp/Metab Acidosis
Temp instability	Dry Crackles
Hypotension	See-saw breathing
Hypotonia	↓ Lung Compliance
Edema (pulm/peripheral)	Negative shake test
L/S ratio < 2 and/or absent phophatidylglycerol	see page 1-3

CXR

Ground glass (diffuse reticulogranular pattern)
  Air bronchograms
  ↓ Lung volume
  ↑ Pulmonary vasculature

RDS Scoring System

	Score		
Variable	**0**	**1**	**2**
Birth weight (g)	> 2000	1500-2000	< 1500
FiO$_2$ needed to keep skin pink	≤ 49	50-65	≥ 65
Venous carbon dioxide pressure (PCO$_2$)	< 40	40-45	> 45
Hydrogen ion concentration (pH)	≥ 7.35	7.34-7.30	< 7.30
Clinical score (see below)	≤ 3	4-5	≥ 6

	0	**1**	**2**
Components of Clinical Score (5th variable above) *			
Respiratory rate (per minute)	< 60	60-80	>80 or apneic episodes
Cyanosis	None	In air	In 40% O$_2$
Retractions	None	Mild	Moderate to severe
Grunting	None	Audible with stethoscope	Audible without stethoscope
Crying (air entry)	Clear	Delayed or decreased	Barely audible

* The scores on each of these components are added together to derive the clinical score. That score is one of the variables in the total score for infants with RDS. Scoring is made during first 6-12 hrs. of life.

Score	Respiratory Care Indicated
0-3	O2 therapy
4-5	CPAP
≥ 6	Mechanical ventilation

Reprinted with permission: Peckham GJ et al; *Clin Ped* 18:716-720,1979.

Prevent (if possible):
 Delay premature delivery with tocolytics
 Promote surfactant production:
 Administer corticosteroids (beta or dexamethasone):
 Aminophylline, Thyroxine, Prolactin
 Indicated only if < 34 wks gestation and delivery is expecte
    within 24-72 hrs.
 Do not give if delivery will be immediate.
 Less effective in male newborns

Support until spontaneous resolution occurs:
 Provide O_2 (most important part of management)
 Maintain PaO_2 50-80 mmHg, SpO_2 85-92 %
 Prevent hypoxemia (< 50 torr) & hyperoxia (> 80 torr).
 Use continuous SpO_2 monitoring
 Provide CPAP (Ch 9) and/or mechanical ventilation as
    needed (Ch 10)
 Surfactant replacement therapy (pg 11-73 and AARC CPG
    in Appendix)
 Maintain temp (critical aspect) & glucose
 Maintain fluid & electrolytes (avoid fluid overload)
 Maintain proper ABGs (see below)
 Maintain BP & HCT (40-45%)
 Minimize handling
 Avoid nipple feeding with tachypnea or dyspnea
 Treat with antibiotics (until Group B strep is ruled out)
 Provide PD, percussion and vibration
    (often not recommended in first 48 hrs.)
 Sx PRN (esp. after 48 hrs.)
 Provide sedation if fighting the ventilator
    (morphine, chloral hydrate, diazepam)
 Paralyze if fighting vent (controversial)?
 HFV — if failing conventional MV or severe pneumothorax,
    PIE or BP fistula?
 ECMO — if severe and failing MV?

CPAP

Indications

PaO$_2$ < 50 mmHg on FiO$_2$ 0.4-0.6
and PaCO$_2$ < 50-60 mmHg with no apnea

> Some clinicians do not recommend CPAP (except during weaning from vent support) for infants < 1500 gm due to the ↑ WOB and ↑ O$_2$ consumption. They proceed directly to low rate IMV and then extubation.

Method — See Chapter 9 for details

Nasal prongs or nasal mask (NCPAP or NM-CPAP)
NPCPAP (if not severe & likely won't need MV)
ETT (if severe & likely will need MV — ETT < 3.5 not recommended)

Initial setup — 5 cmH$_2$O at same FiO$_2$

Increase by 2 cmH$_2$O until PaO$_2$ > 50 mmHg (max 10 cmH$_2$O). Titrate by observing RR, retractions, and O$_2$ Sat.

Weaning from CPAP

↓ FiO$_2$ to 0.4 (by 0.05 increments)
↓ CPAP (by 1-2 cmH$_2$O increments) to 3-4 cmH$_2$O
Extubate
Decrease FiO$_2$ by 0.02-0.03 increments when FiO$_2$ < .3
As the lung improves, CPAP may be too high if:
   ↑ PaCO$_2$ or ↓ PaO$_2$
Failure to wean — see complications next page

Mechanical Ventilation

Indications

PaO$_2$ < 50 mmHg on FiO$_2$ ≥ 0.6
PaCO$_2$ > 55-60 mmHg (or rising > 5 mmHg/hr)
Severe apnea
Earlier in course for infants < 1500 gms

Initial setup (One possible pattern) (see Page 10-23)

> Optimal method is controversial. Different methods may be indicated depending on infant maturity, size and stability. Overall goal is to provide lowest level of ventilator support possible to maintain "adequate" (not necessarily normal) gases and minimize mechanical baro/volutrauma and O$_2$ toxicity. Volume ventilation is preferred.

Treatment (RDS continued)

Where to Maintain ABG's

	Small Premies	Near Term	PPHN
PaO_2	45-65	70-80	> 100
$PaCO_2$	40-55	35-50	25-35

Note: Some clinicians are accepting "adequate" gases (slightly higher $PaCO_2$ and slightly lower PaO_2) in small infants in order to keep ventilating parameters "lower".

Weaning (One possible pattern. See Page 10-28)

Most clinicians advocate extubation from low rate IMV (6-15 bpm) to avoid ↑ WOB and ↑ resistance with CPAP, expecially in infants < 1500 gms.

Complications to watch for with RDS (may cause acute changes or failure to wean conditions).

Respiratory failure	CHF	PDA(L-R or R-L shunt)	ROP
Air Leaks	Pulmonary edema	IVH	PPHN
Hypothermia	Anemia	NEC	Sepsis
Hypoglycemia	Recurrent apnea	BPD	Muscle fatigue
Metabolic acidosis	Atelectasis		(major factor in small
↓ BP			infants)

Surfactant Replacement Therapy for Respiratory Distress in the Preterm and Term Neonate*

1. Surfactant replacement, given as prophylaxis or rescue treatment, reduces the incidence and severity of RDS, air leaks, and mortality in preterm infants with surfactant deficiency.

   a. Surfactant should be given to infants with RDS as soon as possible after intubation irrespective of exposure to antenatal steroids or gestational age.

   b. Prophylactic surfactant replacement should be considered for extremely preterm infants at high risk of RDS, especially infants who have not been exposed to antenatal steroids.

   c. Rescue surfactant may be considered for infants with hypoxic respiratory failure attributable to secondary surfactant deficiency (eg, MAS, sepsis/pneumonia, and pulmonary hemorrhage).

   d. Surfactant treatment improves oxygenation and reduces the need for ECMO without an increase in morbidity in neonates with MAS and sepsis/pneumonia. Surfactant treatment may also reduce morbidity and mortality for infants with pulmonary hemorrhage.

   e. Preterm and term neonates who are receiving surfactant should be managed by nursery and transport personnel with the technical and clinical expertise to administer surfactant safely and deal with multi-system illness.

2. Preterm infants at risk of surfactant deficiency benefit from antenatal steroid exposure. Antenatal steroids and postnatal surfactant replacement independently and additively reduce mortality, the severity of RDS, and air leaks in preterm infants.

3. CPAP, with or without exogenous surfactant, may reduce the need for additional surfactant and incidence of BPD without increased morbidity

Extracted from American Academy of Pediatrics Guideline, *PEDIATRICS* Volume 121, Number 2, February 2008

Surfactant Therapy

Prophylatic Therapy: < 28 wks gestation (consider for infants 28-31 wks), especially if no antenatal steroids, known lung immaturity, male sex, and need for intubation in resuscitation.

Rescue Therapy: 28-32 wks gestation when needing MV and > 30-40% O_2.

Prophylactic surfactant should be administered after initial resuscitation of the infant at birth and administration prior to the "first breath" is unnecessary.

In preterm infants who do not receive prophylactic surfactant, the first dose of surfactant should be administered as early as possible either by the referring hospital or the transport team.

Surfactant administration should be given priority over other admission procedures such as radiographs, line placement, or nursing procedures.

Repeated doses of surfactant after the first dose is thought to be useful provided patient has a respiratory deterioration (persistent or worsening signs of RDS), a positive response to the first dose, and a pneumothorax has been eliminated as the cause of deterioration.

Retreatment has led to a decrease in mortality, respiratory support, NEC, and other outcomes.

Recommendations for Treatment

Type of surfactant: Natural preferred, synthetic may be used for mild disease

Timing: Early rather than the late (e.g., $FIO_2 > 0.4$)

Initial dose: 100-200 mg/kg

Retreatment: Flexible (six to 12-hourly) when $FIO_2 > 0.3$ and still on ventilator (MAP > 7 cmH$_2$O)

Action after treatment: For natural surfactants - lower FIO_2 immediately, ↓ Ti, ↓ PIP according to chest wall movement and ABGs. For synthetic surfactant - lower FIO_2 cautiously and maintain PEEP.

Some causes of a poor response:

<u>Wrong diagnosis</u> - lung hypoplasia, pneumonia, ARDS, CHD

<u>Wrong dose</u> - inadequate to overcome surfactant inactivation

<u>Wrong place</u> - given into one lung or into esophagus

<u>Wrong condition</u> - correct hypothermia, acidosis, and hypotension before treatment, treat sepsis.

Causes of early relapse and its management:

Inadequate dose - retreat

PDA - early use of indomethacin

Pneumonia - early treatment with antibiotics

Pulmonary hemorrhage - increase pressures, close PDA, give diuretics, consider retreatment.

Adapted from ***Neonatal Respiratory Disorders***, 2nd Edition, 2003, Edward Arnold Pub.

RESPIRATORY FAILURE (RF)

Def

$PaCO_2$ acutely > 60 mmHg, pH < 7.25. and/or PaO_2 < 50 mmHg or SaO_2 < 80% (no universally accepted definition)

Etiology

Airway
- Asthma
- Bronchiolitis
- Choanal atresia
- Cord paralysis
- Croup (LTB)
- Cystic fibrosis
- Epiglottitis
- Foreign body aspiration
- Malacia
- Pierre Robin Syndrome
- Subglottic stenosis
- Tumors

Cardiovascular
- Anemia
- CHD
- CHF
- PPHN
- Shock
- Vascular ring

Lungs
- Aspiration syndromes
- Atelectasis
- BPD
- Congenital malformation
- Diaphragmatic hernia
- Pleural effusion/ emphysema
- Pneumonia
- Pneumo/hemothorax
- Prematurity
- Pulmonary edema
- Pulmonary emboli
- Pulmonary hemorrhage/ contusion
- RDS (HMD or ARDS)
- Tumors

Other
- Acid-base imbalance
- Burns
- Drowning
- Electrolyte abnormalities
- Hypoglycemia
- Post op
- Renal failure
- Sepsis
- Trauma

Neuromuscular
- Guillian-Barre
- Muscular dystrophy
- Myathenia gravis
- Phrenic nerve palsy
- Poliomyelitis

CNS
- Apnea (or hypoventilation syndrome)
- Asphyxia
- Drugs
- Encephalopathy/ itis
- Intracranial hemorrhage
- Meningitis
- Poisons
- Seizures
- Spinal Cord Injury
- Trauma
- Tumors

CM

General	Respiratory	Neuro
↓ Muscle tone	↓ BS	↓LOC
Fatigue	Apnea	Restless
Sweating	Brady- or tachypnea	Irritable
	Cyanosis in 40% O2	Headache
<u>Cardiac</u>	Retractions*	Confusion
Brady- or tachycardia	Flaring	Convulsions
Hypo or hypertension	Grunting*	Coma
Pulsus paradoxicus (> 10 mmHg)	Wheezing	

*** Ominous Signs of Impending Respiratory Failure**

Tx

Differentiate between cardiac and pulmonary disease (see Pg. 11-31).

Maintain proper PaO_2 and $PaCO_2$.

Treat cause

RETINOPATHY OF PREMATURITY (ROP, RETROLENTAL FIBROPLASIA [RLF])

Def

Retinal dysfunction in newborns

Etiology

Immaturity + (*always*)	**High PaO_2 +** (*often*) (peak level & duration unknown)	**Predisposing Risk Factors** (*variable*):

O_2 therapy	Exchange transfusions?
Vent support	Down's syndrome
$PaCO_2$ changes	Sepsis
pH changes	Congenital anomalies
Vitamin E & A deficiency	Bright light
Hypoxia/apnea	Maternal diabetes
PDA? (indomethicin therapy)	Steroids
Twins	

CM

Complete recovery to blindness

Tx

See O_2 admininistration (Chapter 8)

Administer O_2 to premature infants only when $PaO_2 < 50$ mmHg in room air with or without cyanosis.

Maintain PaO_2 50-80 mmHg, SaO_2 85-93%.

Avoid excess transfusions

? Vitamin E/A

Opth exam of all infants < 36 weeks exposed to O_2

Laser surgery?

SEPSIS

Def

Infection in the bloodstream

Etiology

Every organism is possible.

Risk Factors:

Prematurity	PROM	Maternal fever	Aspiration
Fetal distress	Hypoxia	Invasive procedure	Fetal tachycardia

CM

Neonate	Child
Lethargy	Initial hyperdynamic state:
Feeding difficulty	Tachypnea
(gastric residuals)	Bounding pulse
Vomiting/diarrhea	Mild hypertension
Temp instability (> 1.5° C)	Widened pulse press
Pallor or mottling	↑ Temp
Cyanosis	Warm, flushed skin
Jaundice	Confusion
Resp. distress	Subsequent hypodynamic state:
Apnea or tachypnea	Respiratory distress
Brady- or tachycardia	Tachycardia
Irritable	Faint pulses
Tremors/seizures	Hypotension
Cold, clammy skin	↓ temp
Abdominal distention/ ileus	Cold clammy skin
Hypotonia	Cyanosis/profound hypoxemia
Hypoglycemia	Seizures
Hypotension	↓ LOC
Edema	Metabolic acidosis
Oliguria	↓ Urine output
	↓ capillary refill time

Lab Data	
Leukopenia	> 60% neutrophils
< 5000mm3	Platelets < 100,000 mm3
Leukocytosis	Shift to left - bands/total ≥ 0.2
> 20,000 mm3	

Tx

O_2; Circulatory support; Correct acidosis
Obtain CBC & cultures (blood, urine, CSF, trach)
Antibiotic therapy

11-79

TRACHEAL-ESOPHAGEAL FISTULA (T-E FISTULA)

Def	Abnormal passage between trachea and esophagus
Etiology	Congenital
CM	Three C's — Choking, Coughing, Cyanosis Excess salivation, aspiration Gastric distention
Tx	NPO — Provide parenteral nutrition Position Patient for patent airway and optimum ventilation Aspirate secretions from oropharynx and pouch Prevent aspiration Surgical correction

THORACIC TRAUMA

Def	Blunt or penetrating injury to the thoracic region
Etiology	Numerous (see table for the following): Rib fracture Pericardial tamponade Flail chest Pulmonary contusion Pneumothorax Diaphragmatic rupture Hemothorax Myocardial contusion Aortic injury
CM	See table
Tx	**General:** Perform life-saving measures first: Airway Breathing Circulation Spinal injury Shock Hemorrhage

11-80

Then assess/evaluate/treat other conditions as needed:

TX must be rapid, aggressive, organized and prioritized because children will often deteriorate suddenly and rapidly.

Assess vital signs, LOC and pupils continuously or every few minutes.

Maintain splints/collars — always assume fractures until ruled out.

Maintain body temp during TX.

Remove all clothing to avoid overlooking an injury.

Administer O_2 immediately.

Specific:

Airway

Provide O_2

Position head (sniffing)

Check for patency

Remove foreign debris

Sx as needed

Insert airway: Oral or tracheal

Cervical injury:

Ruled out = oral intubation

Possible = nasal intubation

If unsuccessful, then

> 3 yrs age: cricothyroidotomy

< 3 yrs age: Trach or oral intubation with axial traction (if necessary)

Breathing:

Inspect for:

Breathing rate, pattern and symmetry	Tracheal shift
Dyspnea	Retractions
Cyanosis	Sub Q emphysema
Chest wall stability (eg. flail chest)	External trauma (eg. sucking chest wound)

Palpate for:

Tenderness	Bone crepitus
Tracheal deviation	Sub Q emphysema

11-81

Percuss for:
Resonance (pneumothorax) Dull (Hemothorax)
Auscultate for:
BS — Loudness & symmetry / Adventitious sounds
Provide CPR, O_2, intubation, ventilation as needed.

Circulation
Monitor BP continuously
Watch for pulsus paradoxicus or orthostatic changes,
hypotension
Obtain 12 lead ECG: Watch for arrythmias.
Inspect for: Anterior chest trauma, JVD, PMI
Auscultate for: Muffled heart sounds
Rubs or murmurs
Provide CPR or other support as needed.

Cervical & Thoracic spine
Always assume fractured until ruled out
Immobilize head/neck with sandbags or collar
Maintain supine on a hard stretcher
Palpate column for alignment/tenderness
Look for loss of breathing:
Diaphragmatic loss (hypovent or apnea) = fracture
C-5 or above
Abdominal & intercostal loss = thoracic fracture
Obtain X-ray

Shock & hemorrhage
Determine source of bleeding & correct
Observe for signs of shock:
Tachycardia
Narrowed pulse pressure
Poor perfusion
Establish IV & CVP
TX for shock as needed

Thoracic Injuries

Injury	Clinical Manifestations	Treatment	Complications
Rib Fractures	dyspnea chest pain point tenderness chest compression is painful tachypnea, tachycardia bone crepitus	simple fx: analgesia teach deep breathing exercises Do not use binders, treat complications	pneumothorax hemothorax pulmonary contusion myocardial contusion organ damage
Flail Chest	same as rib fractures, and: paradoxical respiration mediastinal shift (possible) increased dyspnea cyanosis	position at on side of injury or stabilize with sandbags or pos. press. ventilation intubate for shock or resp. failure	pulmonary contusion atelectasis shock respiratory failure
Pneumothorax Simple	*See Air Leak Syndromes*	*See Air Leak syndromes*	tension pneumothorax hemothorax other air leaks
Pneumothorax Tension			hypertension ↓ CO atelectasis, lung collapse respiratory failure cardiac arrest hemothorax other air leaks

Injury	Clinical Manifestations	Treatment	Complications
Hemothorax	If > 25% of blood vol: pallor restlessness anxiety hypotension tachycardia ↓ BS Dull to percussion Blunting of costophrenic angle on x-ray PMI & trachealshift	chest tube (see Pg. 6-30) Immediate if resp. distress or shock (Sx 15-25 cm H_2O) fluid therapy	hypotension hypovolemic shock respiratory failure pulmonary contusion
Pericardial Tampnade	hypotension JVD (↑CVP) (if not in shock) tachycardia muffled heart sounds narrowed pulse pressure poor perfusion agitated paradoxical pulse (>10 mmHg) bradycardia (arrest is likely)	insert CVP fluid therapy pericardiocentesis (see Pg. 6-34) (Only after ruling out tension pneumo) mast trousers? thoracotomy? surgery?	hypovolemic shock cardiogenic shock

Injury	Clinical Manifestations	Treatment	Complications
Pulmonary Contusion	dyspnea cyanosis tachycardia, tachypnea anxiety restlessness hypotension localized crackles or wheezing ↓BS consolidation on x-ray	provide oxygenation & ventilation as needed CPAP or NIPPV may be of benefit	respiratory failure pneumonia
Diaphragmatic Rupture	asymptomatic to severe respiratory distress acute or delayed onset dyspnea vomiting nausea pain (abdominal &/or chest) tachycardia, tachypnea abdomen scaphoid or distended PMI shift ↓ BS (ipsilateral) tympany (ipsilateral) bowel sounds in chest	NG tube to decompress stomach free resp. distress surgery	bowel obstruction x-ray reveals elevated diaphragm, bowel in chest, atelectasis

Injury	Clinical Manifestations	Treatment	Complications
Myocardial Contusion	persistent unexplained tachycardia chest pain/tenderness tachypnea murmur crackles (late)	analgesics treat complications	↓ CO arrhythmias cardiac arrest/shock cardiac tamponade
Aortic Injury	retrosternal or interscapular pain dyspnea stridor dysphagia harsh systolic murmur hypertension x-ray reveals widened mediastinum, blurring of aortic knob & left pleural effusion	immediate thoracic surgical consult	hypovolemic shock death

TRANSIENT TACHYPNEA OF NEWBORN
(TTN) (WET LUNG, TYPE II RDS)

Def

Respiratory distress at birth due to delayed reabsorption of fetal lung fluid, characterized by ↑ RR and mild cyanosis

Etiology

Delayed reabsorption of fetal lung fluid
Myocardial failure (in some cases)?
PPHN (in some cases)
Predisposing factors:

C-section	Oversedated mothers
IDM	Polycythemia
Asphyxia	Delayed cord clamp
Near-term	Epidure. hypotension

CM

Presents within first two days

Tachypnea	Flaring
Mild Cyanosis	Self-limiting (some cases go on to 2°
Grunting	surfactant deficiency and severe PPHN)

CXR

Prominent vascular masking (perihilar streaking)
Fluid in fissures

Tx

Supportive:

O$_2$ for hypoxemia (usually F$_{i}$O$_2$ < .40 is needed)
Gavage feeding to avoid aspiration
If more respiratory support is needed, then probably another disorder is present.
Rule out other causes of resp. distress, esp. Group B strep, RDS, PPHN.

12   Pharmacology

Pharmacology

Clinical Note

Always check manufacturers' inserts for changes in drug information to include dosages, indications, warnings, precautions and contraindications.

This table is not all-inclusive, and dosages listed are adult dosages, unless indicated. Adult dose is often suitable for children > 12 years of age or > 40kg.

RESPIRATORY MEDICATION INDEX (PAGE FOUND IN CHAPTER)

Anti-Asthma		Bronchodilator			
Mast Cell Stabilizers (13)	Anti-Leuko trienes (14)	SABA (15)	LABA (18)	Anti-Chol inergics (20)	Xanthines (21)
cromolyn Na (Intal)	montelukast (Singular)	albuterol (Accuneb, Proventil, Ventolin, Volmax, Vospire)	arformoteral tartrate (Brovana)	ipratropium bromide (Atrovent)	aminophylline caffeine citrate
nedocromil Na (Tilade)	zafirlukast (Accolate)	bitolterol (Tornalate)	formoterol fumarate (Foradil, Perforomist)	tiotropium bromide (Spiriva)	
	zileuton (Zyflo)	levalbuterol (Xopenex)	salmeterol (Serevent)		
		metaproterenol sulfate (Alupent, Metaprel)			
		pirbuterol acetate (Maxair)			
		terbutaline (Brethine)			

Alpha-1 Antitrypsin (22)	Anti-Foamant (22)	Anti-Infective (23)	IgE Blockers (24)	Mucoactives (25)
alpha 1 proteinase inhibitor	alcohol (Vodka)	colistimethate Na (Colistin, Coly-Mycin)	omalizumab (Xolair)	acetylcysteine (Mucomyst)
		pentamidine isethionate (Nebupent, Pentam 300)		dornase alfa-DNase (Pulmozyme)
		ribavirin (Virazole)		
		tobramycin (Tobi)		

Racemic Epinephrine (25)	Smoking Cessation (27)		Steroids (29)
racemic epinephrine (AsthmaNefrin, MicroNefrin, VapoNefrin)	varenicline (Chantix)	Nicotrol patch (Nicoderm CQ)	beclomethasone (QVAR, Vanceril)
	bupropion (Zyban)	Nicorette Gum (Commit Lozenge)	budesonide (Pulmicort Turbuhaler, Pulmicort Respules)
	nasal spray (Nicotrol NS)	Nicotrol Oral Inhaler	flunisolide (Aerobid, Aerobid-M)
			fluticasone (Flovent)
			mometasone furoate (Asmanex)
			triamcinolone (Azmacort)

Anti-Cholinergic & SABA (26)	Corticosteroid & LABA (30)	Wetting Agents (31)
ipratropium bromide & albuterol (Combivent, Duoneb)	budesonide & formoterol (Symbicort)	water
	fluticasone and salmeterol (Advair)	saline - hypotonic
		saline - isotonic
		saline - hypertonic

12-3

Abbreviations used in Prescriptions

Aa, aa	of each	IM	intra-muscular	Qid	4x/day
ac	before meals	IV	intra-vascular	Q2h	every 2 hours
ad	to, up to	I&O	intake & output	q3h	every 3 hours
ad lib	as much as needed	L	liter/left	q4h	every 4 hours
aq dist	distilled H2O	m	mix	qs, QS	as much as required
bid	2x/day	mixt	mixture	qt	quart
c	with	mL	milliliter	Rx	take
caps	capsule	nebul	spray	s	without
dil	dilute	non rep	not to be repeated	sig	write
el, elix	elixir	NPO	nothing by mouth	sol	solution
emuls	emulsion	ol	oil	solv	dissolve
et	and	p	after	sos	if needed (1x)
ext	extract	part acq	equal parts	ss	half
fl, fld	fluid	pc	after meals	stat	immediately
Ft, ft	make	po	by mouth	syr	syrup
gel	gel, jelly	prn	as needed	tab	tablet(s)
g, gm	gram	rect	rectally	tid	3x/day
fr	grain	pulv	powder	tinct	tincture
gtt	drop	q	every	ung	ointment
ht	hypodermic tablet	qh	every hour	ut dict	as directed

Note: JCAHO has come out with an official "Do Not Use" list. The following chart lists excluded abbreviations, symbols and acronyms along with recommended and accepted terms or abbreviations to use.

Check JCAHO.org for updates

Medication Abbreviation Do-Not-Use List

Excluded Abbreviations	Recommendation
qd, QD	daily
qod, QOD	every other day
U, IU	Unit, International Unit
cc	mL, ml or milliliters
QN	every night, nightly
Q HS	Use "HS" of "at bedtime"
µg	micrograms or mcg
trailing zero, as in 1.0 mg	write 1 mg
No leading zero, as in .1mg	write 0.1 mg
degree sign for hours	spell out "hours"
/ when used in a handwritten prescription or order	spell out "per"
MS, MSIR, MSO4	write "morphine"
MgSO4	write "magnesium sulfate"
ZnSO4	write "zinc sulfate"
Apothecary symbol (e.g. grains)	write metric symbol (e.g. mg)
ss	spell out "sliding scale" or 1/2
per os	use "by mouth," "orally," or "PO"
D/C	Use discharge
Roman Numerals	Use arabic (4, 100, etc.)
> and <	Use "greater than" or "less than"
sq or sub q	use subcut

Percentage Concentration of Solutions
(weight to volume)

%	Ratios	g/L	g/100mL	g/mL	mg/100mL	mg/mL
100	1:1	1000	100	1	100,000	1000
10	1:10	100	10	0.1	10,000	100
5	1:20	50	5	0.05	5,000	50
1	1:100	10	1	0.01	1,000	10
0.5	1:200	5	0.5	0.005	500	5
0.1	1:1000	1	0.1	0.001	100	1

Medication Administration Procedures

Every time you administer medications, you should be following these procedures:

1. Review patient chart, verifying doctor's orders, code status, allergies, etc.
2. Assure you have the **right medication**.
3. Assure you have the **right dose** (including concentation).
4. Assure you have the **right time**.
5. Assure you have the **right route** (MDI vs. DPI vs. Neb).
6. Verify **right patient** (check I.D. bracelet, DOB).
7. Complete an adequate pre-, mid-, and post assessment.

(Major) Red Flag Drugs

These drugs have a high potential for drug-drug interactions

- Aspirin
- Cimetidine
- Penytoin
- Theophylline
- Warfarin

Solving Dosage of Liquids, Tablets, and Capsules

1. Convert all measurements to the same unit

$$\frac{\text{Original Strength}}{\text{Amount Supplied}} = \frac{\text{Desired Strength (dosage)}}{\text{Unknown amount to be supplied}}$$

Example 1:	Example 2:
How many mL of a drug must be given to deliver 75,000 units (50,000 units/mL)?	How many mLs of a drug, at a concent. of 25 mg/mL of solution, would be needed to provide 100 mg?

Example 1:

$$\frac{50,000}{mL} = \frac{75,000}{X \text{ mL}}$$

$$X = \frac{75,000}{50,000} = 1.5 \text{ mL}$$

Example 2:

$$\frac{25 \text{ mg}}{mL} = \frac{100 \text{ mg}}{X \text{ mL}}$$

$$X = \frac{100 \text{mg}}{25 \text{ mg}} = 4 \text{ mL}$$

Calculating Solution and Dosage Problems

Concert 1:500 solution into mg/mL

1:500 = 1 gm/500 gm
= 1 gm/500 mL
= 1000 mg/500 mL
= 2 mg/mL

$$W/W\% = \frac{\text{grams solute}}{100 \text{ gm solution}}$$

What % solution is 2 mg/mL

2 mg/mL = 200 mg/100 mL
= 0.2 gm/100 mL
= 0.2 gm/100 gm
= 0.2% solution

$$W/V\% = \frac{\text{grams solute}}{100 \text{ mL solution}}$$

**Find mg of drug if 0.25 mL
(1:200) is diluted in 2.5 mL saline**

1:200 = 1g/200 mL
= 1000mg/200mL
= 5mg/mL
0.25 mL x 5mg/mL
= 1.25 mg of drug delivered
in 2.75 mL solution

$$V/V\% = \frac{\text{m solute}}{100 \text{ mL solution}}$$

1 mL H2O = 1 gm H2O (specific gravity 1.0)   1 gm = 1,000 mg

12-7

Conversion within Same System

Set up a proportion:	How many mg are in 5 g?
$\dfrac{gm}{mg} = \dfrac{gm}{mg}$	$\dfrac{1\ gm}{1000\ mg} = \dfrac{5\ gm}{X}$

Conversion between Systems

Set up a proportion:	How many grains in 5 g?
$\dfrac{one\ system}{other\ system} = \dfrac{one\ system}{other\ system}$	$\dfrac{metric}{apothecary} = \dfrac{metric}{apothecary}$
	$\dfrac{1\ gm}{15\ grains} = \dfrac{5\ gm}{X}$

Approximate Dosage Equivalents

METRIC		AVOIRDUPOIS	
1 mg	0.015 grain	1 lb	454 gm
1 gm	15 grains	1 ounce	28.4 gm
1 kg	2.2 lbs		
1 mL	16 drops (gtts)		
APOTHECARY		**HOUSEHOLD**	
1 grain	60 mg	1 teaspoon	5 mL
1 ounce	30 gm	1 tablespoon	15 mL
1 fl ounce	30 mL	1 cup	240 mL, 8 fl ounces
1 pint	500 mL		
1 quart	1000 mL		
1 gallon	4000 mL		
1 minim	1 drop (gtt)		

Adjusting for Pediatric Dosages

Remember that recommended dosages are only estimates. Dosages should be individualized - adjust for variations in maturity, metabolism, temperature, obesity, edema, illness and individual tolerances.

Current literature supports BSA as the most consistent and accurate method of drug dosing over a wide range of body sizes. However, for small children (< 10 kg) dosing should be made on a mg/kg basis as BSA increases disproportionately as weight decreases.

Most drugs are dosed on a mg/kg basis in children. Due to differences in distribution, metabolism, and elimination, children require higher mg/kg dose than adults. While this works well for younger children, in older larger children and adolescents (>40 kg), when dosed by this method, adult doses can often be exceeded.

For this reason:
**never give a child a dose greater
than the usual adult dose,
regardless of height or weight.**

Body Surface Area (Clark's BSA) Rule

Estimated child's dose = $\dfrac{\textbf{Child's BSA (m}^2\textbf{) x Adult dose}}{\textbf{1.73}}$

$$BSA (m2) = \sqrt{\dfrac{\textbf{height(cm) x weight(kg)}}{\textbf{3600}}}$$

Lamb, TK, Leung, D. More on Simplified Calculation of Body Surface Area. New England Journal of Medicine 1988: 318:1130

Estimation of BSA for Children of "Normal Height and Weight"

Weight		Approximate	Surface Area
kg	lb	Age	(sq m)
3	6.6	Newborn	0.2
6	13.2	3 months	0.3
10	22	1 year	0.45
20	44	5.5 years	0.8
30	66	9 years	1
40	88	12 years	1.3
50	110	14 years	1.5
65	143	Adult	1.7
70	154	Adult	1.76

adapted from West's nomogram

Body Weight Rules

Clark's Rule (patients > 2 yrs)

Child's dose = $\dfrac{\text{Body Wt (lbs) x adult dose}}{150}$

Weight-Based Dosing:

Dose = pediatric dose/kg x child's weight (kg)

Age Rules (less accurate than BSA or weight-based)

Fried's Rule (infants up to 24 mos)

Infant's dose = $\dfrac{\text{age (mos) x adult dose}}{150}$

Young's Rule (2-12 yrs)

Child's dose = $\dfrac{\text{age (yrs) x adult dose}}{\text{age (yrs) + 12}}$

Bronchodilators

Adrenoreceptor Responses

Receptor	Target
alpha-1	Dilates pupils, contracts smooth muscle
beta-1	Stimulates force/rate of heart
beta-2	Bronchodilator of lungs, causes voluntary muscle tremors

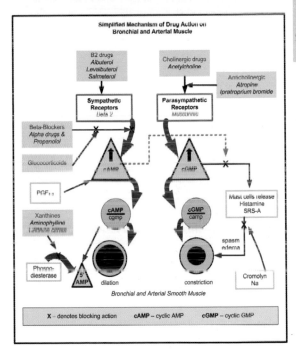

Simplified Mechanism of Drug Action on
Bronchial and Arterial Muscle

B2 drugs
Albuterol
Levalbuterol
Salmeterol

Cholinergic drugs
Acetylcholine

Anticholinergic
Atropine
Ipratropium bromide

Sympathetic Receptors
Beta 2

Parasympathetic Receptors
Muscarinic

Beta-Blockers
Alpha drugs &
Propanolol

Glucocorticoids

cAMP

cGMP

PGF

cAMP
cgmp

cGMP
camp

Xanthines
Aminophylline

Mast cells release
Histamine
SRS-A

Phospho-diesterase

5'
AMP

dilation

spasm
edema

constriction

Cromolyn
Na

Bronchial and Arterial Smooth Muscle

| X – denotes blocking action | cAMP – cyclic AMP | cGMP – cyclic GMP |

12-11

Bronchodilators: Summary of General Side Effects

Pulmonary	Cardiovascular	CNS	Other
Bronchial irritation and edema	↑BP, ↑HR, anginal pain, coronary insufficiency, palpitations, peripheral vasoconstriction	Anxiety, fear, headache, irritability, insomnia, nervousness, restlessness, tremor, vertigo, weakness	Hypersensitivity, reaction to MDI propellants, tachyphylaxis, urinary retention, vomiting, nausea

See AARC CPG, *Assessing Response to Bronchodilator Therapy*, in Appendix.

Pharmacology

Anti-Asthma - Mast Cell Stabilizers

Medication	Dosage	Indications/Actions	Contraindications/Notes
cromolyn Na Intal Other Generics	AEROSOL 10 mg/mL – 2 mL ampule 2 yr – adult: 20 mg T-Qid MDI: (800 µg/puff) >12 yr: 2-4 puffs T-Qid 5-12 yrs: 1-2 puffs T-Qid **ALLERGEN OR EIA:** Administer single dose 10-15 min, but not >50 min before precipitating event.	- Prophylactic maintenance of mild to moderate asthma. - Not for acute exacerbations. - Prevention of allergen or EIA *Prevents release of inflammatory mediators from inflammatory cell types.*	Adverse: Bronchospasm, cough, local irritation, dry mouth, chest tightness, vertigo, unpleasant taste in mouth. Neb solution (may dilute) may be mixed with albuterol.
nedocromil Na Tilade	MDI: (1.75 mg/puff) 6 yr – adult: 2 puffs Qid, may reduce to Bid once well controlled		

12-13

Anti-asthma - Anti-Leukotrienes

Medication	Dosage	Indications/Actions	Contraindications/Notes
montelukast Singulair	Asthma, seasonal or perennial allergic rhinitis (taken in PM): 6 mos - 5yrs: 4 mg/day 6 yr - 14 yr: 5 mg/day Adults: 10 mg/day Bronchoconstriction, EIA (prevention): Adults: 10 mg 2 hrs prior to exercise Granules: 4 mg/packet Chewable Tablet: 4 mg, 5 mg Tablet: 10 mg	Seasonal/perennial allergic rhinitis, prophylaxis and chronic treatment of asthma, prevention of exercise-induced bronchospasm *Leukotriene receptor antagonist blocks inflammatory mediators*	Adverse: Headache, dizziness, dyspepsia, fatigue. May increase liver function test.
zafirlukast Accolate	≥ 12 yr: 20 mg Bid 5-11 yr: 10 mg Bi d (10, 20 mg tabs)	*Prophylaxis/chronic treatment of asthma*	Same as above Admin 1 hr before or 2 hr after meals.
zileuton Zyflo	≥ 12 yr: 600 mg Qid (600 mg tabs)	*Leukotriene inhibitor: Prevents formation of inflammatory mediators*	Headache, dizziness, dyspepsia, fatigue, elevated ALT's

12-14

Bronchodilators: Beta Agonists SABA

Medication	Dosage	Indications, Actions	Contraindications/None
albuterol AccuNeb ProAir HFA Proventil HFA Ventolin Vospire ER	See Chart Below	**Bronchoconstriction, Acute and Maintenance** Stimulates β1 (minor), β2 (strong) Onset: 5 min. Peak: 30-60 min Duration: 3-8 hours	**Adverse:** Slight CV and CNS May mix with cromolyn or ipratropium net soln. **Adverse:** Hyperglycemia, hypokalemia, tremors

ACUTE EXACERBATION (NIH GUIDELINES)

NEBULIZER:
Child: 0.15 mg/kg (minimum 2.5 mg), q 20 min x 3 doses, then 0.15-0.3 mg/kg (up to 10 mg), q 1-4 hrs prn **or** 0.5 mg/kg/hr by continuous neb.
Adult: 2.5-5 mg, q 20 min x 3 doses, then 2.5-10 mg, q 1-4 hrs prn or 10-15 mg/hr by continuous neb.

MDI:
Child: 4-8 puffs, q 20 min x 3 doses, then q 1-4 hrs prn.
Adult: 4-8 puffs, q 20 min for up to 4 hrs, then q 1-4 hrs pm.
MDI (HFA): 90 mcg/puff
Neb. Soln: 5mg/mL (0.5%); 2.5mg/3mL (0.083%), 1.25mg/3mL (0.042%), 0.63mg/3mL (0.02-%)
Syrup: 2mg/5mL; Tabs: 2, 4 mg; Extended release tabs: 4, 8 mg

NON-ACUTE (MAINTENANCE)

NEBULIZER:
Child < 12 yrs: 0.15-0.25mg/kg (max 5 mg), q 4-6 hrs prn
Child > 12 yrs – Adult: 2.5 - 5.0 mg, q 4-6 hrs prn

MDI:
Child < 12 yrs: 1-2 puffs qid
Child > 12 yrs – Adult: 2-4 puffs, q 4-6 hrs (max 12 puffs/day)

ORAL:
2-6 yrs: 0.1-0.2 mg/kg/dose, tid (max 12 mg/day)
6-12 yrs: 2 mg/dose, T-Qid, extended release 4 mg, Bid (max 24 mg/day)
≥ 12 yrs – Adults: 2-4 mg/dose, T-Qid, extended release 4-8 mg, Bid (max 32 mg/day)

Bronchodilators: Beta Agonists SABA

Medication	Dosage	Indications/Actions	Contraindications/Notes
bitolterol Tornalate	**Aerosol: 1-2 mg in 2-4 mL total vol of NS**, TID-QID (max 8mg/day) 1mg/0.5mL, 0.2% **MDI: 0.37 mg/puff** 12 + yrs: 2 puffs, q 8 hours (max: 3 puffs, q 6 hr or 2 puffs q 4 hr)	**Bronchoconstriction** *Stimulates Beta-2 (mod)* **Onset:** 3-4 min **Peak:** 30-60 min **Dur:** 5-8 hrs	Do not mix solutions with other drugs Mild effects
lev albuterol Xopenex Xopenex HFA	**Aerosol: 0.31 mg/3 ml; 0.63 mg/3 ml; 1.25 mg/ 0.5 ml; 1.25 mg/3 mL** **6-11 yrs:** 0.31 mg TID (max 0.63 mg TID) **12 + yrs:** 0.63-1.25 mg TID **MDI: 45 mcg/puff** 4 + yrs: 1-2 puffs q 4-6 hr	**Bronchoconstriction** *R-isomer form of albuterol, stimulates Beta-2 (strong)* **Onset:** 15 min **Peak:** 1.5 hr **Dur:** 5-8 hrs	Slight CV and CNS effects, When using concentrated form (1.25mg/0.5mL), dilution is necessary

Bronchodilators: Beta Agonists SABA

Medication	Dosage	Indications/Actions	Contraindications/Notes
metaproterenol sulfate Alupent Metaprel	AEROSOL: (50 mg/mL (5%), 4 mg/mL (0.4%) in 2.5 mL NS, 6 mg/mL (0.6%) in 2.5 mL NS 2.5 mL NS – Adult: 0.2-0.3 mL (5%) 10-15 mg in 2-3 mL NS prn. > 12 yrs 0.1-0.2 mL (5%), 5-10 mg in 2-3 mL NS, q 4-6 hrs prn. 6-12 yrs: 0.5 mg/kg/dose (max 15 mg) in 2-3 mL NS, q 4-6 hrs prn. < 6 yrs: Infants: 6 mg/dose over 5 min (chronic lung) MDI: (0.65 mg/puff) >12 yrs: 2-3 puffs, q4 hr (max 12 puffs/day)	Bronchoconstriction Stimulates β-1 (mild), β-2 (strong) Onset: 5 min Peak: ½ - 1 hr Dur: 1-6 hrs	Mild CV effects, tremors, headache
pirbuterol acetate Maxair	MDI: 0.2 mg/puff 12 + yrs: 2 puffs, q 4-6 hr (max 12 puff/day)	Bronchoconstriction Stimulates β-1 (mild), β-2 (mod) Onset: 5 min Peak: ½ - 1 hr Dur: 3-5 hrs	Same as Above

Pharmacology

12-17

Bronchodilators: Beta Agonists SABA

Medication	Dosage	Indications/Actions	Contraindications/Notes
terbutaline	**MD:** 200 mg/puff	**Bronchoconstriction**	Adverse Effects: tachycardia, hypertension, nervousness, restlessness, increase in serum glucose and potassium.
Brethine	12+ years: 1-2 puffs q. 4-6h	*Stimulates β-1 (mild), β-2 (moderate)*	
		Onset: 5-30 min **Peak:** 30-60 min **Dur:** 3-6 hrs	

Bronchodilators: Beta Agonists LABA

Medication	Dosage	Indications/Actions	Contraindications/Notes
arformoterol tartrate	**AEROSOL:** 15 mcg /2 mL	**Maintenance treatment of COPD**	NOT indicated for acute constriction
Brovana	Adults: 15 mcg BID (do not exceed 30 mcg/day)	*Selective long-acting β2-adrenergic receptor agonist*	**SEE INSERT FOR BLACK BOX WARNING**

Bronchodilators: Beta Agonists LABA

Medication	Dosage	Indications/Actions	
formoterol fumarate Foradil Perforomist	**Powder/Inhalation:** 12 mcg/capsule (Foradil) **Maintenance Asthma (> 5yr)** Inhale contents of 1 capsule (12 mcg) BID, 12 hrs apart (max 24 mcg/24 hrs) **EIA, prophylaxis (>5 yr)** inhale contents of 1 cap 15 minutes before exercise. Don't repeat within 12 hours **COPD maintenance treatment (Adults)** inhale contents of 1 cap EID (Max 24 mcg/24 hrs)	**Bronchoconstriction** *Long acting selective β2 agonist.* **Onset:** 1-3 min **Peak:** 30-50 min **Duration:** 12 hrs.	Do not use with a spacer. **SEE INSERT FOR BLACK BOX WARNING**
Nebulizer (20 mcg/2 mL) Perforomist -- COPD (maintenance) (Adults) 20 mcg BID, max dose 40 mcg/24 hrs			
salmeterol Serevent	**POWDER:** (50 mcg/dose) > 4 yrs 1 puff, BID, 12 hrs apart max Asthma (>4 yrs; mainten and prevention) COPD adults **PREVENTION OF EIA (> 4yrs):** 1 puff (50 mcg) at least 30 minutes prior to exercise. Don't repeat within 12 hrs, and not to be used by patients on salmeterol BID	**Long-Term management: of Bronchoconstriction** *Long acting selective β2 agonist.* **Onset:** 10-20 min **Peak:** 3 hrs. **Duration:** 12 hrs.	Not for acute management Diskus not for use with spacer **SEE INSERT FOR BLACK BOX WARNING**

Pharmacology

Anti-Cholinergics

Medication	Dosage	Indications/Actions	Contraindications/Notes
ipratropium bromide Atrovent Atrovent HFA	AEROSOL: (0.02%) (500 mcg/2.5 mL) > 12 yr: 250-500 mcg, T-Qid Child: 250 mcg, Tid Infant: 125-250 mcg, Tid Neonate: 25 mcg/kg/dose, Tid, max 250 mcg MDI: (18 mcg/puff) < 12 yr: 1-2 puffs, Tid (max 6/day) > 12 yr: 2-3 puffs, Qid (max 12/day)	Treatment of broncho-spasm associated with COPD, bronchitis/emphy-sema *Anticholinergic: blocks acetyl-choline + potentiates β2 stim.* ACUTE EXACERBATION: > 12 yrs: 500 mcg, q 20 min x 3 doses, then q 2-4 hrs. < 12 yrs: 250 mcg, q 20 min x 3 doses, then q 2-4 hrs. MDI: (all ages) (NIH Guidelines): 4-8 puffs, q 20 minutes as needed for up to 3 hrs	Adverse: mucus viscosity, local inflammation, dry mouth, pupil dilation May mix with Albuterol (See page 12-30) **Not to be used as a rescue inhaler**
tiotropium bromide *Spiriva (HandiHaler)*	DPI: 18 mcg 1 inhalation/day	Maintenance tx of COPD Action same as Atrovent Onset: 30 min Peak: 3 hrs Duration: >24 hrs	Adverse: dry mouth, urinary reten-tion, constipation, increased HR, blurred vision, glaucoma **Not to be used as a rescue inhaler**

Xanthines

Medication	Dosage	Indications/Actions	Contraindications/Notes
aminophylline	**NEONATAL APNEA:** Load: 5 mg/kg over 30" (IV or PO) Maintenance: 5 mg/kg/day, q 12 hrs **BRONCHODILATION:** Load: 6 mg/kg over 20-30 min (IV) Maintenance: Neonate: 0.2mg/kg/hr. 6 wk - 6 mo: 0.5mg/kg/hr 6mo–12mo: 0.6-0.7 mg/kg/hr	Bronchoconstriction Neonatal apnea Bronchodilation (inhibits phospho-di- esterase) *Stimulates rate and depth of respiration, pulmonary vasodilation* 1-9 yrs: 1-1.2 mg/kg/hr 9-12 y's: 0.9 mg/kg/hr (+ young smokers) >12 yrs: 0.7 mg/kg/hr (+ older nonsmokers)	↑CV and CNS effects, many systemic effects Toxicity > 20 mg/L (> 15 mg/L in neonates)
caffeine citrate	AEROSOL: > 6 yr: 300 mg, q 12 hr (300 mg/5 mL) repeat in cycles of 28 days on, 28 days off.	Neonatal apnea *Stimulates CNS, inotropic, increases force of muscle contraction*	Fewer CV and CNS adverse effects in neonates than aminophylline Caution in neonates with renal or hepatic impairment

Alpha-1 Antitrypsin Disorder

Medication	Dosage	Indications/Actions	Contraindications/Notes
Alpha 1 Proteinase Inhibitor	60 mg/kg once weekly For IV use only, infuse over 30 min.	**Congenital alpha 1- antitrypsin deficiency.**	Hypersensitivity and anaphylactic reactions
Human	**Aralast, Prolastin, Azalast NP**: 500 mg, 1000 mg vials	*Replaces enzymes lost in patients with this disorder*	**Adverse:** ↑ALT, AST, Headache, Musculoskeletal discomfort, pharyngitis, allergic reactions, fever, light headedness
	Zemaira: 1000 mg		

Anti-Foamants

Medication	Dosage	Indications/Actions	Contraindications/Notes
alcohol	**Aerosol:**	**Foaming Pulmon. Edema**	Mucosal irritation, flammable
Vodka	3-15 mL of 30-50%	*Decrease surface tension of mucoid secretions*	

Medication	Dosage	Indications/Actions	Contraindications/Notes
colistimethate Na	Aerosol: 75mg/mL	Management of P. aeruginosa	Dilute dose in NS to 4 mL
Colistin Coly-Mycin	37.5–50mg q 8-12 hrs	Antibiotic for G-activity (pseudomonal activity)	Administer via Pari LC plus nebulizer & filter valve set
			Mix immediately before admin.
pentamidine isethionate	- 5–y's: 300 mg (1 vial), q 3-4 wks	Prophylaxis of Pneumocystis pneumonia	Do not mix with other drugs
NebuPent Pentam 300	- <5 y's: 8 mg/kg/dose (up to 300mg)	Anti-protozoan	Mix 300 mg (1 vial) w/ 6mL sterile water
	- Deliver via Respirgard II neb at 5-7 LPM at 50 PSI until gone		Administer bronchodilator prior to tx
			Adverse Reactions: irritation, cough, fatigue, SOB, bronchospasm, metallic taste, systemic effects

Note: Caregiver precautions - administer or mix in an isolated room with separate air circulating system and neg. pressure. Minimize environmental drug exposure. Wear gown, gloves, mask and goggles. Nebulize to <3 µm MMAD.

Anti-Infectives

Medication	Dosage	Indications/Actions	Contraindications/Notes
ribavirin Virazole	**AEROSOL:** 2 grams over 2 hrs 3x/day (60 mg/mL - 6 grams reconstituted w/ 100 mL of sterile, preservatitve-free water, for 3-7 days. May cause adverse effects in healthcare workers (especially for pregnant women). Use of neg. pressure room, scavenging devices, and resp. masks is recommended.	**Severe lower respiratory tract infection (bronchiolitis, viral pneumonia)** *Antiviral (RSV/influenza A & B)* Watch for acute respiratory deterioration + CV effects. Deliver aerosol into mask or hood, (not ET tube and/or vent).	Not recommended for intubated patients Do not mix with other drugs Deliver with SPAG-2
tobramycin Tobi	**AEROSOL:** > 6 yr: 300 mg, q 12 hr (300 mg/5 mL), repeat in cycles of 28 days on, 28 days off. <6yr: 100 mg, q 12h	**Management of P. aeruginosa infections in cystic fibrosis patients.** *Antibiotic for G- activity (Pseudomonal activity)*	Don't dilute/mix w/ other drugs. Admin via Pari®LC plus nebulizer + filter valve set Adverse Reactions: multiple (review mfr insert)

IgE Blockers

omalizumab Xolair	**>12 yrs:** 150 - 375 mg, subcutaneous q. 2-4 weeks (varies according to Ige level/wgt)	**Mod-Sev persistent asthma /inadeq. control w/ steroids** *Humanized IgG1 monoclonal antibody*	Bruising, erythema See **Black Box Warning** for this medication

Mucoactives

Medication	Dosage			Indications/Actions	Contraindications/Notes
acetylcysteine Mucomyst	**AEROSOL:** T-Qid			**Tenacious mucous** *Breaks mucus disulfide bonds. Decreases mucous viscosity.*	**Adverse:** Bronchospasm (administer bronchodilator before use), stomatitis, nausea, rhinitis, unpleasant odor/taste. Overmobilization of secretions
	Age	10%	20%		
	>12 yr	10 mL	5 mL	Peak: 5-10 min	
	Child:	6-10 mL	3-5 mL	Duration: > 1 hr	
	Infant:	2-4 mL	1-2 mL		
	20% is diluted 1:1 with H2O or NS				
INSTILLATION: q 1-4 hrs, prn	1-2 mL (20%) [200 mg/mL] 2-4 mL (10%) [100 mg/mL]				
dornase alfa-dnase Pulmozyme	**AEROSOL:** > 5 yr - ac ult: 2.5 mg, 1-2 x/day (1 mg/mL, 2.5 mL amp)			**Tenacious mucus** (decreases infection) *Dornase alpha recombinant, decrease viscocity*	Same as acetylcysteine -- Do not mix or dilute with other drugs.

Racemic Epinephrine

Medication	Dosage	Indications/Actions	Contraindications/Notes
racemic epinephrine AsthmaNefrin MicroNefrin VapoNefrin	Aerosol: 22.5 mg/mL (2.25%) 0.25-0.5 ml (2.25%) in 2.5 ml diluent **CROUP:** < 5 kg: 0.25 mL/dose > 5 kg: 0.5 mL/dose	**Bronchoconstriction** **Tracheobronchial inflammation** (post extubation, etc), nasal congestion *Stimulates:* *alpha (mild)* *beta-1 (medium)* *beta-2 (mild)*	Milder effects than epinephrine Rebound airway edema, cardiac arrhythmias, chest pain, trembling, dizziness, headache Duration: ½-2 hrs Use min # doses to get response

Pharmacology

5 A's of Smoking

ASK	every patient should be asked if they use tobacco every time you see them
ADVISE	non-judgmentally, advise all smokers to quit
ASSESS	assess the smoker for motivation (are they ready to quit?)
ASSIST	develop a plan with the smoker to quit, discuss pharmacological options, recommend counseling, provide adequate materials
ARRANGE	directly follow-up on regular intervals, or arrange for adequate follow-up

Fagerstrom Test for Nicotine Dependence

How soon after you wake up do you smoke your first cigarette?	5 min or less	*3 points*
	6-30 minutes	*2 points*
	31-60 minutes	*1 point*
	60+ minutes	*0 points*
Do you find it hard to refrain from smoking in places where it is forbidden?	Yes	*1 point*
	No	*0 points*
What cigarette would you hate most to give up?	First Morning	*1 point*
	Any other	*0 point*
How many cigarettes per day do you smoke?	10 or less	*0 points*
	11-20	*1 point*
	21-30	*2 points*
	31 or more	*3 points*
Do you smoke more during the first hours after waking?	Yes	*1 point*
	No	*0 points*
Do you smoke if you are so ill you can't get out of bed?	Yes	*1 point*
	No	*0 points*

≥6 indicates a high level of dependence

Smoking Cessation

Medication	Dosage	Summary of Action	Contraindications/Notes
varenicline Chantix	**Start Chantix 1 week prior to quit date.** -1mg BID following a 1 week titration: Days 1-3: 0.5mg qd Days 4-7: 0.5mg bid Day 8+: 1mg bid 12 wk course of treatment then another 12 weeks if success during 1st course	*Binds with neuronal nicotinic acetylcholine receptors. Produces agonist activity (blocks the reward/reinforcement a person may feel as a result of smoking)*	**Side Effects may be common: serious neuropsychiatric symptoms, including changes in behavior, agitation, depressed mood, suicidal ideation and suicidal behavior** nausea (mild-moderate, persistent), sleep disturbance, flatulence, constipation.
bupropion Zyban	**Tablets (150 mg)** Start 2-wks before quitting 150 mg/day x 3 days *then* 150mg BID for 7-12 weeks	*Unknown, may have noradrenergic or dopaminic effects (decreases some of the cravings for cigarettes)*	Should not be taken with MAO Inhibitors, or people with seizure disorders. **See insert for Black Box Warning**
Nasal Spray Nicotrol NS	Nasal Spray (0.5mg nicotine per spray) 1-2 doses per hour, not to exceed 40mg (80 sprays) per day	*Nicotine Replacement therapies decrease withdrawal symptoms by giving measured, smaller doses of nicotine*	Patient should be instructed to not smoke concurrently Use should not exceed 6 mos.

Smoking Cessation

Medication	Dosage	Summary of Action	Contraindications/Notes
Transdermal patch Nicotrol	**15 mg/patch for 6 weeks** **>10 cigarettes/day:** Apply 1 patch in the A.M.; remove before bed (don't wear overnight)	*Nicotine Replacement therapies decrease withdrawal symptoms by giving measured, smaller doses of nicotine*	**Adverse:** skin irritation, insomnia **Precautions:** pregnancy, heart disease
Transdermal Patch Nicoderm CQ	**Patch 7, 14, 21 mg/ patch** <10 cig/day: 14mg for 16-24hr x 6wk *then* 7mg for 16-24hr x 2 wk >10 cig/day: 21mg for 16-24hr *then* 14mg for 16-24hr x 2 wk *then* 7mg for 16-24hr x 2 wk		
Gum/ Lozenges Nicorette Gum, Commit Lozenge	**Gum:** 2, 4 mg (max: 30 pcs/day) **Lozenges:** 2, 4 mg (max: 20 loz/day) 2-4 mg over 30 min q 1-2 hr x 6wk, *then* q. 2-4 hr x 3 wk, *then* q. 4-8 hr x 3 wk		Dentures Pregnancy Heart Disease
Oral Inhaler Nicotrol	10mg cartridges, 4mg delivered 6-16 cartridges per day Patient should be instructed in controlling depth and frequency of inhalation		**Adverse:** dyspepsia, cough, mouth irritation/burning Avoid in COPD, asthma, pregnancy and heart disease

Medication	Dosage	Summary of Action	Contraindications/Notes
beclomethasone (QVAR, Vanceril) budesonide (Pulmicort Turbuhaler, Flexhaler Pulmicort Respules) flunisolide (Aerobid, Aerobid-M) fluticasone (Flovent) mometasone furoate (Asmanex) triamcinolone (Azmacort)	See insert for dosing information	*Anti-inflammatory for maintenance with prophylactic treatment of asthma*	Cough, sneezing, dysphonia, pharyngitis, voice alteration, headache, dyspepsia, nasal congestion, and oral candidiasis. Rinsing the mouth with water after use will help minimize dry mouth, hoarseness, and oral candidiasis.

Combination: Anti-Cholinergic and SABA

Medication	Dosage	Indications/Actions	Contraindications/Notes
ipratropium bromide and albuterol Duoneb	AEROSOL (0.5 mg ipratropium/2.5 mg albuterol) 3 mL nebulized QID, with 2 additional doses if needed	COPD with bronchospasm	Do not administered with sympathomimetics/MAO inhibitors Paradoxical Bronchospasm
ipratropium bromide and albuterol Combivent	MDI: 18 mcg ipratropium bromide and 103 mcg albuterol sulfate 2 inhalations QID, not to exceed 12 inhalations a day	*SABA and anticholinergic combined effects, which are thought to have a greater effect than either drug independently*	Caution with glaucoma, prostatic hypertrophy

Combination: Corticosteroid and LABA

Medication	Dosage	Summary of Action	Contraindication/Adverse
budesonide and formoterol Symbicort	Inhalation: 80mcg budesonide/ 4.5 formoterol 2 inhalations BID Inhalation: 160 mcg budesonide/ 4.5 mcg formoterol 2 inhalations BID	Long-term maintenance treatment of asthma in persons over 12 years old, who are not easily controlled with corticosteroid and occassional use of a SABA. *Combines action of systemic corticosteroid and LABA*	**SEE BLACK BOX WARNING** SYMBICORT: Instruct patients to shake inhaler for a full 5 seconds prior to using, to mix medications. Rinse mouth after use Adverse: sore nose/throat, headache, stomach irritation, sinusitis, cardiovascular side effects
fluticasone and salmeterol Advair	DPI: 100/50, 250/50, 500/50 (fluticasone/salmeterol) Asthma (100/50, 250/50) COPD (250/50) 1 inhalation BID, max 2/day HFA (LT maint.): (45/21, 115/21, 230/21) >12 yrs: 2 inh. BID, max 4/day	LT maintenance treatment of asthma in persons > 12 yrs Maintenance treatment (250/50)of airway obstruction associated with Chronic Bronchitis	Contraindicated as a rescue inhaler
See insert for recommended dosages for Asthma pts not adequately controlled by corticosteroids			

Wetting Agents

Medication	Dosage	Indications/Actions	Contraindications/Notes
water sterile, distilled	Intermittent or continuous nebulization	**Thick Secretions** *Humidify/thin/liquefy secretions*	Potential mucosal irritation, overhydration, bronchospasm
Saline: Hypotonic (0.45% NaCl)		*Diluent of drugs*	Same as above Less irritating than H_2O
Saline: Isotonic (0.9%)			Bronchospasm
Saline: Hypertonic	**Aerosol:** intermittent only (2-5 mL)	**Sputum Induction** *Same as above, plus osmotic transudation*	Bronchospasm, mucosal irritation, edema, ↑ blood Na^+

12-31

Medications Affecting Ventilation

Respiratory Depression	Respiratory Stimulation

Ethyl alcohol
Hallucinogens (PCP, angel dust)
Narcotics:
  codeine, heroin, propoxyphene (Darvon), oxycodone (Percodan), fentanyl (Sublimaze), hydromorphone (Dialaudid), meperidine (Demerol), morphine
Sedatives/Hypnotics:
  chloral hydrate, diazepam (Valium), lorazepam (Ativan), midazolan (Versed), zolpidem (Ambien)
Barbiturates:
  phenobarbital, pentobarbital, thiopental (Pentothal)
Anesthetics:
  Propofol (Diprivan)
	Acids (CO2, HCl, NH3Cl)
	Adrenergic agents: amphe amine, ephedrine, norep nephrine
	Alcohol: ethylene glycol (antifreeze)
	Analeptics: doxapram (Dopram)
	Benzodiazepine antagonists: flumazenil (Romazicon)
	Diuretics: carbonic anhydrase inhibitors: acetazolamide (Diamox)
	Hormones: ACTH, estrogen, insulin, progesterone, thyroxine
	Irritants: ammonia, ether
	Narcotic antagonist: naloxone (Narcan)
	Salicylates: aspirin
	Xanthines: aminophylline, caffeine, theophylline

Paralytics (Neuromuscular Blocking Agents)

atracurium (Tracrium) cisatracurium (Nimbex) doxacurium (Neuromax) mivacurium (Mivacron)	**pancuronium (Pavulon)** **rocuronium (Zemuron) *** **succinylcholine (Anectine) #** **vercuronium (Norcuron)**

* Used for rapid sequence induction when succinylcholine is contraindicated.

Depolarizing agent used primarily for intubation – all the others are non-depolarizing

Paralytic Reversal Agents

Endrophodium (Tensilon), Neostigmine (Prostigmin), and Pyridostigmine (Mestinon) are antidotes for nondepolarizing agents. Give atropine to offset bronchial secretions and bradycardia caused by antidotes.
There is no antidote for succinylcholine.

See Oakes' *Ventilator Management: A Bedside Reference Guide*, for further details about many of the above drugs

Common Cardiovascular Drugs

Anti-arrhythmics	Vasodilators
	Vessel Dilation
adenosine (Adenocard)	captopril (Capoten)
atropine	enalapril (Vasotec)
diltiazem (Cardizem)	fenoldopam (Corlopam)
fosphenytoin (Cerebyx)	isoproterenol (Isuprel)
ibutilide (Corvert)	hydralazine (Apresoline)
lidocaine (Xylocaine)	labetalol (Nomodyne, Trandate)
phenytoin (Dilantin)	
procainamide (Procan, Pronestyl)	nicardipine (Cardene)
propafenone (Rhythmol)	nitroglycerin
propranolol (Inderal)	phentolamine (Regitime)
quinidine (Cardoquin)	sodium nitroprusside (Nipride, Nitropress)
tocainide (Tonocard)	
verapamil (Calan, Isoptin)	tolazoline (Priscoline)

Inotropics	Vasopressors
↑ *Cardiac Contractility*	*Vessel Constriction*
amrinone (Inocor)	ephedrine (Bofedrol, Ephed)
digoxin (Lanoxin)	metaraminol bitartate (Aramine)
dobutamine (Dobutrex)	
dopamine (Intropin)	norepinephrine or levarterenol (Levophed)
epinephrine (Adrenalin)	
isoproterenol (Isuprel)	phenylephrine (Neosynephrine)
milrinone (Primacor)	

See Oakes' *Hemodynamic Monitoring: A Bedside Reference Manual*, for further details about many of the above drugs

Diuretics (Increased kidney output)
- furosemide (Lasix) — acetazolamide (Diamox)
- bumetanide (Bumex) — torsemide (Demadex)

Anticoagulants (decreased clotting)
- dicumarol — warfarin (Coumadin)
- enoxaparin (Lovenox) heparin

13 CPR

CPR

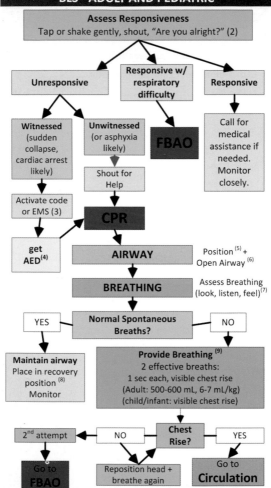

BLS - ADULT AND PEDIATRIC[1]

Assess Responsiveness
Tap or shake gently, shout, "Are you alright?" (2)

Unresponsive

Responsive w/ respiratory difficulty

Responsive

Witnessed (sudden collapse, cardiac arrest likely)

Unwitnessed (or asphyxia likely)

FBAO

Call for medical assistance if needed. Monitor closely.

Activate code or EMS (3)

Shout for Help

get AED[4]

CPR

AIRWAY — Position [5] + Open Airway [6]

BREATHING — Assess Breathing (look, listen, feel) [7]

Normal Spontaneous Breaths?

YES

NO

Maintain airway Place in recovery position [8] Monitor

Provide Breathing [9]
2 effective breaths:
1 sec each, visible chest rise
(Adult: 500-600 mL, 6-7 mL/kg)
(child/infant: visible chest rise)

Chest Rise?

NO

YES

2nd attempt

Go to FBAO

Reposition head + breathe again

Go to Circulation

CPR

CIRCULATION

Assess Signs of Circulation [10]

≤ 10 sec { Check for coughing, breathing, movement
{ Check pulse: Adult + Child: carotid or femoral; < 1yr: brachial

Definite Pulse (confident)	**No Pulse (or not confident)**
Ventilate as needed	or
1 sec each	Child/Infant w/ HR<60 + poor perfusion
Visible chest rise	
Adult: 10-12/min (q. 5-6 sec)	**Provide Chest Compressions** [11]
Child/Infant: 12-20/min (q 3-5 sec)	
Activate EMS (if not already)	
Reassess pulse q. 2 mins (< 10 sec)	

		Infant (< 1yr)	Child (1yr-puberty)	Adult
Push Hard -	Technique	2 fingers (1 rescuer) 2 thumb-encircling hands (2 rescuers)	1 or 2 hands	2 hands
Push Fast -	Place	Just below nipple line	At nipple line (center of chest)	
	Depth	1/3-1/2 depth of chest		1 1/2 - 2 in (4-5 cm)
Allow full recoil	Rate	100/min (approx)		
	Ratio	Unsecured airway 30/2 : 1 rescuer 15/2 : 2 rescuers		Unsecured airway 30/2 1 or 2 rescuers
		Secured airway & 2 rescuers 8-10 breaths/min (q 6-7 sec) (No pause or synchronization for breaths)		

Perform 5 cycles (approx 2 min) [12]
(minimize interruptions)

Activate Code or EMS (if not already)
Get AED (if available) or Use AED (if already have) [13]
Reassess breathing + circulation (take ≤ 10 sec)
Continue CPR + Reasses q. 2 min (5 cycles)

CPR

FOOTNOTES

(1) Algorithms and Footnotes - Pertain to adults and pediatrics (infants [< 1 yr] and children [1 yr – 12 to14 yrs; puberty].
All notes pertain to adults, unless otherwise indicated.
(See also "Neonatal Resuscitation")

(2) Assess for Safety and Response - First ensure scene is safe. Suspected head or neck injury: do not shake; move only if necessary.

(3) 2 Rescuers - One rescuer begins CPR, while the other activates the code (or EMS) and retrieves an AED (if available).

(4) Get AED - If readily available; use as appropriate (See AED section)

(5) Position - Victim: supine, arms alongside on firm, flat surface.
Move head, shoulders, and torso as one unit without twisting.
Rescuer: kneeling beside victim's thorax (Fig 13).

(6) Open Airway -
Head tilt – chin lift: preferred when no evidence of head or neck trauma (Fig 1).
Jaw thrust: use when suspect cervical spine injury. Do not tilt head back or sideways (Fig 2). Use spinal motion restriction rather than immobilization devices. Note: if jaw thrust does not open the airway: use head tilt – chin lift.
Open mouth and remove any visible foreign material, vomitus, or loose dentures (Fig 20).

(7) Assess Breathing - Place ear next to victim's mouth and nose and observe chest for ≤ 10 secs:

> *Look* – for chest to rise and fall
> *Listen* – for air escaping during exhalation
> *Feel* – for air flow

Note: distinguish adequate from inadequate (weak or agonal [reflex gasping]) breathing.

(8) Recovery Position -
Unresponsive victims with normal breathing and effective circulation.
Place victim as near as possible to a true and stable lateral position (lower arm in front of body) with head dependent, no pressure on chest, and good observation/access to airway (Fig 3).
Suspected spinal injury: move to recovery position only if open airway cannot be maintained (eg., lone rescuer must leave victim to get help). May opt for lower arm above head, with head on arm and knees bent.

FOOTNOTES (CON'T)

(9) Breathing - Avoid large, rapid or forceful breaths. Do not deliver more volume or force than is needed to produce visible chest rise. Use mouth to mouth/nose for infants (See ACLS Section)

(10) Signs of Circulation - do not delay chest compressions to locate a pulse (10 sec max).

(11) Chest Compressions - Equal compression/relaxation ratio. Allow chest to return to normal position without lifting hands from chest.

2 Rescuers:
Unsecured airway - Pause compressions for ventilations. Begin compressions at peak inspiration of 2nd breath.

Secured airway - Do not pause or synchronize for ventilations.

Note: Do not monitor and/or gauge chest compression force as adequate by palpable carotid or femoral pulse (may be venous).

(12) Two rescuers should change compressor/ventilator roles approximately every 2 minutes (5 cycles)

(13) Shockable rhythm (child and adult only)
Give 1 shock, immediately resume CPR (beginning with compressions), do not check pulse.
After 5 cycles, analyze rhythm, deliver another shock if indicated.
Infants (< 1 yr) – do not use AED, continue CPR
Children   2 J/kg first attempt; 4 J/kg subsequent attempts
Ages 1- 8 yrs – use pediatric dose-attenuator system, if avail
(See AED section)

FBAO - FOREIGN BODY AIRWAY OBSTRUCTION

CPR

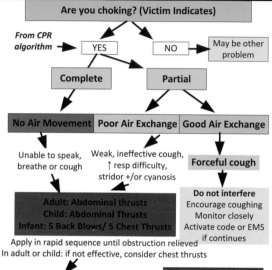

Are you choking? (Victim Indicates)

From CPR algorithm → YES NO → May be other problem

Complete **Partial**

No Air Movement | **Poor Air Exchange** | **Good Air Exchange**

Unable to speak, breathe or cough

Weak, ineffective cough, ↑ resp difficulty, stridor +/or cyanosis

Forceful cough

Adult: Abdominal thrusts
Child: Abdominal Thrusts
Infant: 5 Back Blows/ 5 Chest Thrusts

Apply in rapid sequence until obstruction relieved
In adult or child: if not effective, consider chest thrusts

Do not interfere
Encourage coughing
Monitor closely
Activate code or EMS
if continues

Victim Becomes Unconscious
Lower victim to ground (supine)
Activate code or EMS

Begin CPR
Go to BLS - Airway

Look into mouth before giving breaths – finger sweep ONLY if you see solid material

Notes:

Infant/child –

5 Back blows/5 Chest thrusts: one every sec as needed, same location and technique as chest compressions
Abdominal thrusts not recommended for infants (<1 yr)

Sudden respiratory distress (coughing, gagging, and/or stridor) accompanied by fever, congestion, hoarseness, drooling or lethargy are indicative of infections such as epiglottitis or croup. The child must be taken immediately to an emergency facility because back blows or chest thrusts will not relieve the obstruction.

Late pregnancy – use chest thrusts

Obesity – use chest thrusts (if rescuer cannot encircle abdomen)

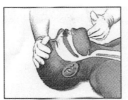

Fig. 1. Head tilt-chin lift

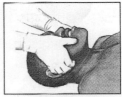

Fig. 2. Jaw thrust (without head tilt)

Fig. 3. Recovery position

Fig. 4. Mouth-to-mouth rescue breathing

Fig. 5. Mouth-to-nose rescue breathing

Fig. 6. Mouth-to-stoma rescue breathing

Fig. 7. Mouth-to-mask cephalic technique

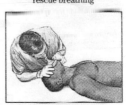

Fig. 8. Mouth-to-mask lateral technique

Fig. 9. Two rescuer use
of the bag mask

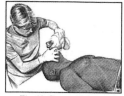

Fig. 10. One rescuer use
of the bag mask

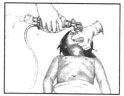

Fig. 11. Bag-mask ventilation for child victim
A, 1 rescuer; B, 2 rescuers

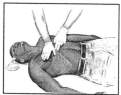

Fig. 12. Positioning of rescuer's
hands for chest compressions

Fig. 13. Position of rescuer
for chest compressions

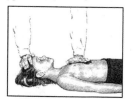

Fig. 14. One hand chest
compression in child

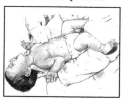

Fig. 15. One rescuer
infant CPR while carrying

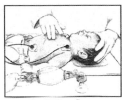

Fig. 16. Two finger
chest compression

Fig. 17. Two thumb-encircling
hands chest compression

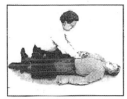

Fig. 18. Heimlich maneuver
in unresponsive victim

Fig. 19. Heimlich maneuver,
victim standing

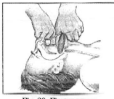

Fig. 20. Finger sweep

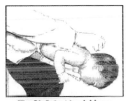

Fig. 21. Infant back blows

AED - AUTOMATED EXTERNAL DEFIBRILLATOR

Witnessed Arrest	Unwitnessed Arrest
Use AED ASAP	Give 5 cycles CPR (2 min), then use AED

Shockable rhythm: Give one shock, immediately resume CPR
(beginning with compressions), do not check pulse.
After 5 cycles, analyze rhythm, deliver another shock if indicated.

Notes: Rescuers must practice minimizing the time between
compressions to give a shock.
   Infants (< 1 yr) – no recommendation for use (optional)
   Children – Use 2 J/kg first attempt; 4 J/kg subsequent attempts
   Ages 1- 8 yrs – use pediatric dose-attenuator system, if available.

ACLS + PALS
ADVANCED CARDIAC LIFE SUPPORT
PEDIATRIC ADVANCED LIFE SUPPORT

AIRWAY

AIRWAY ADJUNCTS

▶ **Oropharyngeal Airway** – Use only in unconscious (unresponsive) patients with no cough or gag reflex.
Should be inserted only by trained personnel.
Note: Incorrect insertion can displace the tongue into hypopharynx.

▶ **Nasopharyngeal airway** – Useful in patients with (or at risk of developing) airway obstruction (particularly clenched jaw).
May be better tolerated than oropharyngeal in patients not deeply unconscious.
Caution in patients with severe cranial facial injury.
May be easily obstructed by secretions in infants

ADVANCED AIRWAYS

Notes:

Advantages: Isolation of airway, reduced risk of aspiration, and more reliable ventilation.

Disadvantage: Insertion may require interruption of chest compressions – weigh the need for compressions vs. the need for an advanced airway. May defer insertion until patient fails to respond to initial CPR or demonstrates ROSC.

Optimal method (bag-mask, ET tube, Combitube, or LMA) depends on rescuer experience, patient's condition, and system.

Healthcare providers must maintain knowledge and skills through frequent practice with these devices.

Once advanced airway is in place, 2 rescuers no longer deliver cycles of CPR.

Infants and children: In out-of-hospital setting, bag and mask ventilation preferred over intubation, if transport is short.

Endotracheal Tube (ET tube)

Indications:

Inability to ventilate unconscious patient with bag and mask
Absence of airway protective reflexes (coma, cardiac arrest)

Advantages:

Patent airway   Permits suctioning
High O$_2$ delivery   Drug admin. route
Specific V$_T$ delivery   Cuff protection

Insertion:

Inserter must be trained and experienced.

Minimize interruption of chest compressions (be fully prepared to insert when compressing rescuer pauses). Compressions should resume as soon as the tube passes through the vocal cords. Provide adequate ventilation/compressions between attempts.

Pulse oximetry and ECG should be monitored continuously during intubation of patient with a perfusing rhythm. Interrupt attempt if oxygenation/ventilation is needed.

Verify tube position:

Auscultation:	Chest expansion
Lungs – BS equal + bilateral	End-tidal CO$_2$ detector or
Epigastrum – BS absent	esophageal detector

Notes:

No one single confirmation technique is completely reliable (including H$_2$O vapor). *If any doubt*: Use laryngoscope to visualize tube passing through vocal cords. If still doubt, remove tube.

Remove tube at once if hear stomach gurgling and see no chest expansion.

Children:

ET tube size (ID) (1–10yrs): Body length is most reliable (use tape)

    Alternate tech: *uncuffed* = age (yrs)/4 + 4;

                     cuffed = age (yrs)/4 +3;

Keep cuff pressure < 20 cm H$_2$O.

Combitube

Acceptable alternative to ET tube
Confirmation of tube placement is essential.

Laryngeal Mask Airway (LMA)

Acceptable alternative to ET tube
Advantages over ET tube when:
    Access to patient is limited
    Unstable neck injury
    Positioning of patient for intubation is impossible

End-tidal CO_2 Detector

CO_2 detected: Tube is most likely in trachea*
*May rarely detect CO_2 if tube in esophagus and large amounts of carbonated fluid ingested prior to arrest. CO_2 will disappear after a few ventilations if in esophagus, it will continue if in trachea.

> Typical Color: *Yellow = Yes* (probable successful intubation)
> *Purple = Problem* (see below)

CO_2 not detected:
1) Tube is in esophagus
2) Tube may be in trachea
> ↓ CO_2 *in* lungs: poor blood flow to lungs
>> Arrest
>> Pulmonary embolus
>> IV bolus of epinephrine
>
> ↓ CO_2 *from* lungs:
>> Airway obstruction (eg., status asthmaticus)
>> Pulmonary edema
>
> *Use another method to confirm (direct visualization or esophageal detector)*

3) Detector contaminated with gastric contents or acidic drug (eg., tracheal admin. epinephrine)

Infants and children: use if child has a perfusing rhythm

Esophageal Detector Device
May use as one method of confirmation of ET tube placement.
Children: use only if child > 20 kg and has a perfusing rhythm
Caution: may be misleading in morbid obesity, late pregnancy, status asthmaticus, or copious secretions

BREATHING
MOUTH BREATHING
Give 2 breaths (1 sec each)
Take "regular" (not deep) breaths
Breaths should be sufficient for chest rise
If no chest rise with breath 1, do head tilt-chin lift and give 2nd.

BAG VENTILATION
▶ **Unsecured Airway (bag-mask)**
Give 2 breaths (1 sec each) during compression pause (3-4 sec)

▶ **Secured Airway (with two rescuers)**
8-10 breaths/min (q 6-7 sec), 1 sec each
Do not pause or synchronize with compressions

Adult	Infant/Child
500-600 mL (6-7 mL/kg)	**Visible chest rise**
1 L adult bag: 1/2 - 2/3 vol	Bag size should be at least
2 L adult bag: 1/3 vol	450 – 500mL

(All volumes must be sufficient for visible chest rise. Do not deliver breaths greater than needed to produce visible chest rise.)

In patients w/: *Perfusing rhythm (no compressions) -*
  10- 12 breaths/min (q 5-6 sec)
  COPD, ↑ Raw, and/or hypovolemia -
  6- 8 breaths/min (q 7-10 sec) to avoid auto PEEP

Notes:

Use O_2 @ 10-15 L/min (when available; 100% O_2 is preferred)

Bag – mask ventilation is most effective when 2 rescuers work together – 1 opens airway and seals mask, while the other squeezes bag. Both rescuers watch for visible chest rise.

Giving > 12 breaths/min (>q 5 sec) → ↑ PIT, ↓venous return, ↓CO, and ↓ coronary and cerebral perfusion.

Gastric inflation. Giving large/forceful breaths may cause regurgitation, aspiration, ↑diaphragm, ↓ lung movement, and ↓ CL.

Cricoid pressure – May help prevent gastric inflation. Use only if victim is deeply unconscious (no cough or gag reflex). Usually requires third rescuer.

If regurgitation occurs – Turn victim to side, wipe out mouth, return to supine, and continue CPR.

MONITORING

Pulses: Carotid pulsations during the CPR *do not* indicate the efficacy of coronary, myocardial or cerebral perfusion. Femoral pulsations may indicate *venous* rather than arterial flow
  Coronary Perfusion Pressure (CPP = aortic dia – R atrial dia)
  CPP ≥ 15 mm Hg predictive of ROSC
  If A-line monitor: maximize BP dia (ideally ≥30 – 10 = 20 mmHg)

ABGs : Not a reliable indicator of the severity of tissue hypoxemia, hypercarbia (ie., ventilation), or tissue acidosis during arrest

Oximetry: Pulse oximetry saturation does not insure adequate systemic O_2 delivery. May be unreliable in patients with poor peripheral perfusion. In children, monitor O_2 Sat continuously.

End – Tidal CO_2 Monitoring:

Safe and effective indicator of CO (+ maybe ROSC) during CPR
  If ventilation is reasonably constant: Δ CO_2 ≈ Δ CO
  After CPR – use to guide ventil. (along w/ ABG) + ET tube position

ANAPHYLAXIS

SIGNS & SYMPTOMS

Multisystem involvement – consider anaphylaxis when responses are from two more body systems:

Respiratory: laryngeal edema and/or asthma (stridor, wheezing)

Rhinitis is often an early sign of respiratory involvement.

Cardiovascular collapse

Neurologic: agitated or anxious

GI: abdominal pain, vomiting, and diarrhea

Cutaneous: either flushed or pale

> Note: The shorter the time between exposure and reaction, the more likely to be severe. Fatal anaphylaxis can occur within 10-15 min.

A number of disease processes produce some of the same signs and symptoms; failure to identify and appropriately treat can be fatal (e.g., asthma).

THERAPIES

Early recognition – urgent support of ABCs are essential

Anticipate deterioration – patient can deteriorate quickly

Oxygen – give high flows

Epinephrine – IM favored; IV if life-threatening

Inhaled β - adrenergic agents – albuterol for bronchospasm (ipratropium for patients receiving β -blockers)

Intubation – early elective intubation is recommended when patient begins to develop hoarseness, stridor, lingual swelling, or oropharyngeal swelling.

> Note: Once these signs progress, either LMA or Combitube will be ineffective and ET intubation and cricothyrotomy may be difficult or impossible. Intubation may only further increase laryngeal edema or cause trauma to the airway.

ASTHMA (NEAR-FATAL)

CLINICAL ASPECTS
Wheezing
Severity does not correlate with a degree of airway obstruction
Absence of wheezing may indicate critical airway obstruction
Increased wheezing may indicate a positive response to broncho-
dilator therapy
Other Causes of Wheezing

Anaphylaxis	Pneumonia
Bronchiectasis	Pulmonary embolism
COPD	Pulmonary edema
Foreign body	Subglottic mass
	Monitor closely for deterioration

PRIMARY THERAPY
Oxygen
Give to all severe asthma patients (even if normal oxygenation)
Titrate to maintain $SaO_2 > 92\%$. Note: SaO_2 may not reflect pro-
gressive hypoventilation, especially if O_2 is being admin.

Inhaled β2 – Agonists
Albuterol (salbutamol): MDI or neb (2.5 or 5 mg, q 15-20 min,
intermittently; 10-15 mg/h, continuous.
Note: MDI-spacer may be difficult in severe asthma; SaO_2 may
initially fall during therapy.

Corticosteroids
Administer as early as possible (onset of effects 6 to 12 hrs)
IV route preferable; inhaled steroids remain controversial

Adjunctive Therapies
Anticholinergics – Ipratropium bromide: adjunct to albuterol
Neb dose 0.5 mg
Onset 20 min; peak 60-90 min
Magnesium sulfate – IV
Epinephrine or terbutaline – subQ
Ketamine – (stimulates copious bronchial secretions)
Heliox – useful for asthma that is refractory to conventional
therapy (cannot be used if patient requires > 30% O_2)

Assisted Ventilation

Intubation

Should be performed if patient deteriorates
Rapid sequence intubation is technique of choice
Use the largest ET tube available

NIPPV – may offer short-term support and delay or eliminate need for ET tube. Requires alert patient with adequate spontaneous respiratory effort.

Mechanical Ventilation (or manual)

Slow rate: 6 - 10 breaths/min   Short T_I
Small V_T: 6 - 8 ml/kg   Long T_E
High flow: adult 80-100 L/min   I:E: 1:4 or 1:5

Watch for auto-PEEP (quickly reduce high PEEP by separating patient from circuit)
Permissive hypercapnia (hypoventilation) = ↓ risk of barotrauma
Sedation often needed to optimize ventilation and ↓ barotraumas
Continue inhaled albuterol treatment through ET tube as needed

DOPE (troubleshooting after intubation)

Acute Deterioration	Troubleshooting
Displacement	Verify position
Obstruction	Eliminate mucous plugs/kinks
Pneumothorax	Decompress
Equipment	Check for leaks/malfunction

DROWNING

BLS - MODIFICATIONS

There is no need to clear the airway of aspirated water
Routine use of abdominal thrusts is not recommended
If hypothermic:

Victim may appear clinically dead – do not withhold lifesaving procedures on the basis of clinical presentation
Pulse and respiration may be slow or difficult to detect –assess for a period of 30 to 45 sec to confirm respiratory arrest, pulseless cardiac arrest, or bradycardia. If any doubt, begin CPR.
AED – If patient does not respond to 1 shock, continue CPR and rewarm patient to 30° - 32° C before repeating defibrillation.

ACLS - MODIFICATIONS

Early intubation recommended

Administer warm, humidified O_2 (42°- 46° C) , if possible

> Note: The theoretical differences between salt and fresh water are not clinically significant.

DRUG - INDUCED

OPIATES POISONING – (HEROIN)

Therapy

1) Support ventilation (bag and mask)
2) Naloxone (to reverse respiratory insufficiency)
3) ET tube intubation (only if needed)

Gastric lavage – recommended only for patients who have ingested potentially lethal amounts within one hour. In comatose or obtunded patients, perform rapid sequence intubation before lavage.

> Note: poisoned patients deteriorate rapidly – frequently assess breathing and protect airway. Prolonged CPR may be warranted in some poisoned patients where CNS is viable.

ELECTRIC SHOCK AND LIGHTNING STRIKES

NOTES.

Vigorous CPR is indicated even for those who appear dead.

Early intubation should be performed for patients with extensive burns, even if patient is breathing spontaneously.

Respiratory arrest due to thoracic muscle spasm and suppression of the respiratory center may continue after ROSC.

PREVENTION OF ARREST

Place patient 15°- 30° back from left lateral position (rolled blanket or object under right hip and lumbar area) or pull gravid uterus to the side.

Give 100% O2

BLS - MODIFICATIONS

Apply continuous cricoid pressure during positive pressure ventilation, if unconscious.

Perform chest compressions higher on the sternum – slightly above center.

ACLS - MODIFICATIONS

Oxygen:

Patients have ↓ FRC and ↑ O2 demand

Intubation:

Secure the airway early

Apply continuous cricoid pressure before and during attempted intubation. Use ET tube 0.5 - 1 mm smaller ID then for a non-pregnant woman (airway edema).

Esophageal detectors may give inaccurate results

Ventilation: May need ↓ VT due to elevated diaphragm

CPR

TRAUMA

BLS – MODIFICATIONS

▶ **Head and neck or multisystem trauma**

Stabilize spine during all BLS maneuvers

Use jaw thrust instead of head tilt – chin lift.

Clear mouth of blood, vomitus, and other secretions

Deliver breaths slowly to reduce risk of gastric inflation

Simultaneous ventilation/compression may result in a tension pneumothorax.

If chest does not expand, rule out tension pneumothorax or hemothorax ($\downarrow$ expansion, $\downarrow$ BS unilateral, $\uparrow$ resistance to ventilation, $\downarrow$ SaO2)

Monitor closely for signs of deterioration

▶ **Infants and children –**

The large head size may require recessing the occiput or elevating the torso to avoid cervical flexion.

Do not over ventilate, even with head injury.

Brief hyperventilation may be used temporarily when observe signs of impending brain herniation (sudden rise in intracranial pressure, dilated pupils not responding to light, bradycardia, hypertension).

ACLS – MODIFICATIONS

Oxygen – provide high O2 even if adequate oxygenation

Intubation – Indications

Respiratory arrest or apnea

Respiratory failure

Severe head injury

Thoracic injuries (eg, flail chest)

Inability to protect upper airway (loss of gag reflex, $\downarrow$ LOC)

Injuries with potential airway obstruction

* Avoid nasotracheal intubation with severe maxilla facial injuries
Out-of-hospital ET intubation is either harmful or at best ineffective for most EMS patients.

POSTRESUSCITATION SUPPORT

Principal Objective – Reestablish effective perfusion of organs and tissues

AFTER THE RETURN OF SPONTANEOUS CIRCULATION (ROSC)
Treat cause or complications

H's	T's
Hypoxia	Toxins
Hypovolemia	Trauma
Hyperthermia	Thrombosis
Hypoglycemia	Tamponade (cardiac)
Hypo/hyperkalemia	Tension pneumothorax
Hydrogen ion (acidosis)	Treat consequences (hypoxia, ischemia, reperfusion)

RESPIRATORY SYSTEM

Perform full physical exam
X-ray (ET tube position, complications)
Ventilatory support (adjust per ABGs, RR, WOB)
Achieve normocarbia – avoid hyperventilation

> **Caution:** after ROSC, there is a brief period (10-30 min) of cerebral hyperemia, followed by a prolonged period of hypoxemia.

Potential detrimental effects of hyperventilation
Cerebral vasoconstriction + ↑ Paw and/or ↑ auto-PEEP → ↑ intracranial pressure, ↓cerebral blood flow, ↑ ischemia

Sedation/NM blockers – no recommendation for defined period of use. Keep NM blockers to a minimum.

WITHDRAWAL OF LIFE SUPPORT

Ethically permissible when:
- No motor response at 24 hrs
- No motor response at 72 hrs
- Absent corneal reflex at 24 hrs
- Absent pupillary response at 24 hrs
- Absent withdrawal response to pain at 24 hrs

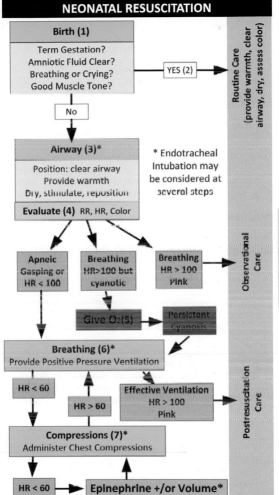

NEONATAL RESUSCITATION

Birth (1)

Term Gestation?
Amniotic Fluid Clear?
Breathing or Crying?
Good Muscle Tone?

YES (2) → **Routine Care** (provide warmth, clear airway, dry, assess color)

No

Airway (3)*

Position: clear airway
Provide warmth
Dry, stimulate, reposition

Evaluate (4) RR, HR, Color

* Endotracheal Intubation may be considered at several steps

| Apneic Gasping or HR < 100 | Breathing HR > 100 but cyanotic | Breathing HR > 100 Pink |

→ **Observational Care**

Give O₂ (5) → Persistent Cyanosis

Breathing (6)*
Provide Positive Pressure Ventilation

HR < 60

HR > 60

Effective Ventilation
HR > 100
Pink

→ **Postresuscitation Care**

Compressions (7)*
Administer Chest Compressions

HR < 60 → **Epinephrine +/or Volume***

CPR

FOOTNOTES

(1) Guidelines apply to neonates at birth and first few months.
   CPR Indications:
   All conditions assoc. with high rate of survival and acceptable
      morbidity (includes ≥ 25 wk gestation [unless fetal compro-
      mise] and most congenital malformations).
   CPR Not Indicated:
   Almost certain death and high morbidity expected (includes < 23
      wk or < 400 g, anencephaly, and chromosomal abnormalities).
   CPR Questionable:
   Uncertain prognosis, survival borderline, and high morbidity and
      burden – support parental desires
   Note: The majority of newborns who will need resuscitation can
      be identified before birth. At least one person who can perform
      a complete resuscitation should be at every delivery. Additional
      skilled personnel should be recruited if resuscitation is antici-
      pated. Special preparations are required for preterm delivery (<
      37 wk). Further info available at www.aap.org/NRP.

(2) Routine Care: Do not separate baby from mother

(3) **AIRWAY**
   Initial steps of resuscitation:
      Place baby under radiant heat
      LBW (< 1500 g) – use additional warming techniques (e.g.,
         plastic wrapping).
      Monitor temperature closely; avoid hyperthermia
      Position head in "sniffing" position to open airway
      Clear airway with bulb syringe or suction catheter
      Dry baby and stimulate breathing

   Meconium staining:
      Routine intrapartum suctioning no longer advised
      Vigorous infant (HR > 100, strong respiratory effort, good
         muscle tone) – do not perform ET suctioning
      Not vigorous – perform ET suctioning immediately after birth

   (4) Evaluate – simultaneous assessment of all 3 (RR, HR, Color
      [in < 30 sec])
      HR is a good indicator of improvement or deterioration
      Reassess all 3 (RR, HR, Color) every 30 sec

(5) *Oxygen*

Indications: PPV or central cyanosis

Dosage:
100% - standard approach and recommended
Room air to 100% - optional and reasonable
Room air - give O_2 if no improvement within 90 sec after birth

Notes:
If no O_2 available, give PPV with room air
Guide administration with pulse oximetry
Avoid excessive O_2 in the premature infant
Healthy term babies may take > 10 min to reach preductal O_2
    Sat > 95% and 1 hr to reach postductal O2 Sat > 95%.
Pallor or mottling may be a sign of ↓ CO, severe anemia, hypo
    volemia, hypothermia, or acidosis.

(6) BREATHING (PPV)

Initial Parameters

Rate: 40 - 60 breaths/min (to achieve/maintain HR > 100)
    (Assess chest wall movement if HR does not improve)
PIP: 30 – 40 cm H_2O
    (Individualize to achieve ↑ HR and/or chest movement)
If monitored, 20 cm H_2O may be effective
If not monitored, use minimum inflation required to achieve
    ↑ HR.

Preterm infants

PIP: 20 to 25 cm H_2O
    Adequate for most
    ↑ if no prompt ↑ in HR or chest movement
    Avoid excessive chest wall movement.
    Monitor PIP if possible
PEEP or CPAP may be beneficial

Endotracheal intubation

INDICATIONS

Bag/mask ineffective or prolonged	Administration of
When chest compressions are	medications
performed	CDH or extremely low
Tracheal suctioning for meconium	birthweight (< 1000 g)

Check tube position:
   Best indicator is ↑ HR
   Chest movement (present or absent)
   Condensation during exhalation
   Confirm visually during intubation
   Confirm with exhale CO_2 detector after intubation

(7) CHEST COMPRESSIONS

   Ensure assisted ventilation is being delivered optimally before starting chest compressions.

   Ventilation/compressions are synchronized (pause compressions)

Method:	Depth: 1/3 of chest A-P dia
2 thumb-encircling technique – recommended	I:E: slightly > 1:1
	Rate: 90 compressions/min
2 finger technique – optional	Ratio: 3:1
	(90 compressions + 30 breaths)
Position: lower 1/3 of sternum	(120 events/min; ½ sec each)

	Continue until HR ≥ 60/min

Discontinuation is justified after 10 min of continuous and adequate resuscitation efforts and no signs of life.

A   Appendix

Metric Measurements

Linear		Weight			
kilometer (km)	$m \times 10^3$	kilogram (kg)	$g \times 10^3$	kiloliter	1×10^3
decameter	$m \times 10$	decagram	$g \times 10$	decaliter	1×10
meter (m)		gram (g)		liter (L)	
decimeter	$m \times 10^{-1}$	decigram	$g \times 10^{-1}$	deciliter (dL)	1×10^{-1}
centimeter (cm)	$m \times 10^{-2}$	centigram	$g \times 10^{-2}$	centiliter	1×10^{-2}
millimeter (mm)	$m \times 10^{-3}$	milligram (mg)	$g \times 10^{-3}$	milliliter (mL)	1×10^{-3}
micrometer (μ or μm)	$m \times 10^{-6}$	microgram (μg)	$g \times 10^{-6}$	microliter (μL)	1×10^{-6}

U.S. Customary and Metric Equivalents

1 inch	2.54 cm	1 ounce (oz)	28.35g	1 ounce (fl)	29.57 mL
1 foot	.0348 m	1 pound	454 g	1 quart	0.9463 L
1 mile	1.609 km	1 gram	0.0352 oz	1 gallon	3.785 L
1 micron	3.937×10^{-5} in	1 kilogram	2.2 lb	cubic inch	16.39 mL
1 centimeter	0.3937 in			cubic foot	28.32 L
1 meter	39.37 in			1 liter	1.057 qt

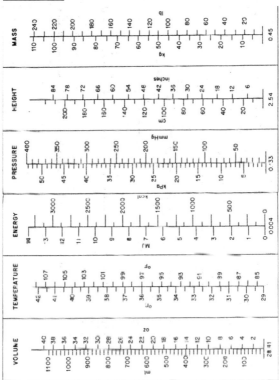

SI = Standard International Unit
Pressure Unit: kPa = mmHg × 0.133; kPa = cm H₂O × 0.098
Compliance Unit: L/kPa = L/cm H₂O × 10.2

Appendix

Appendix

Conversion of pounds to kilograms for pediatric weights

Pounds →	0	1	2	3	4	5	6	7	8	9
0	0.00	0.45	0.90	1.36	1.81	2.26	2.72	3.17	3.62	4.08
10	4.53	4.98	5.44	5.89	6.35	6.80	7.25	7.71	8.16	8.61
20	9.07	9.52	9.97	10.43	10.88	11.34	11.79	12.24	12.70	13.15
30	13.60	14.06	14.51	14.96	15.42	15.87	16.32	16.78	17.23	17.69
40	18.14	18.59	19.05	19.50	19.95	20.41	20.86	21.31	21.77	22.22
50	22.68	23.13	23.58	24.04	24.49	24.94	25.40	25.85	26.30	26.76
60	27.21	27.66	28.12	28.57	29.03	29.48	29.93	30.39	30.84	31.29
70	31.75	32.20	32.65	33.11	33.56	34.02	34.47	34.92	35.38	35.83
80	36.28	36.74	37.19	37.64	38.10	38.55	39.00	39.46	39.91	40.37
90	40.82	41.27	41.73	42.18	42.63	43.09	43.54	43.99	44.45	44.90
100	45.36	45.81	46.26	46.72	47.17	47.62	48.08	48.53	48.98	49.44
110	49.89	50.34	50.80	51.25	51.71	52.16	52.61	53.07	53.52	53.97
120	54.43	54.88	55.33	55.79	56.24	56.70	57.15	57.60	58.06	58.51
130	58.96	59.42	59.87	60.32	60.78	61.23	61.68	62.14	62.59	63.05
140	63.50	63.95	64.41	64.86	65.31	65.77	66.22	66.67	67.13	67.58
150	68.04	68.49	68.94	69.40	69.85	70.30	70.76	71.21	71.66	72.12
160	72.57	73.02	73.48	73.93	74.39	74.84	75.29	75.75	76.20	76.65
170	77.11	77.56	78.01	78.47	78.92	79.38	79.83	80.28	80.74	81.19
180	81.64	82.10	82.55	83.00	83.46	83.91	84.36	84.82	85.27	85.73
190	86.18	86.68	87.09	87.54	87.99	88.45	88.90	89.35	89.81	90.26
200	90.72	91.17	91.62	92.08	92.53	92.98	93.44	93.89	94.34	94.80

POUNDS AND OUNCES TO GRAMS

OUNCES	0 LB	1 LB	2 LB	3 LB	4 LB	5 LB	6 LB	7 LB	8 LB	9 LB	10 LB	11 LB	12 LB
							GRAMS						
0	0	454	907	1361	1814	2268	2722	3175	3629	4082	4536	4990	5443
1	23	482	936	1389	1843	2296	2750	3204	3657	4111	4564	5018	5471
2	57	510	964	1418	1871	2325	2778	3232	3686	4139	4593	5046	5500
3	85	539	992	1446	1899	2353	2807	3260	3714	4167	4621	5075	5528
4	113	567	1021	1474	1928	2381	2835	3288	3742	4196	4649	5103	5557
5	142	595	1049	1503	1956	2410	2863	3317	3771	4224	4678	5131	5585
6	170	624	1077	1531	1985	2438	2892	3345	3799	4252	4706	5160	5613
7	198	652	1106	1559	2013	2466	2920	3374	3827	4281	4734	5188	5642
8	227	680	1134	1588	2041	2495	2948	3402	3856	4309	4763	5216	5670
9	255	709	1162	1616	2070	2523	2977	3430	3884	4337	4791	5245	5698
10	283	737	1191	1644	2098	2552	3005	3459	3912	4366	4819	5273	5727
11	312	765	1219	1673	2126	2580	3033	3487	3941	4394	4848	5301	5755
12	340	794	1247	1701	2155	2608	3062	3515	3969	4423	4876	5330	5783
13	369	822	1276	1729	2183	2637	3090	3544	3997	4451	4904	5358	5812
14	397	851	1304	1758	2211	2665	3119	3572	4026	4479	4933	5386	5840
15	425	879	1332	1785	2240	2693	3147	3600	4054	4508	4961	5415	5866

To convert: 1 pound = 453.59237 grams; 1 ounce = 28.349523 grams; 1,000 grams = 1 kilogram. Example: To obtain grams equivalent to 6 pounds, 8 ounces, read "6" on top scale, "8" on side scale; equivalent is 2948 grams.

Appendix

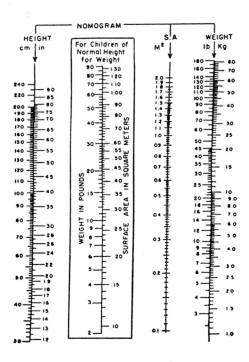

Nomogram for estimation of surface area. The surface area is indicated where a straight line which connects the height and weight levels intersects the surface area column; or the patient is roughly of average size, from the weight alone (enclosed area). (Nomogram modified from data of E. Boyd by C. D. West.)

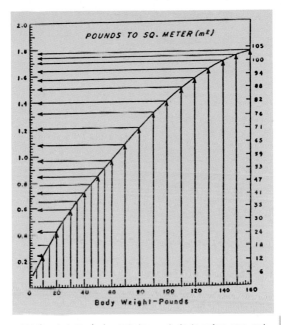

Relations between body weight in pounds, body surface area, and adult dosage. The surface area values correspond to those set forth by Crawford et al. (1950). Note that the 100 per cent adult dose is for a patient weighing about 140 pounds and having a surface area of about 1.7 square meters. (From Talbot, N. B., et al.: *Metabolic Homeostasis – A Syllabus for Those Concerned with the Care of Patients.* Cambridge. Harvard University Press. 1959.)

From Vaughan, V.C., McKay, R.J., and Behrman, R.E.: *Nelson Textbook of Pediatrics*, ed. 11, Philadelphia, 1979, p. 2055, W.B. Saunders Co.

Static Lung Volumes — PFT Values

Static Lung Volumes		Infant (ml/kg)	Adult (ml/kg)
Total lung capacity	(TLC)	63	82
Inspiratory capacity	(IC)	33	52
Thoracic gas volume	(TGV)	30–36	30
Functional residual capacity	(FRC)	30	30
Vital capacity	(VC)	30–40	66
Closing capacity	(CC)	35	23
Tidal volume	(V_T)	6	7
Expiratory reserve volume	(ERV)	7	14
Closing volume	(CV)	12	7
Residual volume	(RV)	23	16
ERV/FRC		0.23	0.47
RV/TLC		0.37	0.20
FRC/TLC		0.48	0.37
V_T/FRC		0.20	0.23

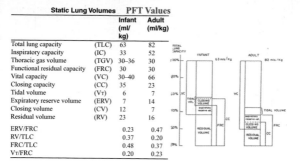

Pulmonary Ventilation

	Symbol	Infant	Adult	Units
Respiratory frequency	(f)	34–35	13	BPM
Tidal volume	(V_T)	6–8	7	ml/kg
Alveolar volume	(V_A)	3.8–5.8	4.8	ml/kg
Dead space volume	(V_D)	2.0–2.2	2.2	ml/kg
Minute ventilation	($\dot{V}_E$)	200–260	90	ml/kg/minute
Alveolar ventilation	($\dot{V}_A$)	100–150	60	ml/kg/minute
Wasted (dead space) ventilation	($\dot{V}_D$)	77–99	30	ml/kg/minute
Dead space/tidal volume	(V_D/V_T)	0.27–0.37	0.3	
Oxygen consumption	($\dot{V}_{O_2}$)	6–8	3.2	ml/kg/minute
Ventilation equivalent	($\dot{V}_A/\dot{V}_{O_2}$)	16–23	19–25	
Alveolar ventilation	($\dot{V}_A$)	2.3	2.4	L/m²/minute

Distribution of Pulmonary Ventilation (V_A) and Perfusion (Q_c) in the Infant

Type of Alveolus $\dot{V}_A/\dot{Q}_c$	% Total Ventilation	% Total Perfusion	
Anatomically shunted	20	10	
Atelectatic, perfused	0	15	0
Trapped gas, perfused	0	10	0
Silent (atelectatic, nonperfused)	0	0	0
Low $\dot{V}_A/\dot{Q}_c$ areas	2 ⎫	5 ⎫	0.4
Normal $\dot{V}_A/\dot{Q}_c$ areas	68 ⎬ 75	58 ⎬ 65	1.2
High $\dot{V}_A/\dot{Q}_c$ areas	5 ⎭	2 ⎭	2.5
Dead space (ventilated, nonperfused)	5	0	∞
Diffusion block	<1	<1	—

Respiratory Gas Differences

	Total Difference	=	Diffusion Component	+	Dead Space Component	+	Distribution Component	+	Shunt Component
	$AaDO_2$	=	$AcDO_2$	+	$aADCO_2$	+	$aADN_2$	+	$caDO_2$
Adult	10 mmHg	=	< 1	+	1	+	7	+	2
Infant	25 mmHg	=	< 1	+	1	+	10	+	14

$AaDO_2$ = alveolar – arterial O_2 difference

$AcDO_2$ = alveolar – capillary O_2 difference

$aADCO_2$ = arterial – alveolar CO_2 difference

$aADN_2$ = arterial – alveolar N_2 difference

$caDO_2$ = capillary – arterial O_2 difference

Reprinted with permission from Avery, G., *Neonatology: Pathophysiology and Management*, 3rd Ed. Copyright 1987 by J.B. Lippincott Co.

Application of Continuous Positive Airway Pressure to Neonates via Nasal Prongs (NCPAP) or Nasopharyngeal Tube (NP-CPAP) *
(AARC CPG)

Description

The application of positive pressure to the airways of a spontaneously breathing patient throughout the respiratory cycle via nasal prongs or nasopharyngeal tube attached to a suitable ventilator, set in the CPAP mode, and delivering a continuous flow of warm, humidified gas.

CPAP maintains inspiratory and expiratory pressure above ambient pressure resulting in:

↑ Paw, FRC, $V_T/\Delta P$, C_L
↓ WOB, Raw, & O_2 requirement
Stabilization of $\dot{V}_E$
Improved V/Q

Contraindications

Bronchiolitis
Congenital diaphragmatic hernia
Need for intubation and MV:
CV instability (impending arrest), respiratory drive unstable (frequent apnea), upper airway abnormalities (choanal atresia, cleft palate, TE fistula, ventilatory failure ($PaCO_2 > 60$ mm Hg and pH < 7.25). †

Indications

ABG's inadequate: $PaO_2 \leq 50$ mm Hg on $FiO_2 \geq 0.6$ (with adequate $\dot{V}_E$: $PaCO_2 < 50$ mm Hg, pH ≥ 7.25)†
Chest radiograph: Poorly expanded or infiltrated lung fields
Physical exam abnormalities: Agitation, grunting, nasal flaring, ↑ RR (30 - 40% above normal), retractions (sub/suprasternal), skin color (pale or cyanotic), ↑WOB.
Certain conditions associated with one of the above indications: Apnea of prematurity, atelectasis, extubation (recent), pulmonary edema, RDS, tracheal malacia, TTN.

Monitoring

Continuous monitoring: Airway pressures (proximal, P_{aw}, PEEP), CO_2 (PetCO₂), O_2 (PtcO₂ and SpO2), ECG, FiO_2, RR.

Periodic monitoring: ABG's (arterial, capillary or venous), chest radiographs, patient-ventilator checks (q 2-4 hrs).

CONTINUED NEXT PAGE

(CPAP continued from previous page)	
Hazards / Complications **Equipment Related** *Alarm inactivation:* Low airway pressure/disconnect – due to ↑ resistance from turbulent flow; low or high airway pressure – due to complete obstruction resulting in continued pressurization; manual breath activation causing gastric insufflation and discomfort. **Patient Related:** Gastric insufflation (potential aspiration) Lung overdistension leading to: air leaks, CO_2 retention, impeded pulmonary blood flow, V/Q mismatch, ↑ WOB. Nasal irritation or mucosal damage (drying) Skin irritation and pressure necrosis **Frequency** Continuous use	**Limitations** Ineffective during mouth breathing Difficult to secure in place **Assessment of Outcome** Initiate CPAP at 4 - 5 cm H_2O and gradually ↑ up to 10 cm H_2O to provide: Chest radiograph improvement FiO_2 stabilized ≤ 0.6 with: PaO_2 > 50 mm Hg, SpO_2 clinically acceptable, $PaCO_2$ ≤ 50 - 60 mm Hg, pH ≥ 7.25 Patient comfort improvement ↓ WOB (evidenced by): ↓ RR 30 – 40%, ↓ retractions, grunting, and nasal flaring **Infection Control** Employ Universal Precautions Sterile suctioning procedures *Ventilator:* Do not change circuits/humidifiers < 48 hrs (≥ 5 days acceptable with humidity other than aerosol); clean external surfaces according to manufacturer recommendations.

* Adapted from AARC Clinical Practice Guideline, ***Respiratory Care***, Vol. 49(9), 2004.

† $PaCO_2$ 60 mm Hg and pH 7.20 is more concurrent with today's "gentile ventilation" and permissive hypercapnia

Assessing Response to Bronchodilator Therapy (AARC CPG) *

Indications

Assessment of airflow and other clinical indicators to:

Confirm therapy inappropriateness

Individualized medication dose &/or frequency

Determine patient status during therapy

Determine need for changes in therapy (dose, frequency, types of medication)

Contraindications

Some assessment maneuvers should be postponed during acute, severe distress.

Hazards/Complications

Airway collapse

Bronchoconstriction

Coughing &/or syncope

Inherent hazards of specific procedures

Frequency

Acute, unstable patient –

Pre-therapy: ABGs, full assessment, baseline values

Pre and Post therapy. BS, side effects, vital signs, PEFR, or FFV1 (freq. is based upon acuteness and severity).

Continuous. SpO2

Stable patient-

Hospital: PEF (pre and post therapy initially, then 2 x/day.

Home. PEF initially 3-4/day than 2x/day, depending on severity of symptoms.

Assessment of Outcome/ Monitoring

Pre-therapy (identify):

Clinical Indications

Contraindications

Respiratory and CV baseline values

During therapy (identify):

Adverse responses

Clinical changes

Post therapy (identify):

Adverse responses

Therapeutic responses

Lack of therapeutic responses

Trend analysis (identify):

Change in baseline

Need to – change therapy, discontinue therapy, modify dose

Document

Patient responses and progress: BS, lung function (PEFR, FEV, FVC), vital signs, symptoms.

CONTINUED NEXT PAGE

(Bronchodilator Response continued from previous page)	
Monitoring	**PFT's:**
Patient observation:	FEV$_1$ &/or FVC (improved by
Accessory muscle use decreased	12% increase and 200mL increase) &/or FEF 25-75%
General appearance improved	improved, ↑PEF.
Sputum expectoration increased	SaO$_2$, SpO$_2$ &/or ABG's improved
	Exercise performance improved
Auscultation:	Ventilator variables improved:
BS improved and volume of air moved is increased	Decreased: auto- PEEP, PIP, Pplat, Raw
Vital signs improved	Increased: expiratory flow
Subjective patient improvement	

Adapted from AARC Clinical Practice Guidelines: Assessing Response
to Bronchodilator Therapy at Point of Care, *Respiratory Care*,
Volume 40, (12), 1995.

Appendix

Capillary Blood Gas Sampling for Neonatal and Pediatric Patients (AARC CPG)

Description

Capillary blood sample to estimate pH and $PaCO_2$ (It is of little value in estimating PaO_2)

Indications

Abnormal noninvasive monitor readings ($PtcO_2$, $PetCO_2$, SpO_2)

Arterial ABG access is not available

Assessment of therapeutic modalities

Monitoring of a disease process

Patient status change (based on history or physical assessment)

Contraindications

Absolute:

Patients less than 24 hrs. old

Site locations not to be used -
  Areas of infection
  Cyanotic or poorly perfused
  Fingers of neonates
  Heel (posterior curvature or callused)
  Inflamed, swollen or edematous tissue
  Peripheral arteries
  Previous puncture sites
  When direct analysis of arterial blood is needed

Relative:

Hypotension

Peripheral vasoconstriction

Polycythemia

Hazards / Complications

Artery laceration

Bleeding

Bone calcification

Bruising

Burns

Inappropriate patient management from reliance of PcO_2

Infection (patient or caregiver)

Nerve damage

Pain

Scarring

Limitations of method

Inadequate warming of site

Second puncture may be needed

Undue squeezing of puncture site

Variability of PcO_2

Limitations of validity

Air contamination

Analysis of sample delayed (> 15 min., room temp; > 60 min., iced)

Clotting

Sample quantity insufficient

Monitoring

Monitor and document.
  Date, time and sampling site
  Ease (or difficulty) of obtaining sample

CONTINUED NEXT PAGE

(Capillary Sampling continued from previous page)	

Free flow of blood (without 'milking')
 Oxygen administration (device, FiO_2 or flow)
 	
 Patient -
   Adverse reactions or complications
   Clinical appearance
   Level of activity or position
   Puncture site appearance
   Respiratory rate
   Temperature
 Results of analysis
 Sample contamination (air or clot)
 Values of noninvasive monitors ($PtcO_2$, $PetCO_2$, SpO_2)
 Ventilator settings
	Frequency
	 No prescribed frequency
	 Dependent upon indications and clinical status of the patient
	
	 Infection Control
	 Aseptic technique
	 Universal precautions

Adapted from AARC Clinical Practice Guideline, *Respiratory Care*, Vol. 46 (5), 2001.

Capnography/Capnometry during Mechanical Ventilation [1,2] (AARC CPG)

Indications

Evaluation of exhaled CO_2 (esp. $PetCO_2$ to assess alveolar ventilation or metabolic rate)

Intubation (verify ET tube placement – tracheal vs. esophageal) [3]

Monitor pulmonary disease: Adequacy of pulmonary, systemic and coronary blood flow, response to therapy, and severity of disease.

Therapeutic administration of CO_2 gas

Ventilatory support: Monitor circuit integrity (including airway), efficiency ($PaCO_2$ – $PetCO_2$ diff), patient-ventilator interface (graphics).

Contraindications:
None

Hazards / Complications

↑ V_D, ↑ weight on artificial airway or line

Monitoring

Ventilatory variables: V_T, f, PEEP, I/E, PIP, FIO_2

Hemodynamic variables: BP (sys & pulm), CO, shunt, V/Q imbalances

Frequency

PRN, during intubation

Limitations

Is not a substitute for assessing $PaCO_2$

Reliability may be affected by: resp. gas mixture, RR, Freon, secretions/condensate, filters, leaks, low CO or V_T.

---

1) Evaluation of CO_2 in respiratory gases on MV patients.

2) Adapted from AARC Clinical Practice Guideline: Capnography / Capnometry during Mechanical Ventilation, 2003 Revision and Update, *Respiratory Care*, Vol. 48, (5), 2003.

3. Low CO may negate its use for this indication.

Endotracheal Suctioning of Mechanically Ventilated Adults and Children * †
(AARC CPG)

Indications

Atelectasis (from secretion retention)

Maintain airway patency

Obtain sputum specimen

Remove accumulated secretions: Evidenced by – ABG deterioration, coarse BS, ↑ WOB, X-ray changes, suspected aspiration, ineffective cough, ventilator changes (↑ PIP, ↓ VT, change in flow), visible secretions in airway.

Contraindications

Relative: Adverse reaction or worsening clinical condition from the procedure.

Frequency

PRN

Hazards/Complications

Atelectasis

Bronchospasm/constriction

Cardiac arrhythmia/arrest

Hemorrhage/bleeding

Hypo/hypertension

Hypoxia/hypoxemia

↑ ICP

Infection (patient or caregiver)

Interruption of MV

Mucosal trauma

Respiratory arrest

Monitoring

ABGs/SaO$_2$, BS, cough effort, CV parameters (BP, HR, EKG), ICP, RR and pattern, skin color, sputum prod (color, volume, consistency, odor), ventilator parameters (PIP, Pplat, VT, graphics, FiO$_2$).

---

* A component of bronchial hygiene therapy involving the mechanical aspiration of pulmonary secretions from a patient with an artificial airway.

† Adapted from the AARC Clinical Practice Guideline: Endotracheal Suction of Mechanically Ventilated Adults and Children with Artificial Airways, *Respiratory Care*, Vol. 38, (5), 1993.

Management of Airway Emergencies[1]
(AARC CPG)

Indications

Conditions requiring general airway management: airway compromise, protection, respiratory failure.

Conditions requiring emergency tracheal intubation, surgical placement or alternative techniques (see the AARC guideline for a list of numerous specific conditions).

Contraindications

Patient's documented desire not to be resuscitated.

Monitoring
Patient:

Clinical signs – airway obstruction (blood, foreign objects, secretions, vomitus), BS, chest movement, epigastric sounds, LOC, nasal flaring, retractions, skin color, upper airway sounds (snoring, stridor), ventilation ease.

Physiologic variables – ABG, pulse ox., CXR, $PeCO_2$, HR, rhythm, f, V_T, Paw.

Tube positioned in trachea.

Confirmed by – chest x-ray, endoscopic visualization, exhaled CO_2

Suggested by – BS (bilateral), chest movement (symmetrical), condensate upon exhalation, epigastrium (absence of ventilation sounds), esophageal detector devices, visualization of passage through vocal cords.

Precautions/Hazards/Complications

Emergency Ventilation:
barotrauma, gastric insufflation/rupture, hypo/hyper ventilation, hypotension, O_2 delivery (inadequate), unstable cervical spine, upper airway obstruction, ventilation (prolonged interruption), vomiting, aspiration.

Trans-Laryngeal intubation, Cricothyroidotomy:
Aspiration, bronchospasm, laryngospasm, bradycardia, tachycardia, dysrhythmia, hypo/hypertension.

ET tube problems:
Cuff herniation, perforation, extubation (inadvertent), pilot tube valve incompetence, size inappropriate, tube kinking, occlusion

Failure to establish patient airway, intubate the trachea, Intubation of bronchi, esophagus

Pneumonia

Trauma – airway, cervical spine, dental, esophagus, eye, nasal, needle cricothyroidotomy (bleeding, esophageal perforation, subcutaneous emphysema), vocal cords.

Ulceration, stenosis, malacia

1) Adapted from the AARC Clinical Practice Guidelines: Management of Airway Emergencies, *Respiratory Care*, Volume 40, (7), 1995.

Appendix

Nasotracheal Suctioning (2004 AARC Revision/Update) [1,2]

Indications
Patient's cough unable to clear secretions or foreign material in the large central airways.
Evidenced by:
Audible or visible secretions in airway
Chest x-ray (retained secretions → atelectasis or consolidation)
Coarse, gurgling BS or ↓ BS
Hypoxemia or hypercarbia
Suspected aspiration
Tactile fremitus
↑WOB
To stimulate cough or for unrelieved coughing
To obtain sputum sample

Contraindications
Absolute: Croup or epiglottitis
Relative: Acute facial, head or neck injury, broncho-spasm, coagulopathy or bleeding disorder, high gastric surgery, irritable air-way, laryngospasm, MI, nasal bleeding, occluded nasal passages, tracheal surgery, URI.

Frequency
Only when indicated and other measures have failed.

Monitoring
(before, during, and after)
BS, cough, CV parameters (HR, BP, EKG), ICP, laryngospasm, oxygen saturation, RR, pattern, SpO2, skin color, sputum (color, volume, consistency, odor), subjective response (pain), trauma, bleeding.

Hazards/Complications
Atelectasis, bronchospasm, CV changes (↓ HR,↑↓BP, arrhyth-mia, arrest), gagging, vomiting, hypoxia, hypoxemia,↑ ICP (IVH, cerebral edema), laryngo-spasm, mechanical trauma (bleeding, irritation, laceration, perforation, tracheitis), misdi-rection of catheter, nosocomial infection, pain, pneumo-thorax, respiratory arrest, uncontrolled coughing.

Assessment of Outcome
Improved BS, improved ABGs or SpO2, secretions removed, ↓WOB (↓RR or dyspnea)

Pressures Sx time should be < 15 sec.

Adult	-100 to -150 mm Hg	Infant	-80 to -100 mm Hg
Child	-100 to -120 mm Hg	Neonate	-60 to -80 mm Hg

1) The insertion of a suction catheter through the nasal passage and pharynx into the trachea (no tracheal tube/tracheostomy) to remove material from the trachea/nasopharynx that can't be removed by the pt's spont. cough.
2) Adapted from the AARC Clinical Practice Guideline: Nasotracheal Suction-ing, *Respiratory Care*, Volume 37, (8), 1992 and 2004 update.

Postural Drainage Therapy [1,2]
(AARC CPG)

Indications

Turning –
Patient unable or unwilling to change positions, ↓ PaO_2 associated with position, atelectasis (present or potential), artificial airway present.

Postural drainage –
Secretion clearance difficult; qty > 23-30 mL/day, retained secretions with artificial airway, atelectasis from mucous plugging
Specific diseases: bronchiectasis, cystic fibrosis, cavitating lung disease, foreign body aspiration.

External manipulation of thorax:
additional assistance needed to move secretions -↑ sputum volume and/or consistency.

Frequency

Turning
Critically ill and ventilated: q 1-2 hrs
Less acute: q 2 hr

Postural drainage therapy
Critical care: q 4-6 hrs as indicated
Spontaneous breathing patients. per response to therapy
Re-evaluate frequency order q 48-72 hrs or with change in patient status.

Contraindications

All positions –

Absolute: head and neck injury until stabilized, active hemorrhage with hemodynamic instability.

Relative: BP fistula, empyema, hemoptysis (active), ICP > 20 mm Hg, pleural effusion (large), pulmonary edema (CHF), pulmonary embolism, rib fracture, spinal injury (acute) or surgery (recent), surgical wound or healing tissue, unable to tolerate position.

Trendelenburg position
Relative: aspiration risk (uncontrolled airway, tube feed or recent meal), distended abdomen, esophageal surgery, hemoptysis (recent & gross), uncontrolled hypertension, ICP > 20 mm Hg or any ↑.

Reverse Trendelenburg position
Relative: hypotension, vasoactive medication

CONTINUED NEXT PAGE

Appendix

Removal of the Endotracheal Tube - 2007*
(AARC CPG)

Indications

Airway control no longer necessary and patient is able to maintain patent airway & adequate spontaneous ventilation (i.e. adequate neuro drive, muscle strength, cough)

Artificial airway obstruction (not able to be cleared rapidly)

Discontinuance of further medical care

Contraindications

No absolute

Hazards/Complications

Hypoxemia (aspiration, atelectasis, bronchospasm, hypoventilation, laryngospasm, low O_2, pulmonary edema)

Hypercapnia (bronchospasm, excessive WOB, muscle weakness, upper airway edema)

Death (discontinuance of medical care)

Assessment of Readiness

Artificial airway no longer needed as indicated by reversal of cause, adequate spontaneous ventilation and meet readiness criteria:

Maintain adequate PaO_2:
$PaO_2/FiO_2 > 150$-200,
$PEEP \leq 5$-8 cm H_2O and
$FIO_2 \leq 0.4$-0.5

Maintain appropriate pH > 7.25 and $PaCO_2$

Cthorax > 25 mL/cmH_2O

$f < 35$/min (adult)

Modified CROP ≥ 0.1-0.15 mL.mmHg/breaths/min/mL/kg

MVV > 2x$\dot{V}E$ (resting)

NIP > - 20-30 cm H_2O

O_2 cost of breathing < 15% total

P0.1 < 6 cm H_2O

PEF ≥ 60 L/min

RSBI ≤ 105 (modified RSBI $\leq$ 8-11 breaths/min.mL.kg)

SMIP > 57.5

Successful SBT (30-120 min) with low CPAP (5 cmH_2O) or low PS (5-7 cmH_2O) (i.e., adequate respiratory pattern, gas exchange, hemo stability and comfort)

VC > 10 mL/kg (ideal)

$V_D/V_T < 0.6$

$\dot{V}E$ (spont) < 10 L/min

WOB < 0.8 J/L.

(continued from previous page)	
Assessment of Outcome/ Monitoring	**Resolution of need for airway protection:**
Assess/monitor: ABGs, adequate spontaneous ventilation & oxygenation, airway patency, chest X-ray, complications, hemodynamics, neuro status, VS, WOB	Adequate airway protective reflexes Easily managed secretions Normal consciousness
	Other Considerations
Note: Attentive monitoring, prompt ID of respiratory distress and maintaining patent airway is essential	Electrolytes Hemodynamics Nutrition Prophylactic meds (lidocaine, steroids) Reintubation need
Infection Control Follow CDC Standard Precautions	Risk factors Upper airway obstruction/ edema

* Adapted from AARC Clinical Practice Guideline: Removal of the Endotracheal Tube – 2007 Revision & Update, *Respiratory Care*, Vol. 52, (1), 2007

Appendix

Selection of an Aerosol Delivery Device for Neonatal and Pediatric Patients (AARC CPG)

Description

A guideline to assist the clinician in selecting an aerosol delivery device based on the patient's ability.

Types of delivery systems

SVN - small volume nebulizer

A continuous jet nebulizer powered by a gas source

Use mouthpiece with extension reservoir for > 3 years of age if able

Use face mask < 3 years old

Use T-connector or trach collar for patients with artificial airways

Use T-connector and inspiratory circuit reservoir for patients on mechanical ventilation

MDI - Metered Dose Inhaler

A pressurized canister with medication

Use spacer device and mouthpiece > 3 years of age

Use spacer device and face mask < 3 years of age

Use spacer device configured for artificial airways or mechanical ventilation

DPI - dry power inhaler

A breath-actuated device with a gelatin capsule of medication

Use for children > 6 years old

LVN - large volume nebulizer

A continuous jet nebulizer used to deliver medication of a long period of time

A face mask is typically used

Limited use in children

Indications

Whenever a medication approved for inhalation is prescribed

Contraindications

Any specific medication contraindications

MDI or DPI - should not be used in patients allergic to medication preservatives or unable to perform the required respiratory maneuver

Hazards/Complications

Aerosol delivery –

Improper technique

Malfunction of device

Medication, propellant, or preservative side effects

Misuse

Overdose/underdose

MDI –

May affect tidal and/or dead space volumes or F_IO_2 in neoates

CONTINUED NEXT PAGE

(Aerosol Devices continued from previous page)

SVN –
May adversely affect the operation of mechanical ventilation when used inline - to include tidal volumes, pressures, flows, triggering, FiO2

Infection

Limitations of Procedure or Device
Many - see original guidelines

Assessment of Need
See Description above and original guidelines

Assessment of Outcome
Desired medication effect is observed in subjective and objective assessments

Monitoring
Observe self-administration technique of patient
SVN - slow deep inhalation with pause
MDI - actuation at end-exhalation followed by slow inspiration with 10 sec breath hold
DPI - rapid inhalation

Observe response to medication subjective and objective
Monitor ventilator effects or problems
Document patient's medical record

Frequency
According to prescribe medication

Infection Control
Universal precautions
All devices are for single patient use
SVN - clean and dry between uses
MDI/DPI - clean or replace when dirty
SVN/LVN - disinfect or sterilize between patients
Aerosol solutions -
Use only sterile solutions
Dispense aseptically
Patients - rinse mouth after inhaled steroids

Adapted from AARC Clinical Practice Guideline, *Respiratory Care*, vol 40 (12) 1995.

Appendix

Selection of an Oxygen Device for Neonatal and Pediatric Patients (*AARC CPG*)

Description
Oxygen Delivery Systems:

Low-Flow System
FdO_2 varies with patient's inspiratory flowrate (variable performance).
Types –
Nasal cannula, Nasopharyngeal catheters (not for neonates), Tracheostomy adapter, Transtracheal catheter

Reservoir System
FdO_2 varies with patient's inspiratory flowrate (variable performance).
Types –
Simple O_2 mask, Partial-rebreathing mask, Non-rebreathing mask (not appropriate for neonates)

High-Flow System
Provides a specific FdO_2 at flows that meet or exceed the patient's inspiratory flow requirement (fixed performance).
Types –
Air-entrainment mask, Air-entrainment nebulizer with aerosol mask, face tent, trach collar or T-piece

Enclosure System
Provides controlled FdO_2, temperature and humidity
Types – Oxygen hood, Oxygen tent, Closed incubators (not recommended for O_2 delivery)

Indications
Hypoxemia (documented), Hypoxemia (suspected)

Contraindications
Oxygen delivery - none.
Intubated infants - CPAP is recommended over a T-piece.
Nasal cannula/catheter - nasal obstruction
Nasal catheter - maxillofacial trauma, basal skull fracture (present or suspected), coagulation problems.

Hazards/Precautions/Complications
Physiologic –
Altered respiratory drive (cool O2 on trigeminal nerves).
Compromised blood flow (patients with certain congenital heart lesions).
Hypoxemia or hyperoxemia (inappropriate FdO_2 or flow).

CONTINUED NEXT PAGE

(Hazards/Precautions/Complications cont.)

Pulmonary complications (pulmonary fibrosis, O_2 toxicity).

Retinopathy of prematurity (in preterm infants < 37 week gestation).

Keep $PaO_2 \leq 80$ mmHg.

Equipment –

Nasal cannula
Allergic reaction to tubing
Inadvertent CPAP
Displacement ($\downarrow FiO_2$)
Nasal obstruction/irritation
Excessive flow (irritation)
Skin irritation

Nasopharyngeal catheter
Allergic reaction to tubing
Inadvertent CPAP
↑ Risk of infection/complications
Pneumocephalus
Gagging
Skin irritation
Mucosal inflammation
Trauma
Occlusion of distal openings

Mask
Aspiration of vomitus
Rebreathing of CO_2 (inadequate O_2 flow)
Skin irritation

Air-entrainment nebulizer
Bronchoreactivity (nonisotonic solution)
Cold stress in neonates (unheated O_2)
Contamination
Hearing impairment (high noise environment)
Inadvertent extubation or decannulation
Inadvertent lavage (condensate in tubing)

Hood
Apnea (overheating)
Cold stress
Fungal infection (prolonged humidified O_2)
Hypoxia/hypercapnia (inadequate O_2 flow)
Skin irritation

Trach adaptor
Inadvertent decannulation from unwanted torque
HME (↑ WOB in patients < 8 Kg)

General –
O_2 fire hazard, Contamination of humidification system

CONTINUED NEXT PAGE

Limitations

Nasal cannula

FIO_2 *fluctuations (positioning, mucus, minute ventilation, etc.)*

Maximum flow in neonates (2 L/min) and infants

Nasopharyngeal catheter

FIO_2 *fluctuations (as with cannula)*

Maximum flowrate (< 3 L/min)

Occlusion of catheter holes

Change nares q 8-12 hrs

Change catheter q daily

Mask

Variable FIO_2 (inspiratory flow, mask size, blocked entrainment ports)

Rebreathing of CO_2 (inadequate O_2 flow)

Interferes with feeding

Not well tolerated

Air-entrainment nebulizer

Same as mask plus temperature effects (cool mist not recommended for infants: keep at environmental temp)

Hood/tent

Variable FIO_2 (measure FIO_2 at nose and mouth)

Keep O_2 flow > 7 L/min (to wash out CO_2)

Confining

Maintain proper noise and temperature control

Assessment of Need

Need is determined by ↓ PaO_2 or SaO_2 or clinical indicators.

Titrate O_2 flow to maintain adequate SpO_2.

Nasal cannula/catheter: low-level O_2 feeding of infants increased mobility

Simple mask: FIO_2 0.35 – 0.5 for short periods of time (eg. transport)

Partial rebreathing mask: FIO_2 0.4 – 0.6 (eg. during transport)

Non-rebreathing mask: FIO_2 ≥ 0.6 or specific concentrations from a blender

Air-entrainment mask: Precise O_2 concentration (0.24-0.4)

Air-entrainment: To provide high humidity or aerosol

Hood: To provide controlled FIO_2 in infant and small child, high humidity and/or patient accessibility

Tent: To provide supplemental O_2 and/or cool, high humidity to patients with LTB, too large for hoods, certain artificial airways

CONTINUED NEXT PAGE

(Oxygen Devices continued from previous page)	

Assessment of Outcome
Appropriate ↑ in SaO_2
Adequate patient monitoring
Appropriate for patient
 	
Monitoring
 	
Patient:
  Clinical: cardiac, pulmonary,
  neurological
  Physiological: PaO_2 or SaO_2
  (within 1 hr for neonate)
 	
Equipment:
O_2 delivery systems q day
  More frequent in patients
  with artificial airways or
  variable O_2
Continuous for hoods
Heated systems - continuous
  temp monitoring
	Frequency
	Continuous unless O_2
	  indicated only for specific
	  situations (eg. exercise)
	
	Infection Control
	Universal precautions
	Change nasal catheters q
	  24 hrs
	  LVN q 24 hrs when ap-
	  plied to artificial airways
	High level disinfection re-
	  quired for between patient
	  use of equipment
	Nebulizer solutions - sterile
	  fluids only and dispense
	  aseptically

Adapted from AARC Clinical Practice Guideline, *Respiratory Care*, vol 47, (6), 2002.

Appendix

Surfactant Replacement Therapy (AARC CPG)

Description

Surfactant is a compound that forms a layer between the alveolar surface and the alveolar gas and reduces alveolar collapse by decreasing surface tension within the alveoli.

Without surfactant, alveoli may never inflat or may collapse on expiration, leading to RDS. The more premature the infant, the higher the probability for RDS.

Direct tracheal instillation of surfactant reduces the mortality and morbidity in infants with RDS.

Two basic strategies:
1) Prophylactic or preventative
2) Rescue or therapeutic

Indications

Prophylactic administration:

High risk RDS (< 32 wks gestation or < 1300 gm)

Surfactant deficiency (laboratory evidence) L/S < 2:1

Bubble stability test

Absence of phosphatidylglycerol

Rescue/therapeutic administration:

RDS confirmed by chest x-ray and Paw ≥ 7cmH$_2$O to main-adequate oxygenation

Contraindications

RDS in infants with mature lungs

Congenital abnormalities incompatible with life beyond the neonatal period

Hazards / Complications

Procedure complications (resulting from administration)

Administer suboptimal dose

Administer to only one lung

Bradycardia (hypoxia)

Tachycardia (agitation)

Hemoglobin desaturation

Pharyngeal deposition

Plugging of ET tube

Physiologic complications

Apnea

Barotrauma (failure to reduce vent settings post-therapy)

Mucous plugs

PDA

Pulmonary hemorrhage

ROP

Monitoring

During administration:

Delivery device (placement and position)

ET tube reflux

Patient
  Chest expansion
  HR
  O$_2$ sat
  Position of head
  Respirations
  Skin (color & vigor)

Ventilator settings & F$_I$O$_2$

Surfactant Replacement Therapy (continued)

Plus requiring mechanical ventilation [due to ↑ WOB (↑ RR, retractions, grunting and nasal flaring) and ↑ O_2 requirements > 0.4 (pale or cyanotic skin, agitation, and ↓ O_2 measurements)]

Assessment of outcome
Decreased FiO_2, WOB and ventilator requirements (PIP, PEEP, Paw)
Improved chest radiograph, pulmonary mechanics (CL, Raw, VT, V̇E), FRC, and a/APO$_2$

Frequency
Dependent upon clinical status of the patient

Infection Control
Aseptic techniques
Universal precautions

After administration:
Patient
ABGs
Breath sounds
Blood pressure
Chest expansion
Chest radiograph
HR
Pulmonary mechanics and volumes
Respirations
Skin (color & vigor)
Ventilator settings and FiO_2

Adapted from AARC Clinical Practice Guideline, *Respiratory Care*, Vol. 39 (8), 1994.

Appendix

Transcutaneous Blood Gas Monitoring for Neonatal & Pediatric Patients—2004 Revision & Update
(AARC CPG)

Description/Definition

Transcutaneous monitoring measures skin-surface PO_2 and PCO_2 to provide estimates of PaO_2 and $PaCO_2$.

Indications:

Monitor adequacy of arterial oxygenation and/or ventilation

Quantitate response to diagnostic and therapeutic interventions

Contraindications:

Patients with poor skin integrity and/or adhesive

Allergy

Hazards/Complications:

False negative and false-positive results may lead to inappropriate treatment of the patient

Tissue injury at measuring site (blisters, burns, erythema, skin tears)

Device Limitations/Validation

Factors affecting readings, precision, performance or application

Technical:

Prolonged stabilization time, improper calibration, trapped air, bubbles, damaged membranes

Clinical:

Hyperoxemia ($PaO_2 > 100$ torr)

Hypoperfused state (shock, acidosis)

Improper electrode placement or application

Patient's skin/subcutaneous tissue (thickness, edema)

Vasoactive drugs

Validation:

Validation should be performed initially and periodically as dictated by the patient's clinical state.

Disparity between transcutaneous, ABG value and patient clinical presentation of the patient, should be explored before results are reported.

CONTINUED NEXT PAGE

(Transcutaneous Blood Gas continued from previous page)	
Monitoring	**Frequency**
Record:	Continuous monitoring
Clinical appearance of patient (patient's position, respiratory rate, activity level) assessment of perfusion, pallor, and skin temperature	
Date/time of measurement, transcutaneous reading and simultaneous ABG results (when available)	
Electrode placement site, temperature, and time of placement	
FiO_2 and type of oxygen delivery device	
Mode, ventilator, or CPAP settings	

Adapted from AARC Clinical Practice Guideline, *Respiratory Care*, Vol. 49 (9), 2004.

Appendix

Bibliography

American Academy of Pediatrics	*Guidelines for Air & Ground Transport of Neonatal & Pediatric Patients, 3rd Ed, 2007*	American Academy of Pediatrics
American Academy of Pediatrics	*Guidelines for Perinatal Care,* 4th Ed, 2007	American Academy of Pediatrics
American Heart Association	*2005 AHA Guidelines for Cardiopulmonary Resuscitation and Emergency Cardiovascular Care*	*Circulation.* 2005;112:IV-1-IV-5
MacDonald, M,. et.al.	*Avery's Neonatology, Pathophysiology and Management,* 6th Ed, 2005	Lippincott – Williams & Wilkins
Kliegman, R., et. al.	*Nelson's Textbook of Pediatrics,* 18th Ed, 2007	Saunders
Brodsky, D., & Martin, C.	*Neonatology Review,* 2003	Hanley & Belfus
Burg.F., et.al.	*Current Pediatric Therapy,* 18th Ed, 2006	Saunders
Cloherty, J., et.al.	*Manual of Neonatal Care,* 7th Ed, 2007	Lippincott Williams & Wilkins
Czervinski, M. & Barnhart, S.	*Perinatal and Pediatric Respiratory Care,* 2nd Ed, 2003	Saunders

Goldsmith, J. & Karotkin, E.	*Assisted Ventilation of the Neonate,* 4th Ed, 2003	Saunders
Robertson, J. & Shilkofske, N.	*The Harriet Lane Handbook,* 18th Ed, 2009	Mosby Inc.
Hay, W. et.al.	*Lange Current Pediatric Diagnosis & Treatment,* 18th Ed, 2007	Lange Medical Books
Klaus, M. & Faranoff, A..	*Care of the High Risk Neonate,* 5th Ed, 2001	Saunders
Merenstein, G. & Gardner, S.	*Handbook of Neonatal Intensive Care,* 6th Ed, 2006	Mosby Inc.
NIH/NHLBI/NAEPP	*Guidelines for the Diagnosis and Management of Asthma, Expert Panel Report 3,* 2007	
Oakes, Dana	*Clinical Practitioner's Pocket Guide To Respiratory Care,* 7th Ed, 2008	Health Educator Publications, Inc
Oakes, Dana	*Hemodynamic Monitoring: A Bedside Reference Manual,* 4th Ed, 2005	Health Educator Publications, Inc
Oakes, Dana	*Ventilator Management: A Bedside Reference Guide,* 3rd Ed, 2009	Health Educator Publications, Inc

Appendix

Pearson, G.	*Handbook of Pediatric Intensive Care,* 2002	Saunders
Sinha, S. & Donn, S.	*Manual of Neonatal Respiratory Care, 2nd Ed,* 2006	Mosby Inc.
Wilkins, R. et.al.	*Egan's Fundamentals of Respiratory Care,* 9th Ed, 2009	Mosby Inc.
Wilson	*Neonatal and Pediatric Respiratory Care,* 3rd Ed, 2002	Mosby Inc.

Appendix

Abbreviations

A   Artery
A-line   Arterial line
A-V   Atrial-ventricular
ABG   Arterial blood gas
Admin   Administration
Adq   Adequate
AGA   Appropriate for gest. age
ALS   Advanced life support
Alv   Alveolar
Assoc   Associated
BD   Base deficit
BLS   Basic life support
BP   Blood pressure
BPD   Bronchopulmonary dysplasia
Bpm   Beats per minute or breaths per minute
Brady   Bradycardia
BS   Breath sounds
BSA   Body surface area
CBF   Cerebral blood flow
CBG   Capillary blood gas
CDH   Congenital diaphragmatic hernia
CF   Cystic fibrosis
CFT   Capillary fill time
CHD   Congenital heart disease

CHF   Congestive heart failure
CI   Cardiac index
Ck   Check
CL   Lung compliance
CLD   Chronic Lung Disease
CM   Clinical manifestations
CNS   Central nervous system
CO   Carbon monoxide
CO   Cardiac output
Comp   Compliance
CPAP   Continuous positive airway pressure
CPP   Cerebral perfusion pressure
CPR   Cardiopulmonary resuscitation
CPT   Chest physical therapy
CSF   Cerebral spinal fluid
CV   Cardiovascular
CVP   Central venous pressure
D   Definition
DIC   Disseminated intravascular coagulation
E   Etiology
EA   Esophageal atresia
ECMO   Extracorporeal membrane oxygenation
EST   Estimated

ET   Endotracheal tube
ETA   Estimated time of arrival
F   Frequency
F or Fr   French
FHR   Fetal heart rate
FO   Foramen ovale
FRC   Functional residual capacity
Fx   Function
Gest   Gestation
GM   Grams
HCT   Hematocrit
HFV   High frequency ventilation
HIE   Hypoxic Ischemic encephalopathy
HMD   Hyaline membrane disease
HOB   Head of bed
HR   Heart rate
HRF   Hypoxic Respiratory Failure
I-O   Intake and output
I/E   Inspiratory time/expiratory time
IC   Intercosta/Intracardiac
ICP   Intracranial pressure
ICU   Intensive care unit
IDM   Infant of diabetic mother
IGR   Intrauterine growth retardation
IM   Intramuscular

IMV   Intermittent mandatory ventilation
IVC   Inferior vena cava
IVH   Intraventricular hemorrhage
JVD   Jugular vein distension
Kg   Kilogram
L-R   Left to right
L/S   Lecithin/sphinomyelin
LA   Left atrium
LAP   Left atrial pressure
LGA   Large for gestational age
LOC   Level of consciousness
LP   Lumbar puncture
LV   Left ventricle
LVEDP   Left ventricular end diastolic pressure
MAP   Mean airway pressure
MAS   Meconium aspiration syndrome
Metab   Metaboli
MI   Myocardial infarct
MV   Mechanical ventilation
N-P   Nasopharyngeal
NEC   Necrotizing enterocolitis
NIF   Negative inspiratory force
NSS   Normal saline solution
NTE   Neutral thermal environment

Appendix

OI Oxygen index
P/L Pressure limit
PA Pulmonary artery
PAL Pulmonary air leak
PAP Pulmonary artery pressure
PaO2 Pressure of arterial O2
Paw Mean airway pressure
PetCO2 Pressure of end tidal CO2
PtcO2 Pressure of transcutaneous CO2
PtcCO2 Pressure of transcutaneous CO2
Pc Pressure of capillary (gas)
PCWP Pulmonary capillary wedge pressure
PD Postural drainage
PDA Patent ductus arteriosus
Pedi Pediatric
PEEP Positive end expiratory pressure
PG Prostaglandin E1, E2
PIE Pulmonary interstitial emphysema
PIP Peak inspiratory pressure
PMI Point of maximal impulse
PND Paroxysmal nocturnal dyspnea
PP Pulse pressure

PPHN Persistent pulmonary hypertension of the newborn
Premie Preterm infant
Press Pressure
PROM Premature rupture of membranes
Pt Patient
Ptc Pressure of transcutaneous
Pulm Pulmonary
PVC Premature ventricular contraction
PVR Pulmonary vascular resistance
QS/QT Shunt
R-L Right to left
RA Right atrium
RAP Right atrial pressure
RAW Airway resistance
RDS Respiratory distress syndrome
Resp Respiration
Resus Resuscitation
RHF Right heart failure
RLF Retrolental fibroplasia
ROP Retinopathy of prematurity
RR Respiratory rate
RSV Respiratory syncytial virus
RV Right ventricle

Rx Treatment
S+S Signs and symptoms
S/D Systolic over diastolic
Sat Saturation
SC Subcutaneous
SGA Small for gestational age
SIDS Sudden infant death syndrome
SIMV Synchronized intermittent mandatory ventilation
SLE Systemic lupus erythematosus
Soln Solution
Spont Spontaneous
Std Standard
SV Stroke volume
SVR Systemic vascular resistance
Sx Suction
TAPVR Total anomalous pulm. venous return
T-E Trachea-esophagus
Tc Transcutaneous
TE Expiratory time
TI Inspiratory time
TTN Transient tachypnea of the newborn
TTOT Total time
TV Tidal volume

Tx Treatment
UA Umbilical artery
UAC Umbilical artery catheter
UV Umbilical vein
UVC Umbilical venous catheter
V-fib Ventricular fibrillation
V̇A Minute alveolar ventilation
VD Deadspace volume
V̇E Minute ventilation
Vent Ventilation or ventilator
VI Flowrate
VIC Intracranial volume
Vol Volume
VS Vital signs
VT Tidal volume
WOB Work of breathing
↓ Decreased
↑ Increased

Appendix